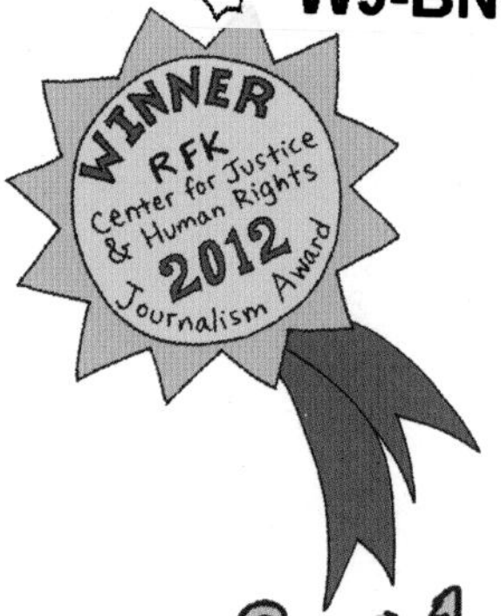
WINNER
RFK
Center for Justice
& Human Rights
2012
Journalism Award

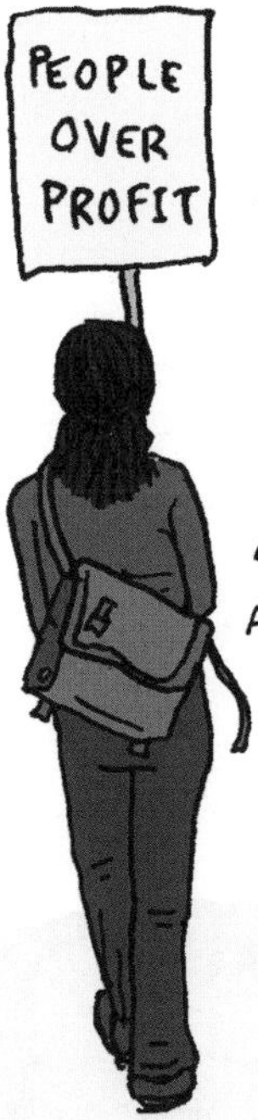
PEOPLE
OVER
PROFIT

The Beginning of the AMERICAN FALL

A COMICS JOURNALIST INSIDE THE OCCUPY WALL STREET MOVEMENT

Stephanie McMillan

Seven Stories Press
NEW YORK

A SEVEN STORIES PRESS FIRST EDITION

SEVEN STORIES PRESS
140 Watts Street
New York, NY 10013
www.sevenstories.com

College professors may order examination copies of Seven Stories Press titles for a free six-month trial period. To order, visit
http://www.sevenstories.com/textbook
or send a fax on school letterhead to (212) 226-1411.

Library of Congress Cataloging-in-Publication Data
McMillan, Stephanie, 1965–
The beginning of the American fall : a comics journalist inside the Occupy Wall Street Movement / Stephanie McMillan.
p. cm.
ISBN 978-1-60980-452-7 (pbk.)
1. Occupy Wall Street (Movement)—Comic books, strips, etc. 2. Protest movements—United States—History—21st century—Comic books, strips, etc. 3. Political participation—United States—History—21st century—Comic books, strips, etc. 4. Counterculture—United States—History—21st century—Comic books, strips, etc. I. Title.
HN59.2.M426 2012
303.48'4—dc23
2012029865

BOOK DESIGN BY STEPHANIE MCMILLAN
PRINTED IN THE UNITED STATES OF AMERICA

A Note to Pirates

Your goals may be noble: everything should be free, including information. Liberating state secrets is a righteous act. But liberating information from the enemy isn't the same as taking content from your friends and allies, especially while we still live in an economy that forces us to pay for food and shelter. If we don't find ways to support our movement's artists, musicians, writers, and independent publishers, then soon we won't have any.

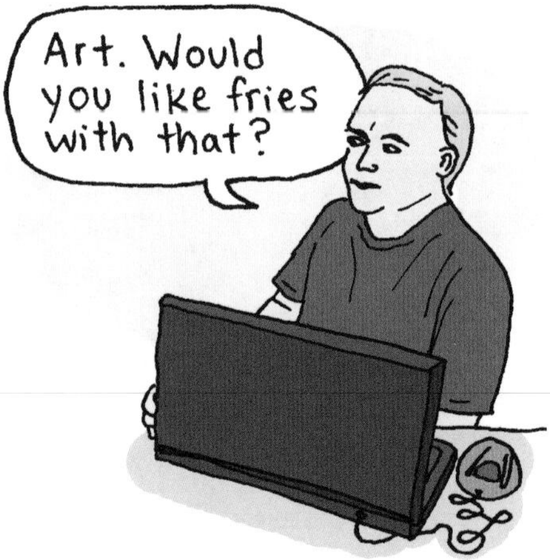
Art. Would you like fries with that?

For each heart
that burns with
the flame of
revolution.

How I Became Politicized

WHEN I was in high school in South Florida, in the early 1980s, I was persuaded to read a book called *Fate of the Earth*, by Jonathan Schell. I opened it very reluctantly, not wanting to know the reality of the destructive power and impulses of the system I lived in (which I didn't understand as a system then). Some part of me realized, deep down, that if I knew the truth, then I'd have to do something about it, and that might divert the course of my life, which was on track to be fairly safe and comfortable.

Anyway, someone bugged me until finally I agreed to read it. It laid out, in gruesome detail, the dangers of nuclear war. The idea that governments would put all of humanity—as well as the planet's very ability to support life—at risk this way was horrifying, a nightmare. I knew I would have to do whatever I could to stop it.

So I did the usual things that people do when they begin to act in the political realm: I looked for people who were already doing something to tell me what to do. I read articles and attended lectures, and learned a lot about the problem. Whenever they would get to the part about what to do, though, it was always the same list: Write a letter to the editor. Write to government representatives. Vote in elections.

Even being the wide-eyed newbie that I was, I understood immediately that these things would never work. I kept asking people: What should we do, for real? Is that all there is? Yes, this is all there is, they would say, handing me a pen to sign another petition.

Until one day when I attended a film showing at a Miami library, after which an activist gave the same old droning speech about pressuring government officials and so on. My friend wandered outside, and after a while returned. He whispered, "This is boring." I agreed. "There's a guy outside in a purple hat," he continued. "He's talking about revolution. Let's go listen to him."

We did, and my life changed. Until someone had pointed out the possibility of revolution in the United States, the concept had never occurred to me. It was, to me, a purely historical phenomenon, safe in the distant past; I had never imagined it as part of the possible future. And then, suddenly there it was. It felt like lightning, this new idea. The answer!

I bought a copy of the newspaper he offered, the *Revolutionary Worker*, and wrestled my way through dense articles with phrases like "proletarian dictatorship" and "bourgeois democracy" and "social imperialism" . . . having no clue what they meant.

It was the beginning of a process that never ends.

A Snapshot: Ten Years Later

In the early 1990s, the Miami group US Hands Off the Haitian People Coalition worked to oppose the US imperialist military and economic domination of Haiti, plus the detention and forced repatriation of emigrants. Eventually it morphed into a new group: One Struggle, widening its focus to address imperialism as a whole. After a couple of years it broke apart and we went our separate ways. I moved to New York to work with the October 22nd Coalition to Stop Police Brutality.

And Now: Thirty Years Later

By October 2010, I'd been back in South Florida for quite a while. Almost exactly a year before Stop the Machine and Occupy Wall Street began, a few of us former One Struggle members talked about whether or not it was time to reactivate it after twenty years of dormancy.

Uprisings were occuring in North Africa and Europe. We sensed storms on the horizon even in the US, and felt a strong urge to prepare to the extent of our ability, to try to build the kind of organizations capable of riding new, huge, historical shifts. The local activist scene that had limped along through the multi-decade Great Political Ebb wasn't going to cut it. It was fragmented, issue-oriented, and dominated by liberal and reformist ideology. Something different was required.

We searched online and at events to locate like-minded people, and had one-on-one discussions with them to determine our level of political unity. We started holding weekly meetings until we were cohesive enough to call ourselves a group and could present compelling enough events to attract fresh forces. At this writing we have a fairly solid collective of about fifteen members.

I have a tendency to be overly optimistic. So when I brought up Stop the Machine in a meeting, I downplayed it a little to compensate for possibly excessive enthusiasm. "It might be a waste of time," I said. "But who knows, it might turn into something." A couple OS'ers rolled their eyes. "It'll be the same old kind of protest," said one skeptic. "An empty gesture."

"But if the revolution starts," someone else said, "let us know. We'll come up and join you."

CONDITIONS IN 2011

- More than 54% of the U.S. discretionary budget was spent on imperialist aggression.
- 6 million Americans had lost their homes.
- A million people annually faced bankruptcy due to medical bills.
- 100,000 in the U.S. died annually by being denied decent medical care.
- Real joblessness spiraled to over 20%.

- Average college tuition in the U.S. had risen by 900% since 1978.
- The average college graduate was $25,000 in debt.

- No 2010 income taxes were paid by corporations that made huge profits or took huge bailouts and subsidies, such as Citicorp, Exxon/Mobil, Bank of America, Wells Fargo, Boeing, Verizon, News Corporation, Merck, and Pfizer.

- 78% of the world's old growth forests were gone.
- 94% of the large fish in the oceans were gone.
- Phytoplankton, the tiny plants that produce half of the oxygen we breathe, had declined by 40% since 1950.
- 200 species per day became extinct.

- Industries produced 400 million tons of hazardous waste each year.
- The water in 89% of U.S. cities tested had been found to contain the carcinogen hexavalent chromium.
- The Earth's average temperature had risen by 1.4 degrees F since 1920.

- There were 56 million active Twitter users.
- 600 million people visited Facebook each month.

WASHINGTON, DC. OCTOBER 2011.

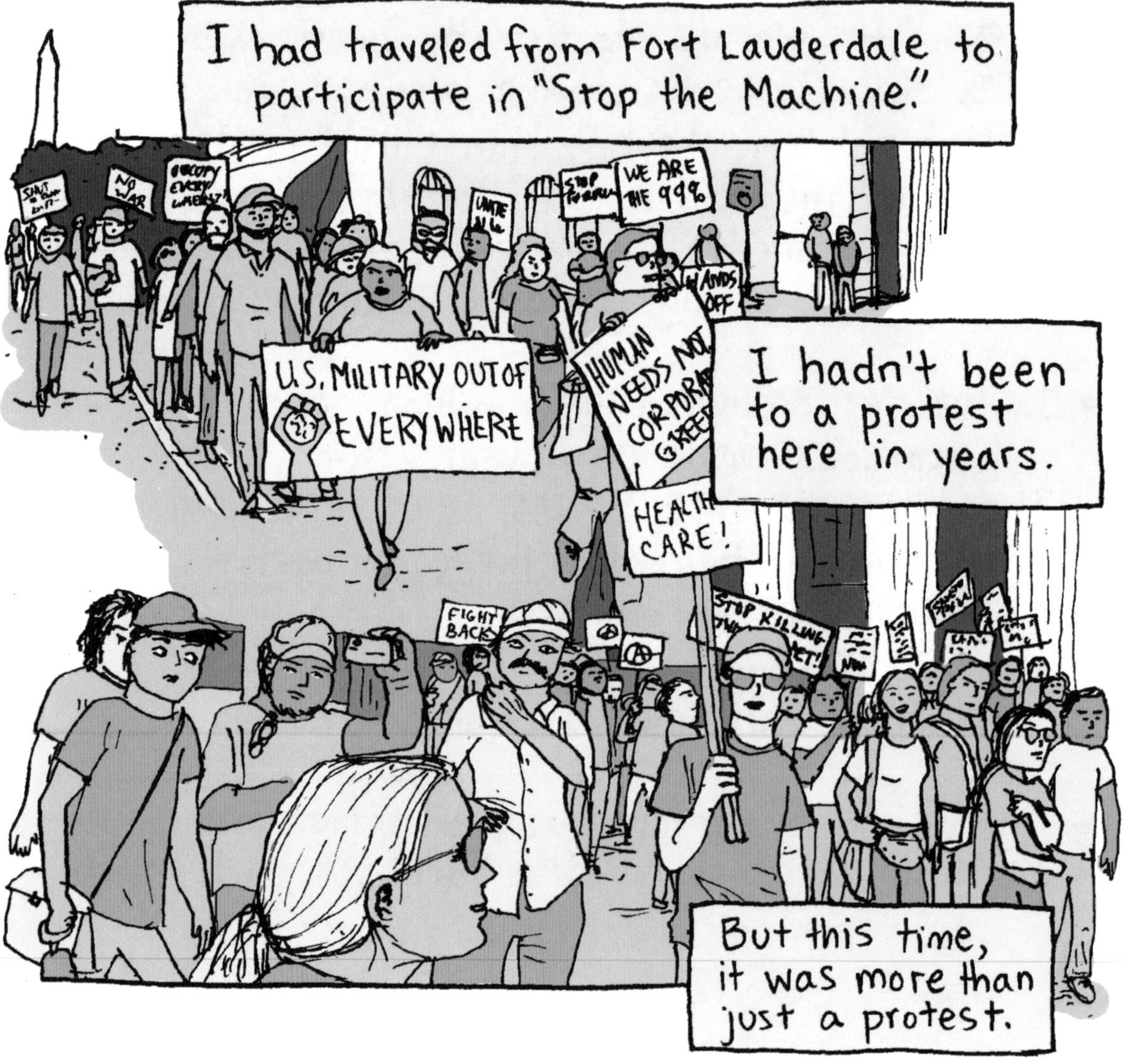
I had traveled from Fort Lauderdale to participate in "Stop the Machine."
NO WAR
WE ARE THE 99%
HANDS OFF
U.S. MILITARY OUT OF EVERYWHERE
HEALTH CARE!
I hadn't been to a protest here in years.
FIGHT BACK
STOP KILLING
But this time, it was more than just a protest.

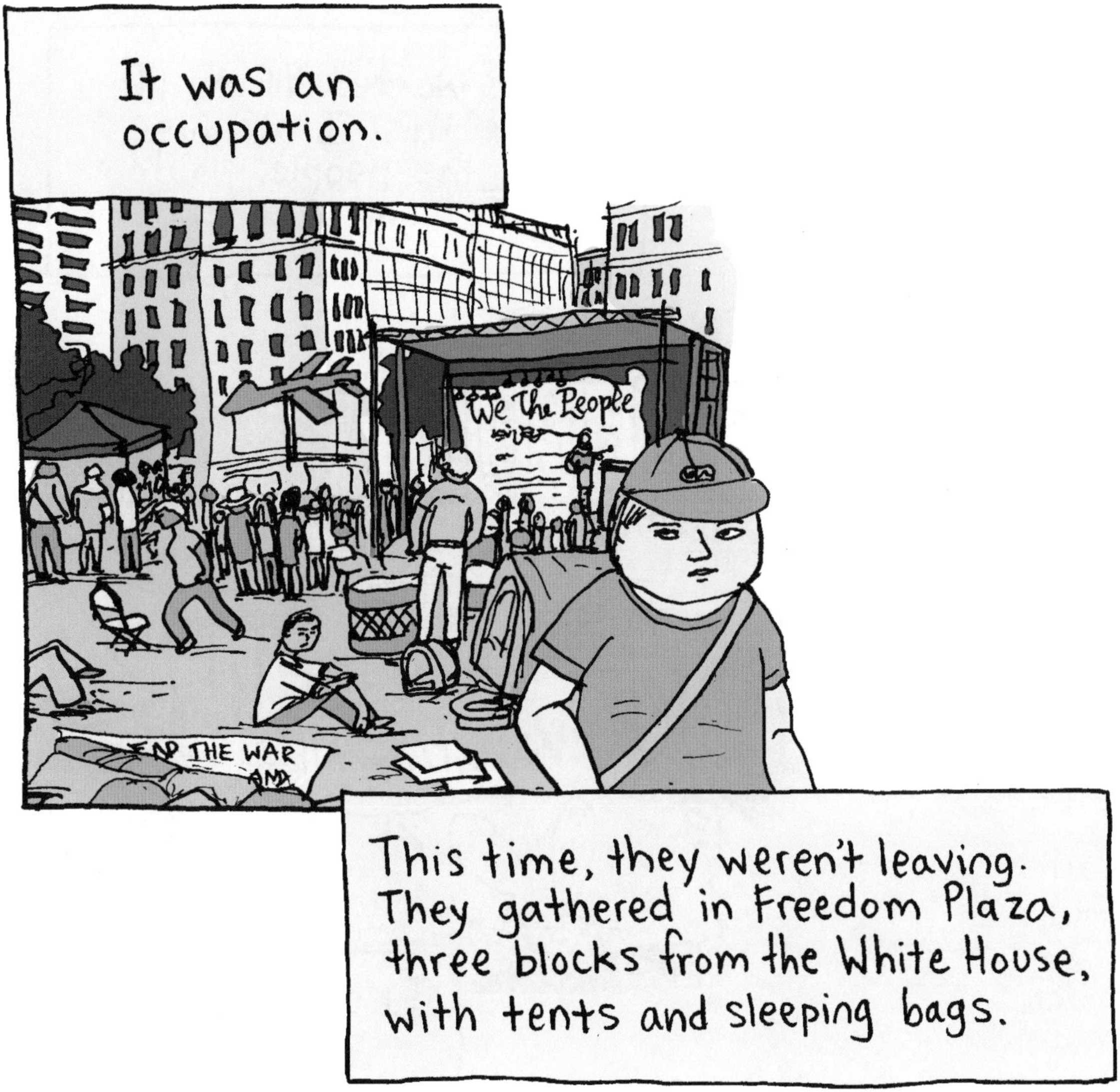
It was an occupation.
We The People
THE WAR
This time, they weren't leaving. They gathered in Freedom Plaza, three blocks from the White House, with tents and sleeping bags.

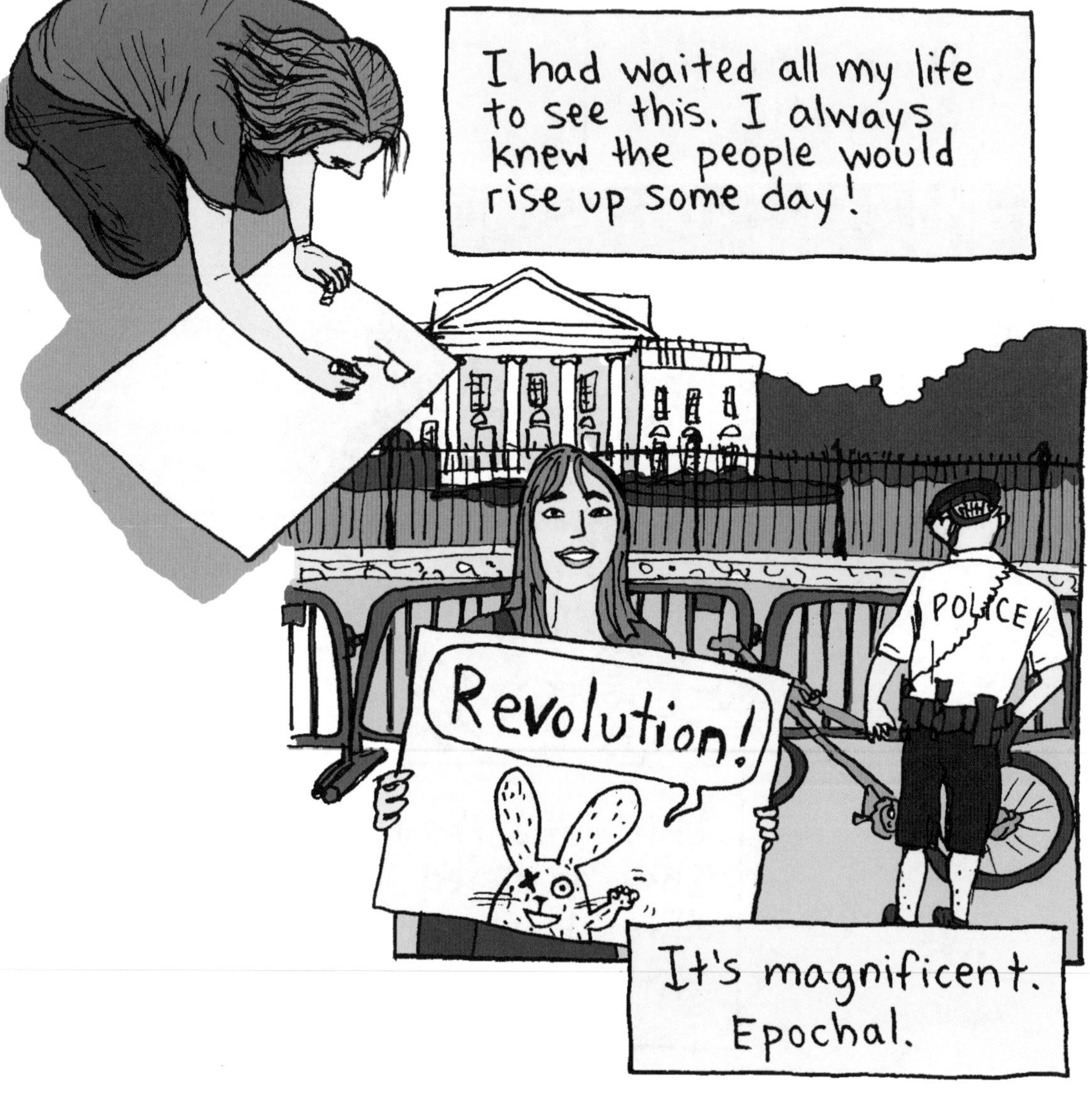
I had waited all my life to see this. I always knew the people would rise up some day!
Revolution!
POLICE
It's magnificent. Epochal.

NEW YORK. OCCUPY WALL STREET.

"Stop the Machine" had been planned since early June. In the meantime, Occupy Wall Street had materialized in lower Manhattan. Starting on September 17, it sputtered for about a week, ignored or ridiculed by mainstream media. Others wondered: would it gain traction, or melt away?

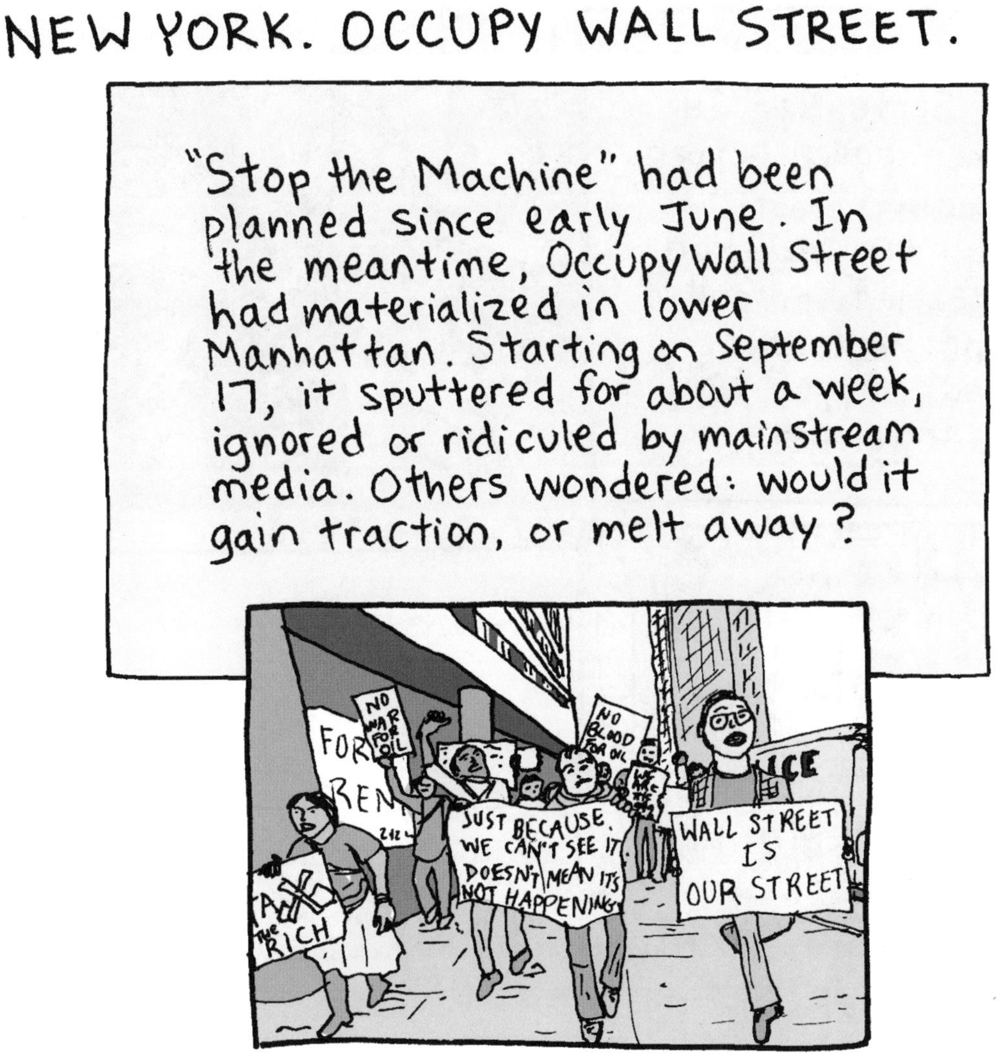
NO WAR FOR OIL
NO BLOOD FOR OIL
JUST BECAUSE WE CAN'T SEE IT DOESN'T MEAN IT'S NOT HAPPENING
WALL STREET IS OUR STREET
THE RICH

The answer came on September 24 when police pepper-sprayed four women they had "kettled," or culled from the crowd and trapped behind orange nets.

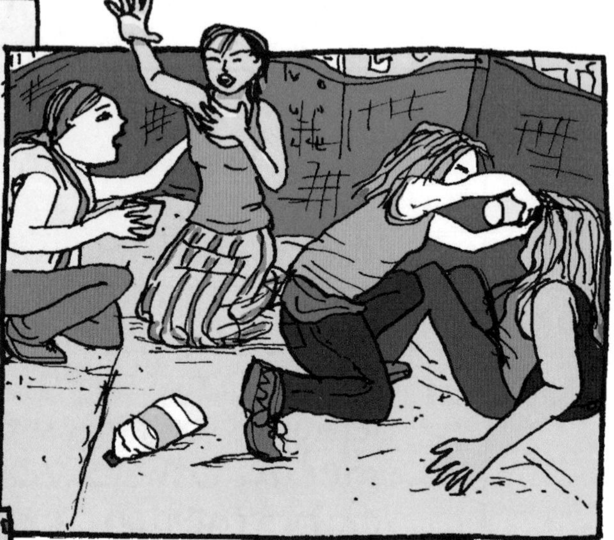

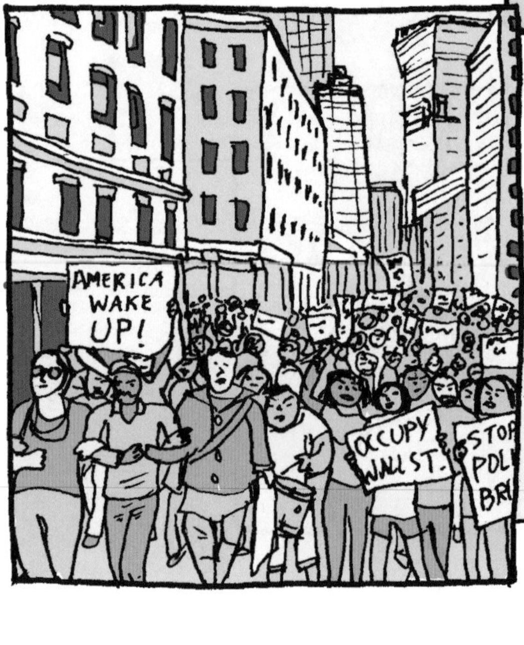
AMERICA WAKE UP!
OCCUPY WALL ST.
STOP

The number of participants surged.

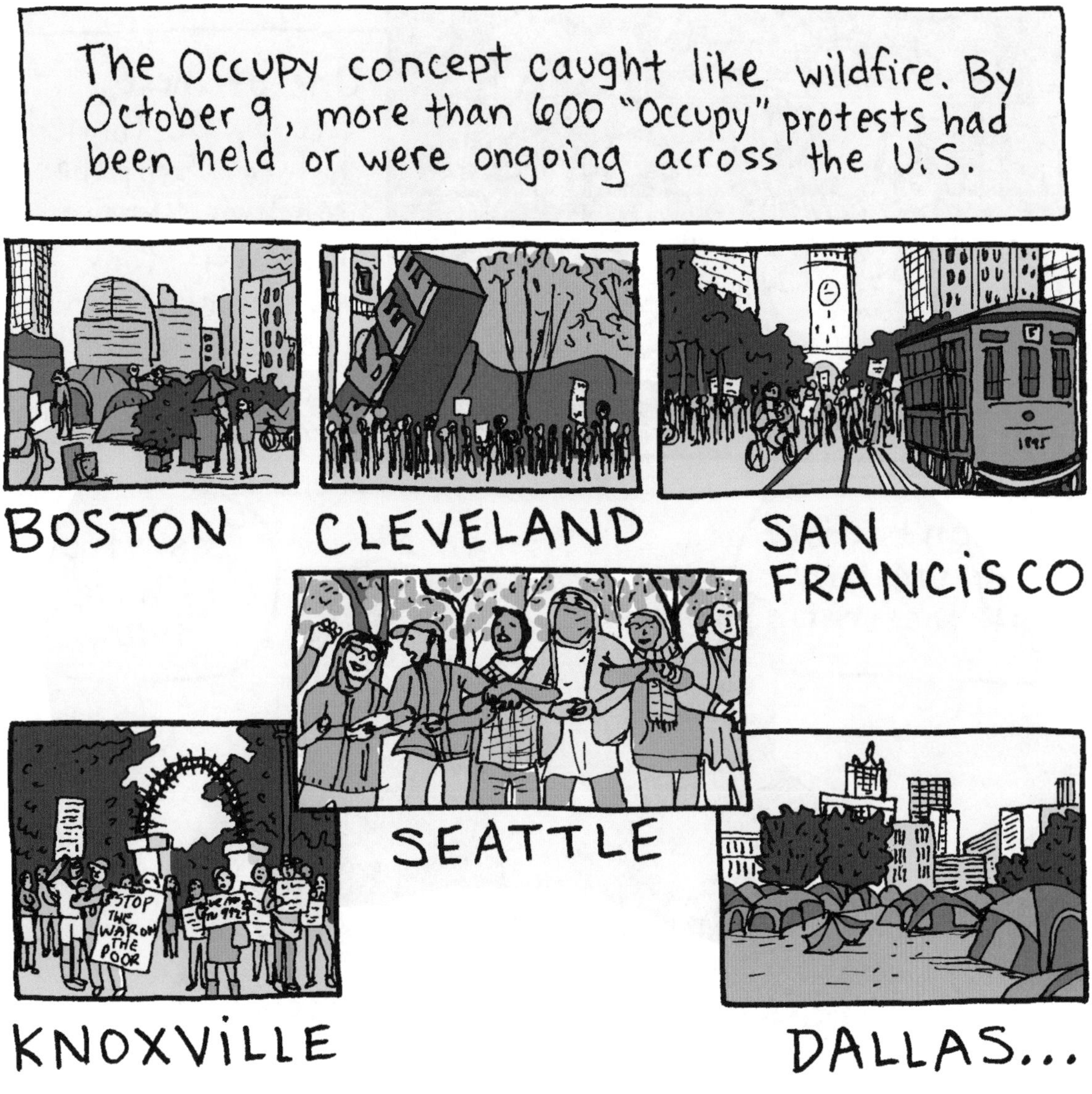
The Occupy concept caught like wildfire. By October 9, more than 600 "Occupy" protests had been held or were ongoing across the U.S.
BOSTON
CLEVELAND
SAN FRANCISCO
SEATTLE
KNOXVILLE
STOP THE WAR ON THE POOR
DALLAS...

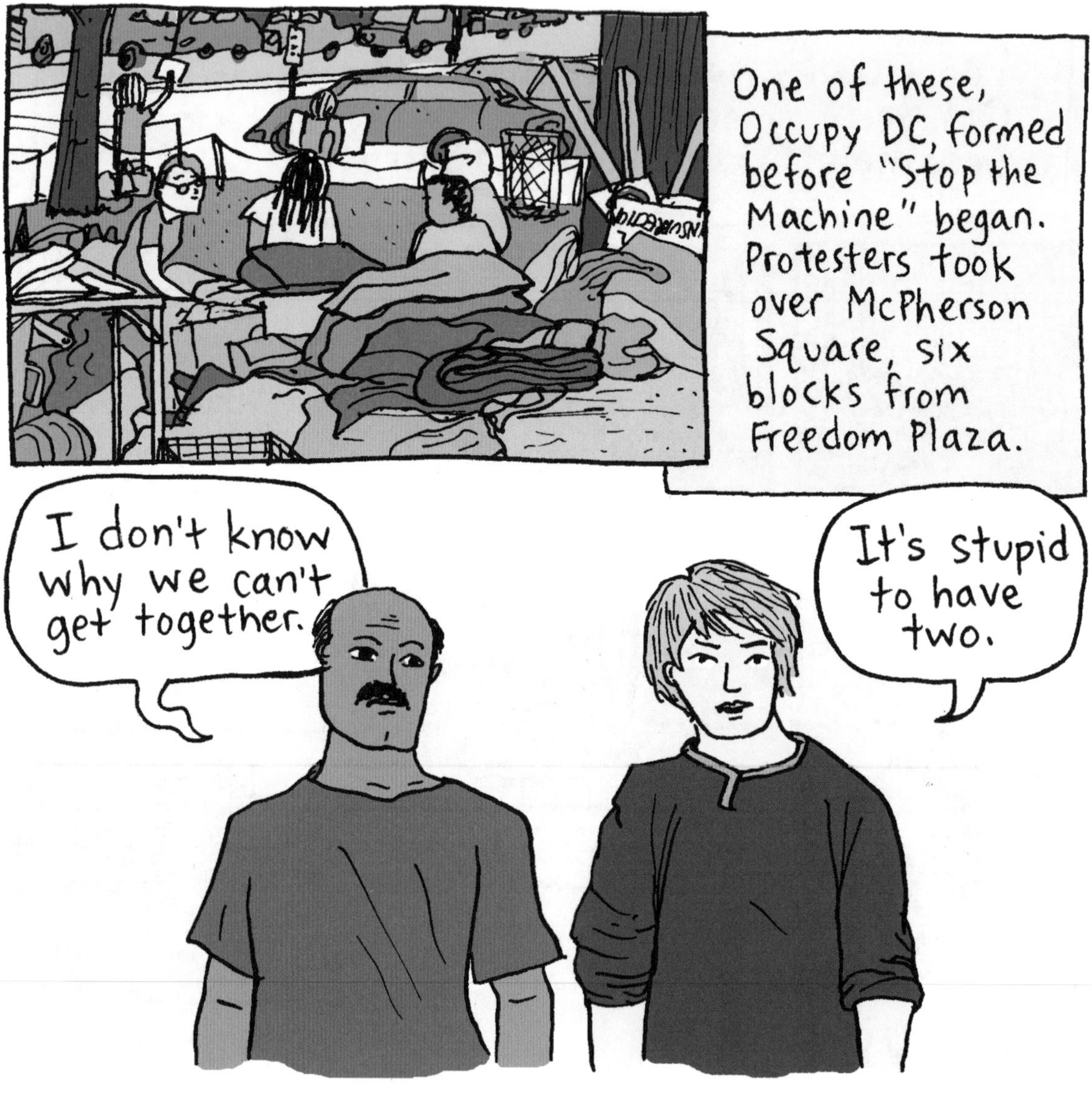
INSURRECTION
One of these, Occupy DC, formed before "Stop the Machine" began. Protesters took over McPherson Square, six blocks from Freedom Plaza.
I don't know why we can't get together.
It's stupid to have two.

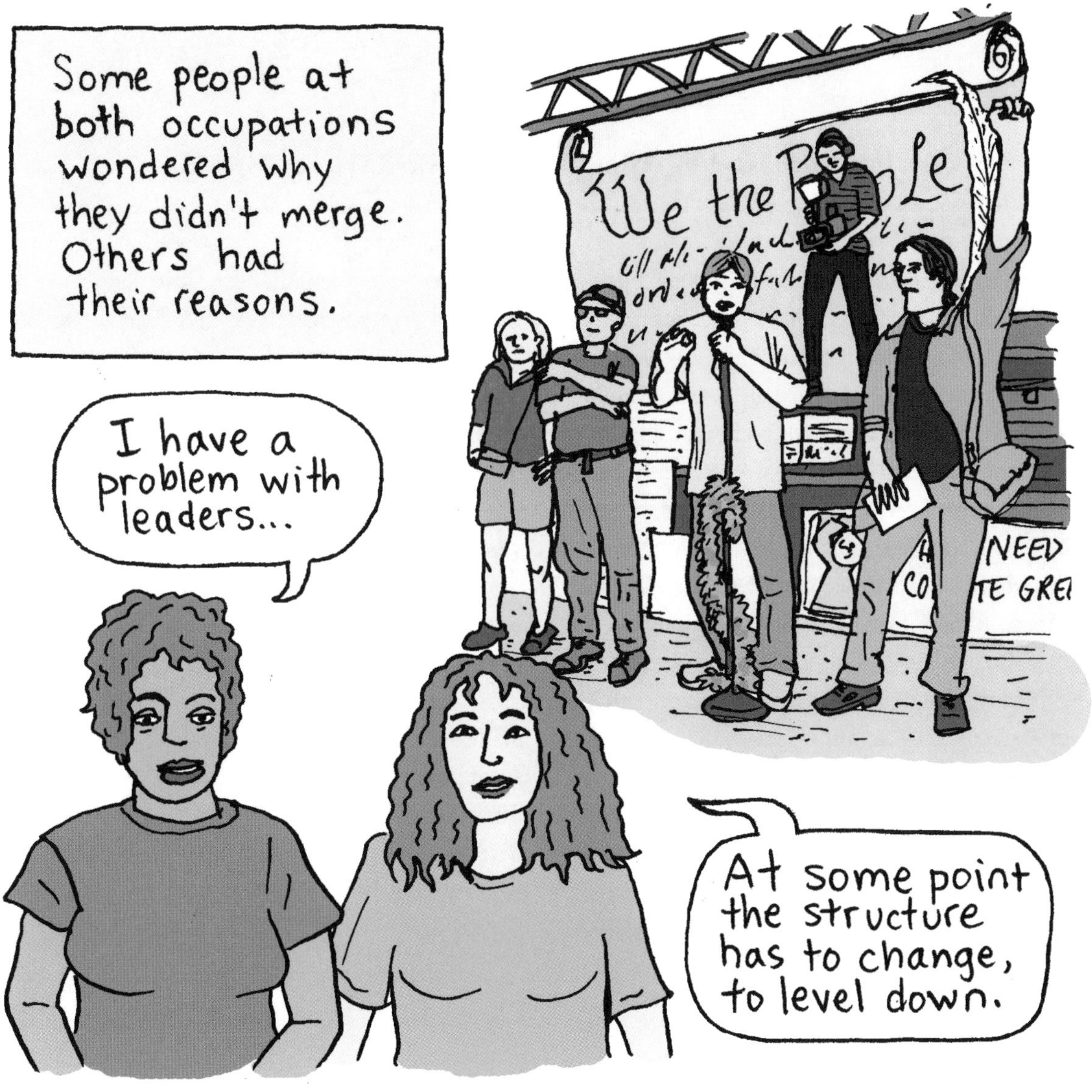
Some people at both occupations wondered why they didn't merge. Others had their reasons.
I have a problem with leaders...
At some point the structure has to change, to level down.

We Need a Whole Movement of Leaders

THE Occupy movement, heavily influenced by anarchism, insisted upon the need for non-hierarchical forms of organization. It followed that some participants were turned off by the prominence and continuing active leadership role of Stop the Machine's initial organizers. A small number of people ran the meetings, got the television interviews, and were generally looked to for answers.

But the problem in most initiatives is not that of too many leaders. Instead, usually not enough people step up to take responsibility. Leaders always emerge organically from collective activities, whether that fact is acknowledged or not. The way to avoid a problematic concentration of power or bureaucratization is to make sure each person is encouraged to participate to her or his fullest ability, and to stretch this to the maximum. We need to foster a culture where each person feels confident to speak, develops a sense of responsibility for what's happening, is equipped to help determine the movement's future direction.

Confidence comes through experience, but it also requires a friendly atmosphere where ideas are not shot down through sectarian labeling ("That's revisionist drivel!") or competition between people who value their own prestige and being right over the development of the collective. This open atmosphere is not the default mode in most groups (quite the opposite), and must be consciously cultivated.

At Stop the Machine, clearly some attempt was made to distribute responsibility, even if its method seemed like a rather mechanical (and exasperated) afterthought. A sign appeared at the media tent: "NO ONE is in charge. If you see something that needs to be done . . . do it!!"

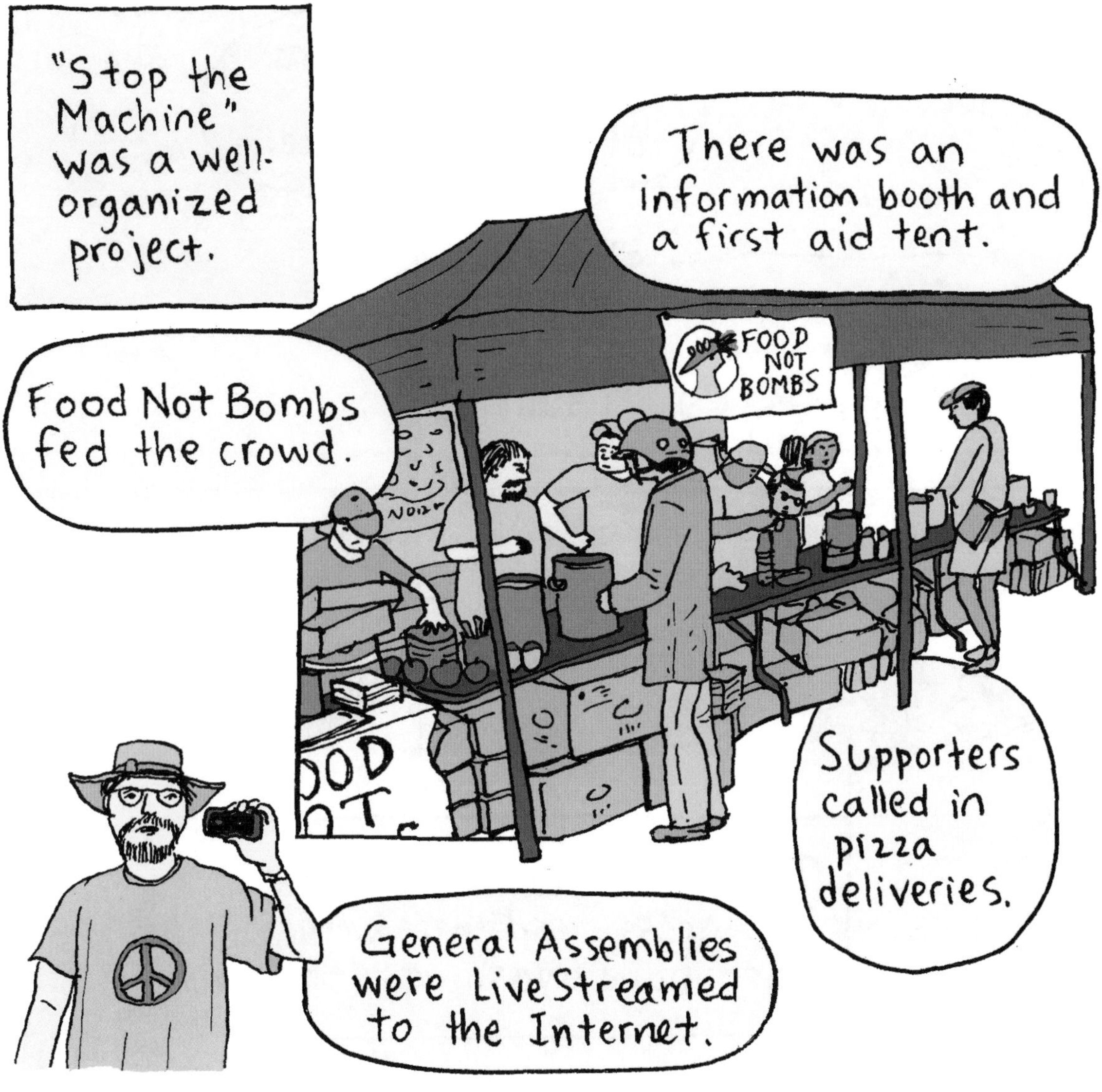
"Stop the Machine" was a well-organized project.
There was an information booth and a first aid tent.
FOOD NOT BOMBS
Food Not Bombs fed the crowd.
Supporters called in pizza deliveries.
General Assemblies were Live Streamed to the Internet.

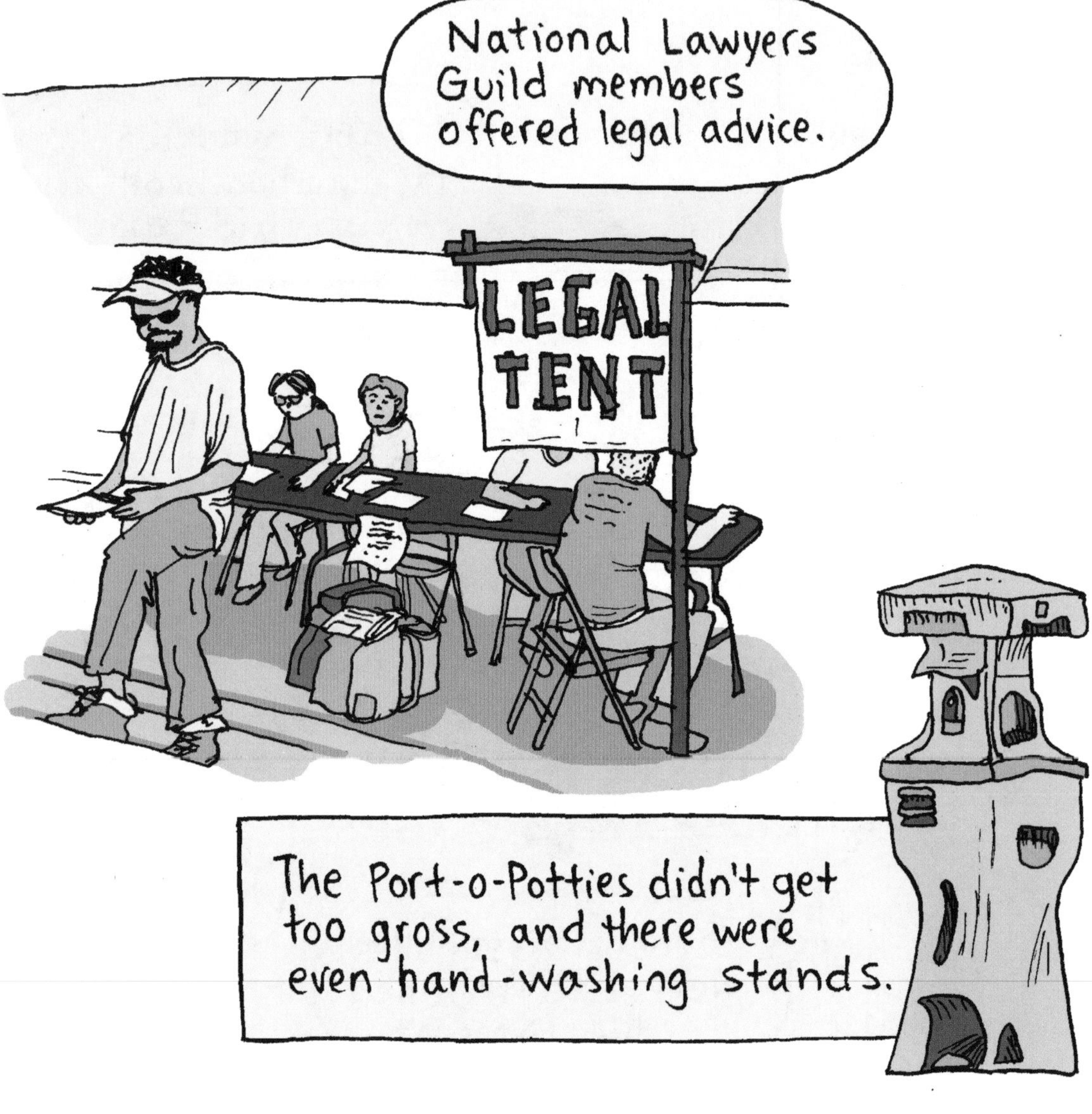
National Lawyers Guild members offered legal advice.
LEGAL TENT
The Port-o-Potties didn't get too gross, and there were even hand-washing stands.

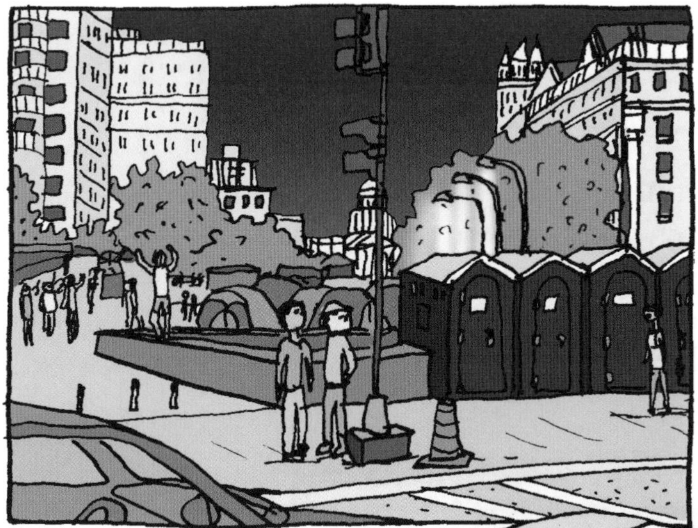

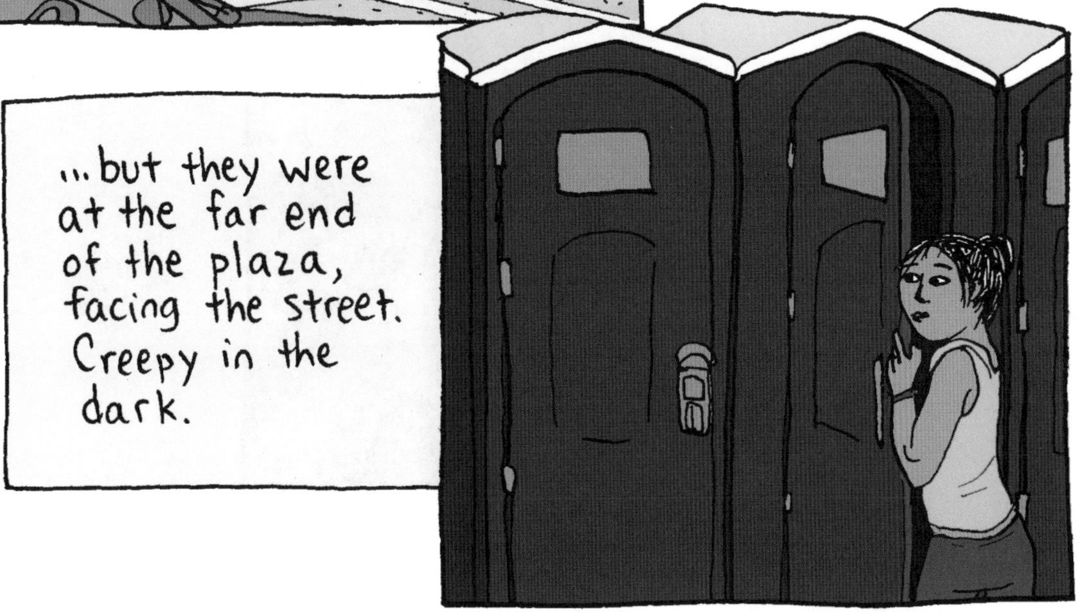
...but they were at the far end of the plaza, facing the street. Creepy in the dark.

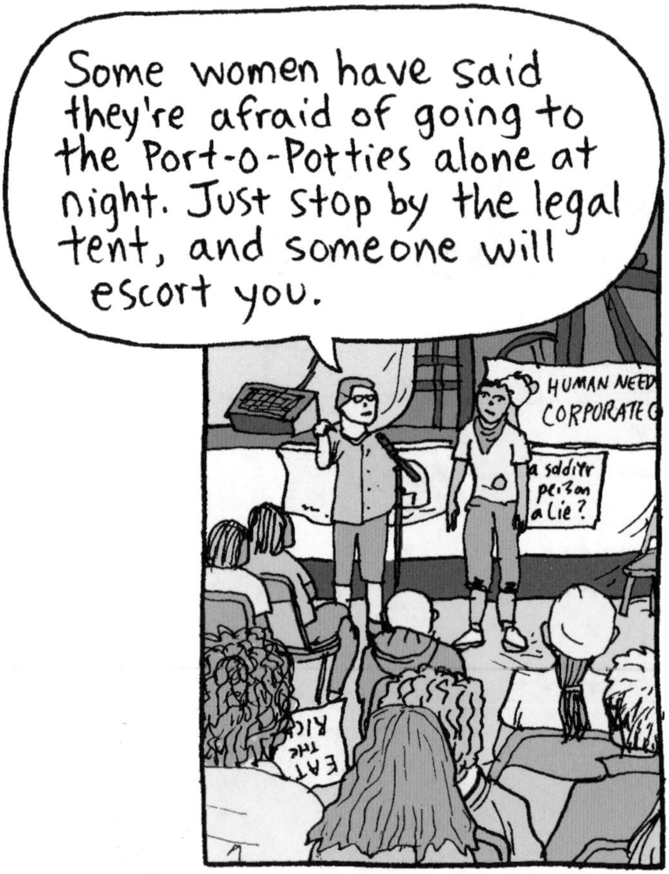
Some women have said they're afraid of going to the Port-o-Potties alone at night. Just stop by the legal tent, and someone will escort you.
HUMAN NEED
CORPORATE

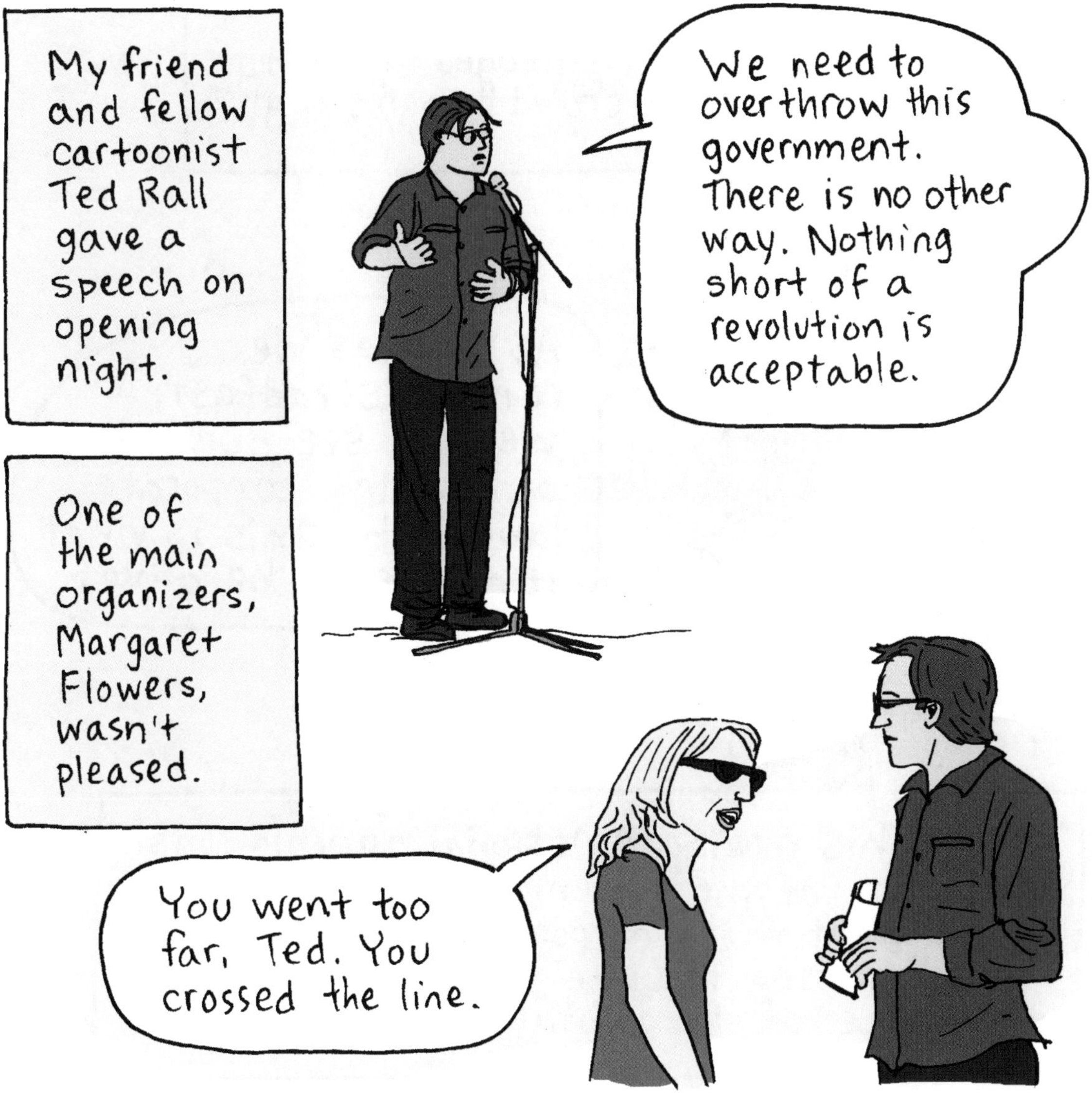
My friend and fellow cartoonist Ted Rall gave a speech on opening night.
We need to overthrow this government. There is no other way. Nothing short of a revolution is acceptable.
One of the main organizers, Margaret Flowers, wasn't pleased.
You went too far, Ted. You crossed the line.

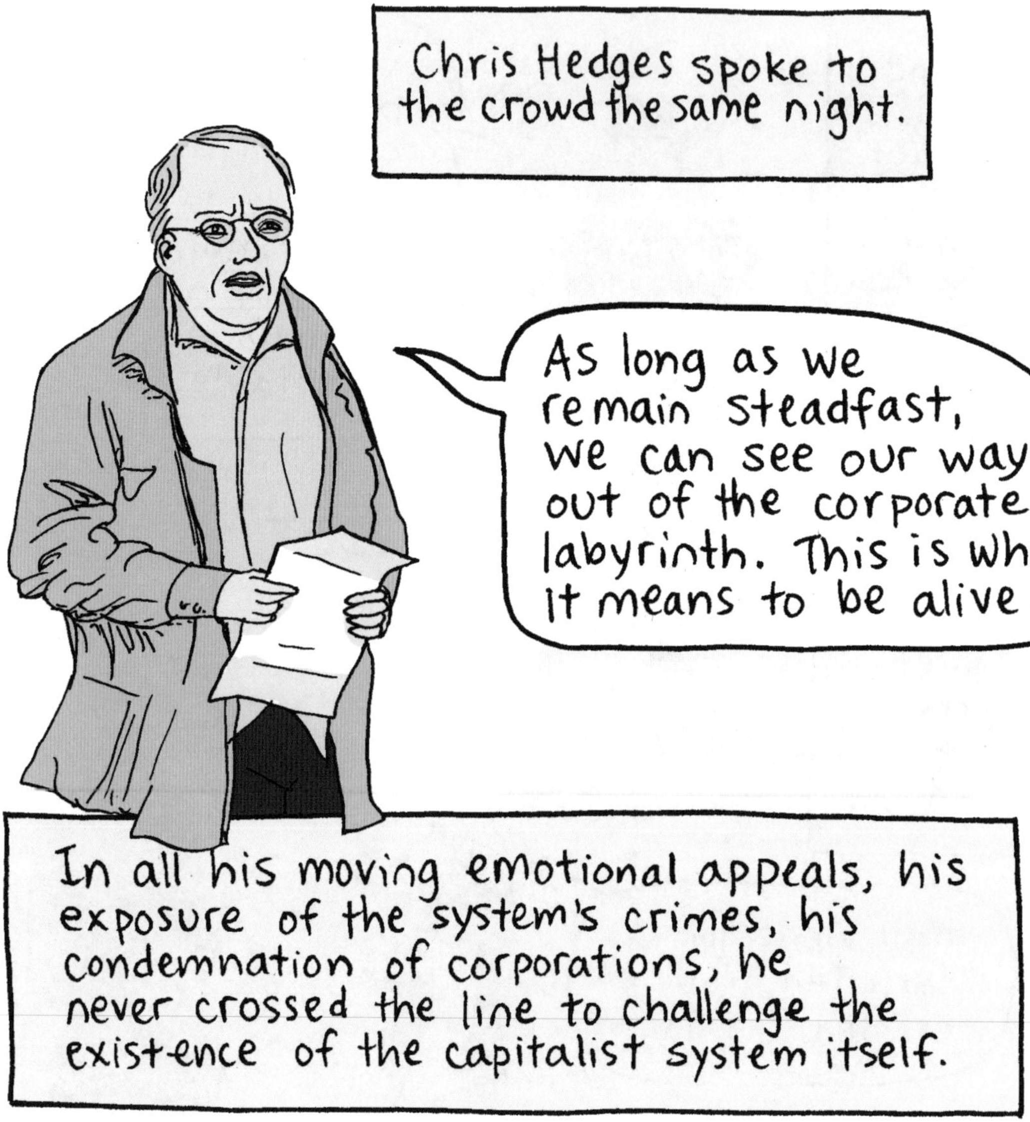

Chris Hedges spoke to the crowd the same night.
As long as we remain steadfast, we can see our way out of the corporate labyrinth. This is what it means to be alive.
In all his moving emotional appeals, his exposure of the system's crimes, his condemnation of corporations, he never crossed the line to challenge the existence of the capitalist system itself.

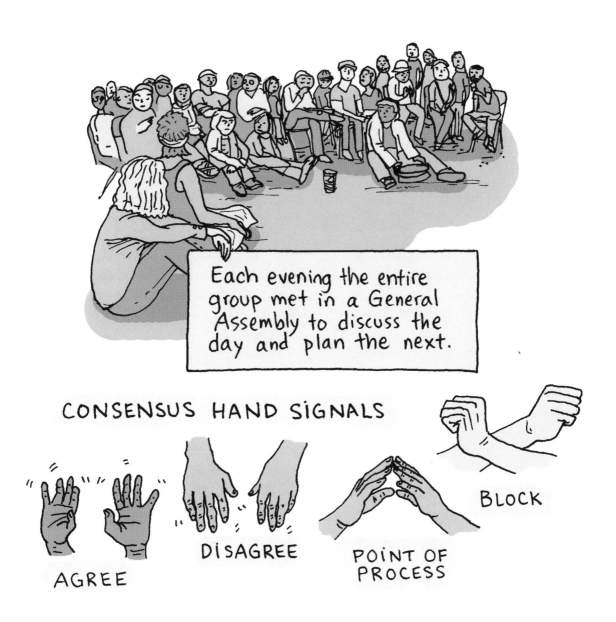

Each evening the entire group met in a General Assembly to discuss the day and plan the next.

CONSENSUS HAND SIGNALS

AGREE

DISAGREE

POINT OF PROCESS

BLOCK

The Frustrations of Consensus

GENERAL Assemblies were the organizational form for making decisions at the new encampments. These evolved from anarchist norms, employing full inclusion and consensus.

For me, having spent much of my political life working in a more structured organizational context, this was hard to get used to.

It was frustrating to sit through endless GAs listening to detailed and rambling proposals, clarifications, concerns (from the major to the trivial to the irrational), revisions and counter-proposals. It seemed terribly inefficient. I wondered how anything would possibly get done.

But as they went on, I warmed up to them. When I thought about it, I couldn't think of a better way to make sure everyone's voice was heard. Intended to pre-figure a future egalitarian and democratic society, the GAs trained people in participation. If you want to be heard, you have to participate.

I developed a real fondness for "progressive stack," a process that assists those who have been socially conditioned to be silent, and who may need more encouragement to talk. Members of oppressed groups were placed first in the speaking order, ahead of those in privileged groups and those who had already spoken. This seemed at least partly effective at preventing the "endlessly pontificating white male" syndrome (AKA "mansplaining").

The General Assembly wouldn't be appropriate for all situations or forms of organization. (Can you imagine members of a People's Army in the process of seizing an airport stopping to discuss whether or not to fire back on the enemy? "We should send a petition asking them to hold their fire . . ." "Block!") But for the purposes of making decisions in the Occupy camps, that approach, with all its limitations, probably worked as well as any other would have.

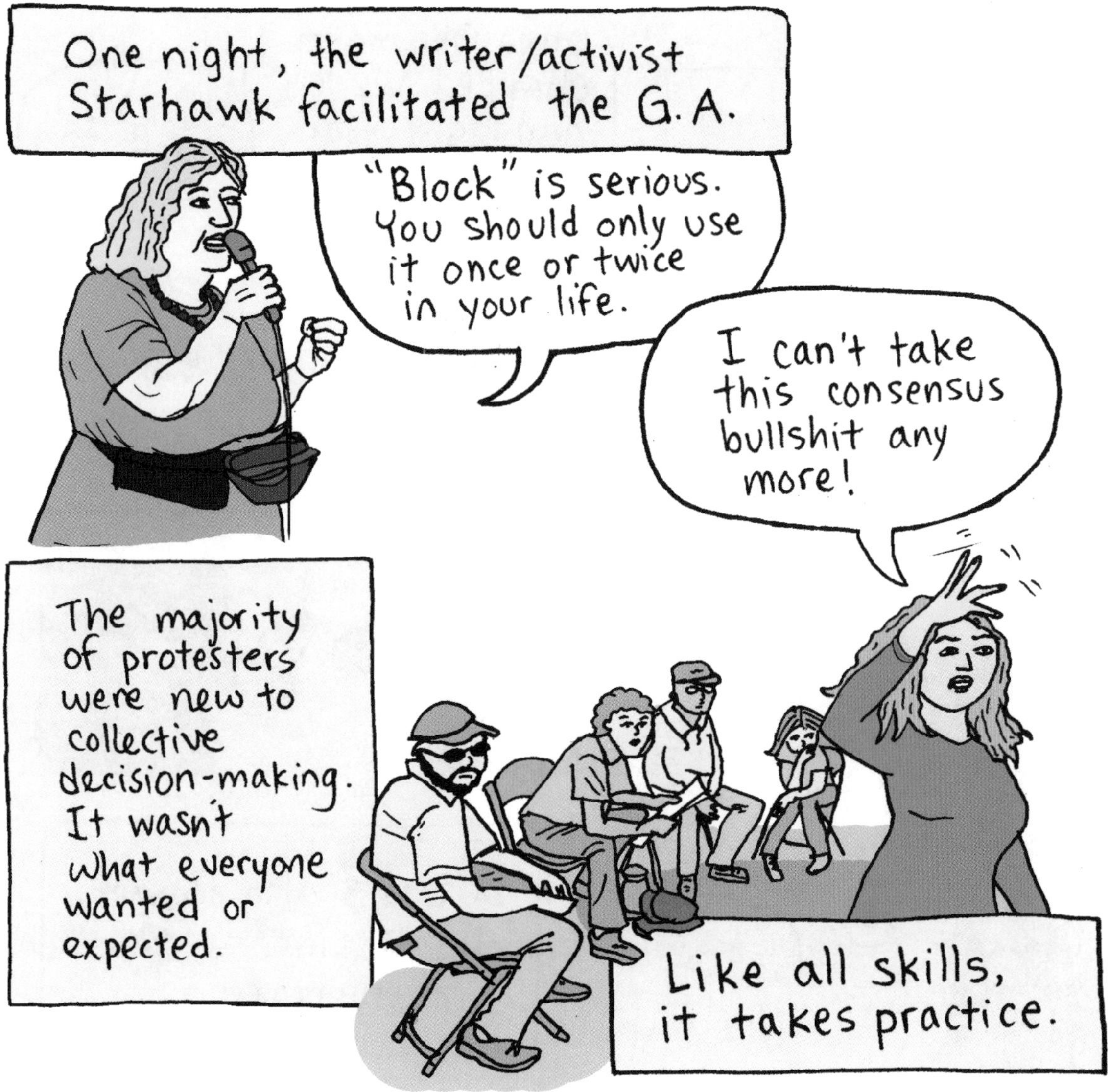
One night, the writer/activist Starhawk facilitated the G.A.
"Block" is serious. You should only use it once or twice in your life.
I can't take this consensus bullshit any more!
The majority of protesters were new to collective decision-making. It wasn't what everyone wanted or expected.
Like all skills, it takes practice.

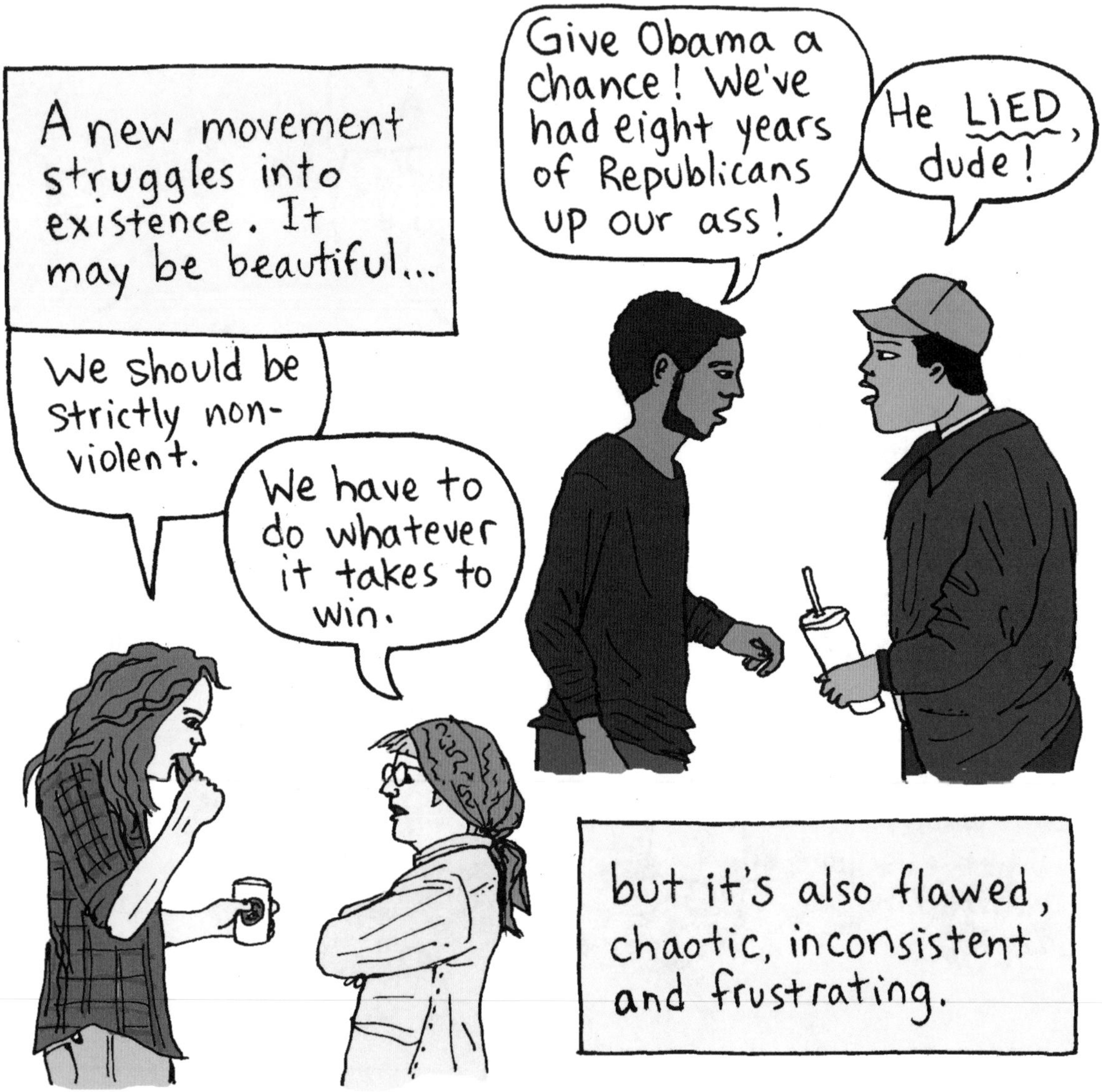
A new movement struggles into existence. It may be beautiful...
We should be strictly non-violent.
We have to do whatever it takes to win.
Give Obama a chance! We've had eight years of Republicans up our ass!
He LIED, dude!
but it's also flawed, chaotic, inconsistent and frustrating.

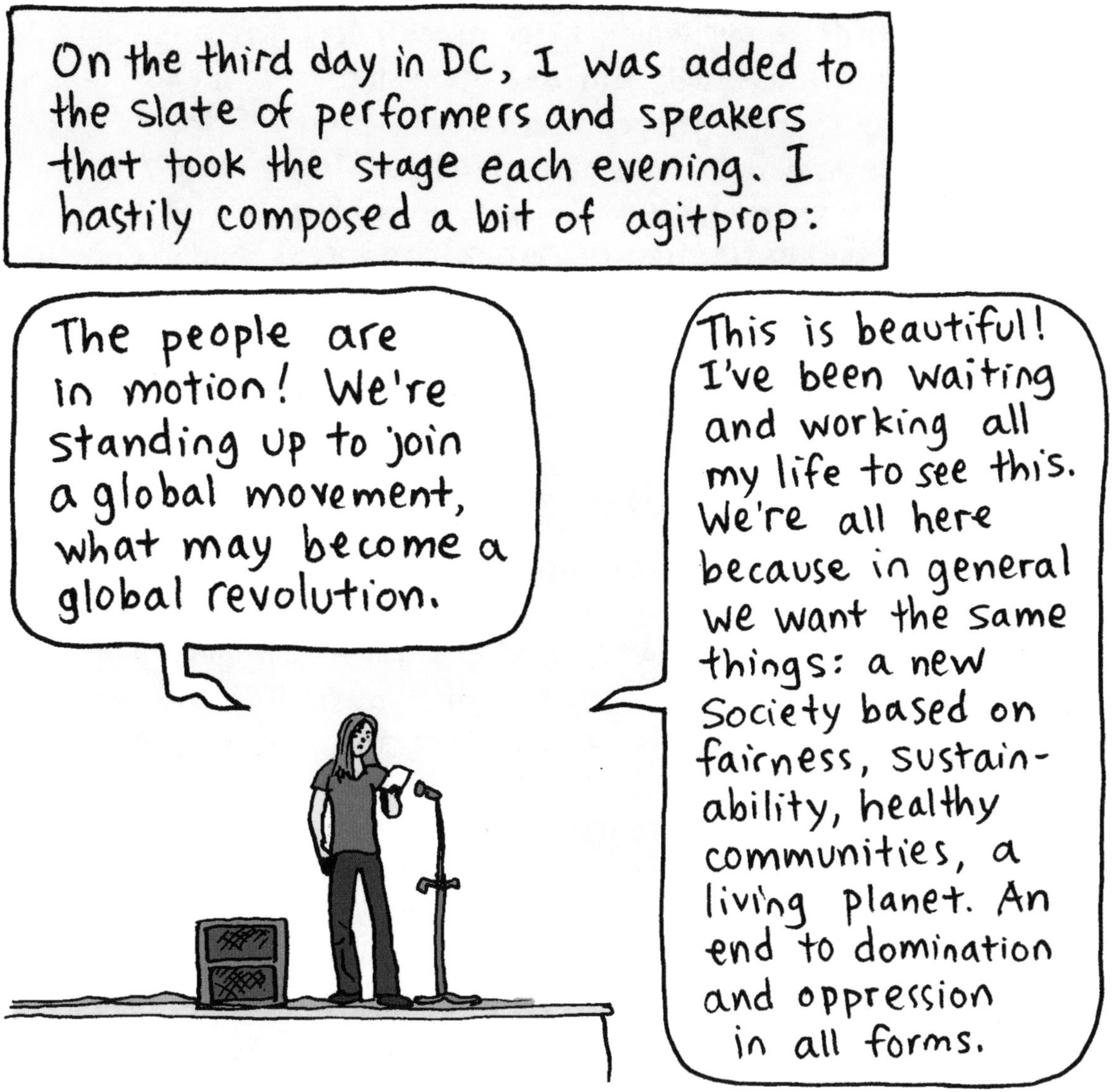
On the third day in DC, I was added to the slate of performers and speakers that took the stage each evening. I hastily composed a bit of agitprop:
The people are in motion! We're standing up to join a global movement, what may become a global revolution.
This is beautiful! I've been waiting and working all my life to see this. We're all here because in general we want the same things: a new Society based on fairness, sustain-ability, healthy communities, a living planet. An end to domination and oppression in all forms.

What stands in our way? Is it greedy corporations that have grown too big and gone too far? It's those, but it goes deeper than that. Profit is the problem. And a whole social/cultural/economic/political system based on accumulating profit, through the extraction of natural resources and the exploitation of labor.

We have an enemy. I'll go ahead and name it: global capitalism.

Capitalism is not a thing, but a process: the conversion of life into commodities into toxic waste.

It's also a social relation, where a small minority owns and controls our means of subsistence and uses this to dominate and exploit the majority of people and the world. Those in power start out by seizing land and destroying traditional land-based and indigenous communities. They push people into labor camps (commonly known as cities), and make them work for food and shelter. Would anyone consent to work in a factory or mine if they had any other way to survive? Would you? I wouldn't.

Capitalism is based on constant expansion, on ever-increasing rates of private accumulation. This means it's structurally unreformable. The nicest capitalist in the world might want to change that, but wouldn't be able to. They must make profit or go out of business.

Global capitalism is in deep crisis. It's played out. Many expect it to collapse. But the truth is, it won't. It's dynamic and adaptable. It could morph into fascism or neo-feudalism. But it will use up everything and keep going until all life on the planet is extinguished.

I don't know about you, but for me that's too late.

We must eliminate it. It's our responsibility. We may be the last generation with the opportunity to do so.

With this action, with this movement, I'm starting to believe it's possible.

I hope to see this grow into a radical mass movement that can unite all who can be united to fight the system, our common enemy. A diverse, non-sectarian movement, mutually supportive, and above all visionary and fearless.

We don't know what's going to happen or what this will become. But we have to keep it going, keep moving hand-in-hand to wherever the demands of our situation may lead us.

Sure, we're chaotic, flawed, unpredictable. This may not be exactly what each of us wants or thinks we need. But the important thing is that we're MOVING. We've woken up. We're challenging the system.

Capitalists, we're coming for you!

Imperialists and war-mongers, we're coming for you!

Exploiters and oppressors, we're coming for you!

Ecocidal maniacs and corporate bloodsuckers, we're coming for you!

We'll fight you, and we'll fight you, and we'll make mistakes along the way, and we'll falter. But we'll keep getting up and we'll fight again, and fight again, and one day we are going to win.

To my relief, the audience responded with enthusiasm.

But not everyone agrees on the most effective ways to go up against the system.

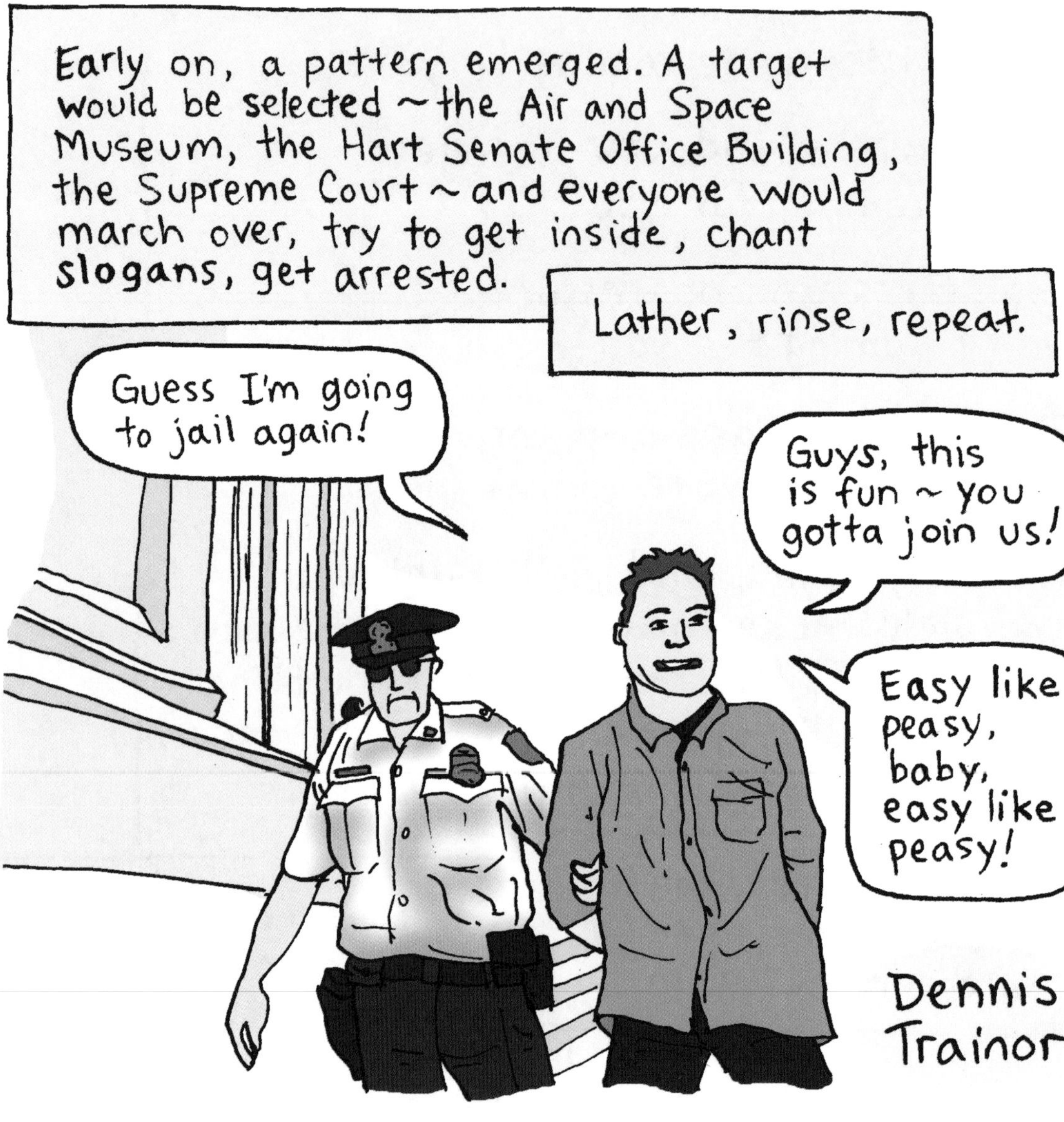
Early on, a pattern emerged. A target would be selected ~ the Air and Space Museum, the Hart Senate Office Building, the Supreme Court ~ and everyone would march over, try to get inside, chant slogans, get arrested.
Lather, rinse, repeat.
Guess I'm going to jail again!
Guys, this is fun ~ you gotta join us!
Easy like peasy, baby, easy like peasy!
Dennis Trainor

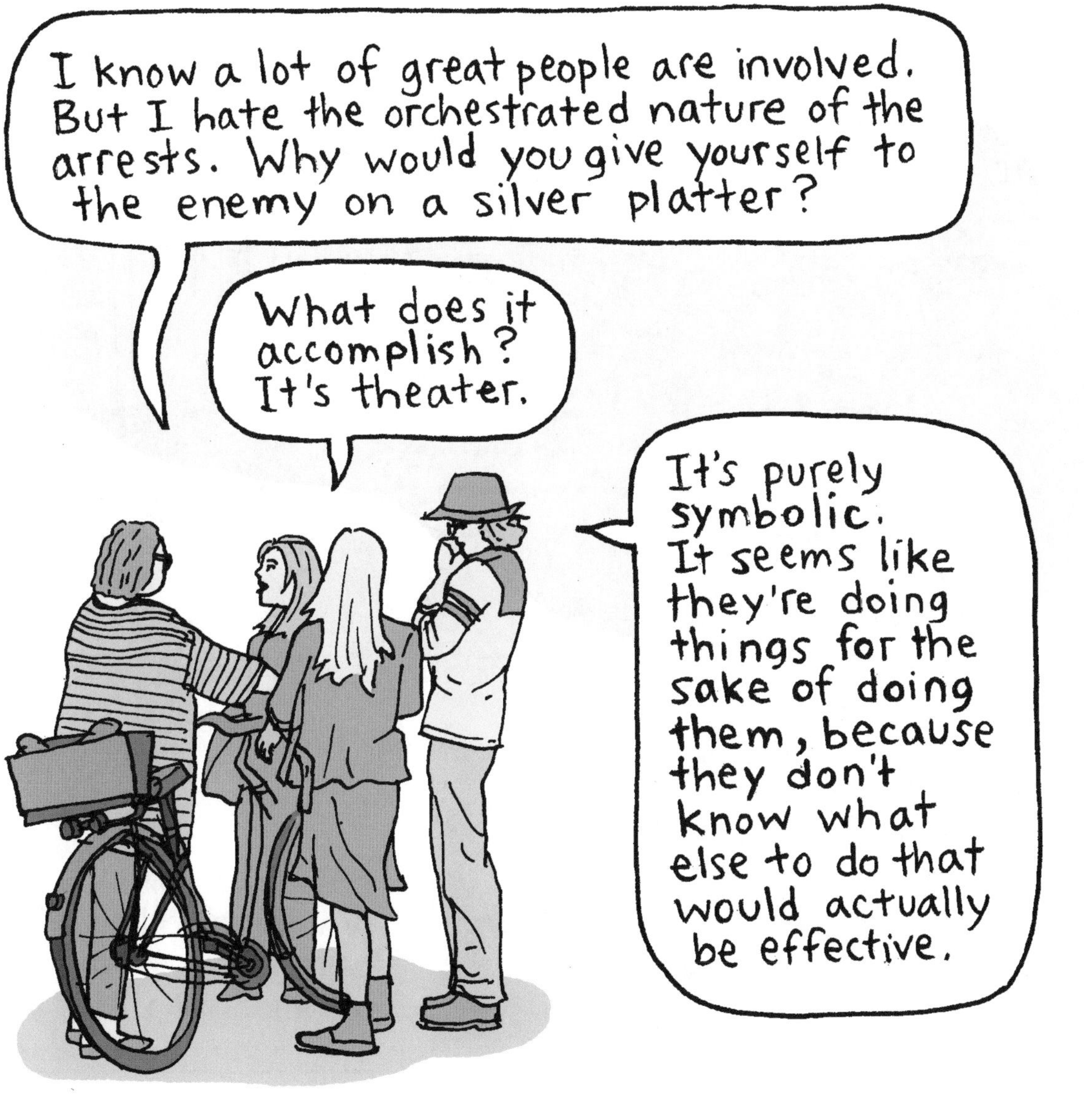
I know a lot of great people are involved. But I hate the orchestrated nature of the arrests. Why would you give yourself to the enemy on a silver platter?
What does it accomplish? It's theater.
It's purely symbolic. It seems like they're doing things for the sake of doing them, because they don't know what else to do that would actually be effective.

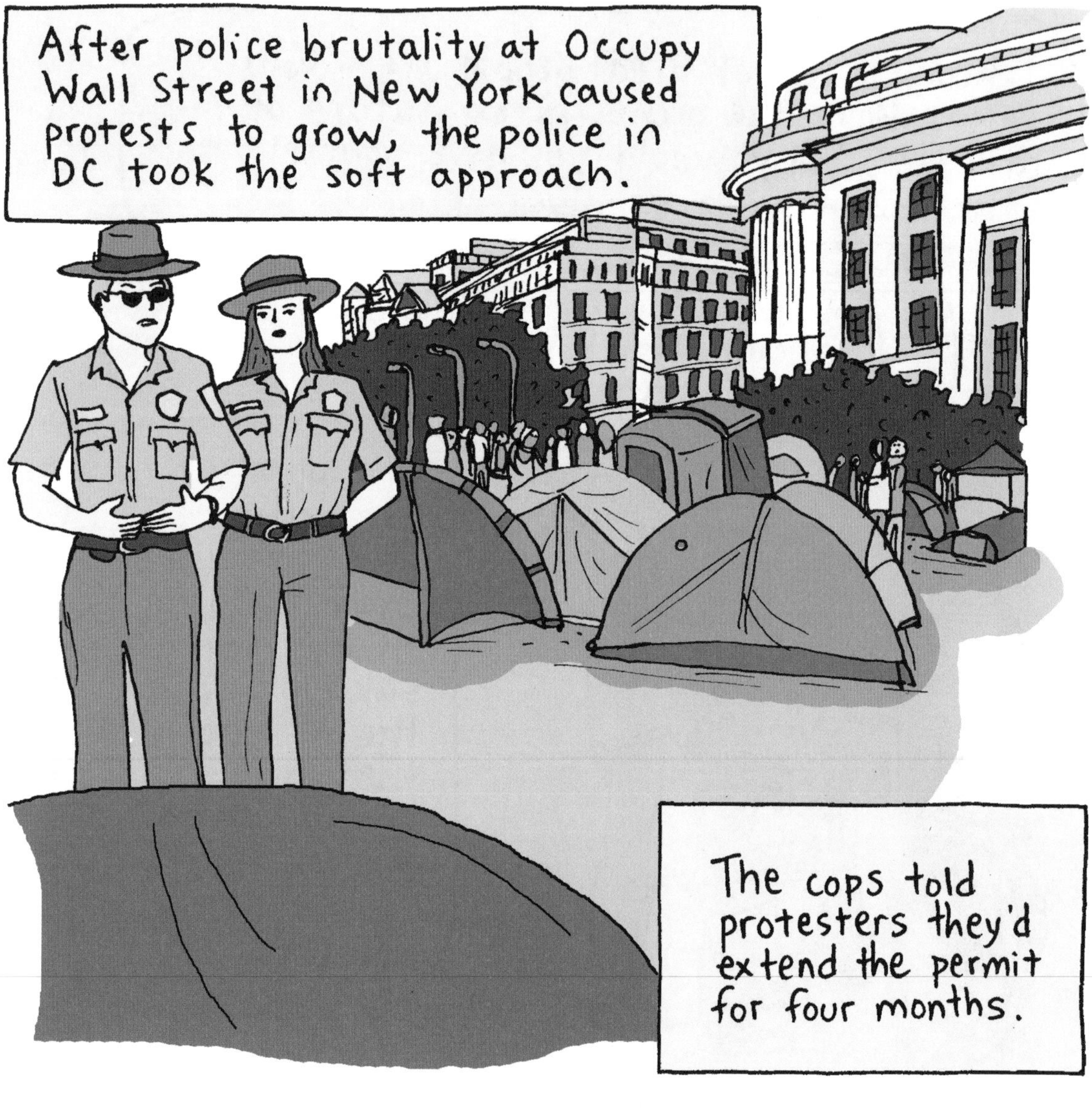
After police brutality at Occupy Wall Street in New York caused protests to grow, the police in DC took the soft approach.
The cops told protesters they'd extend the permit for four months.

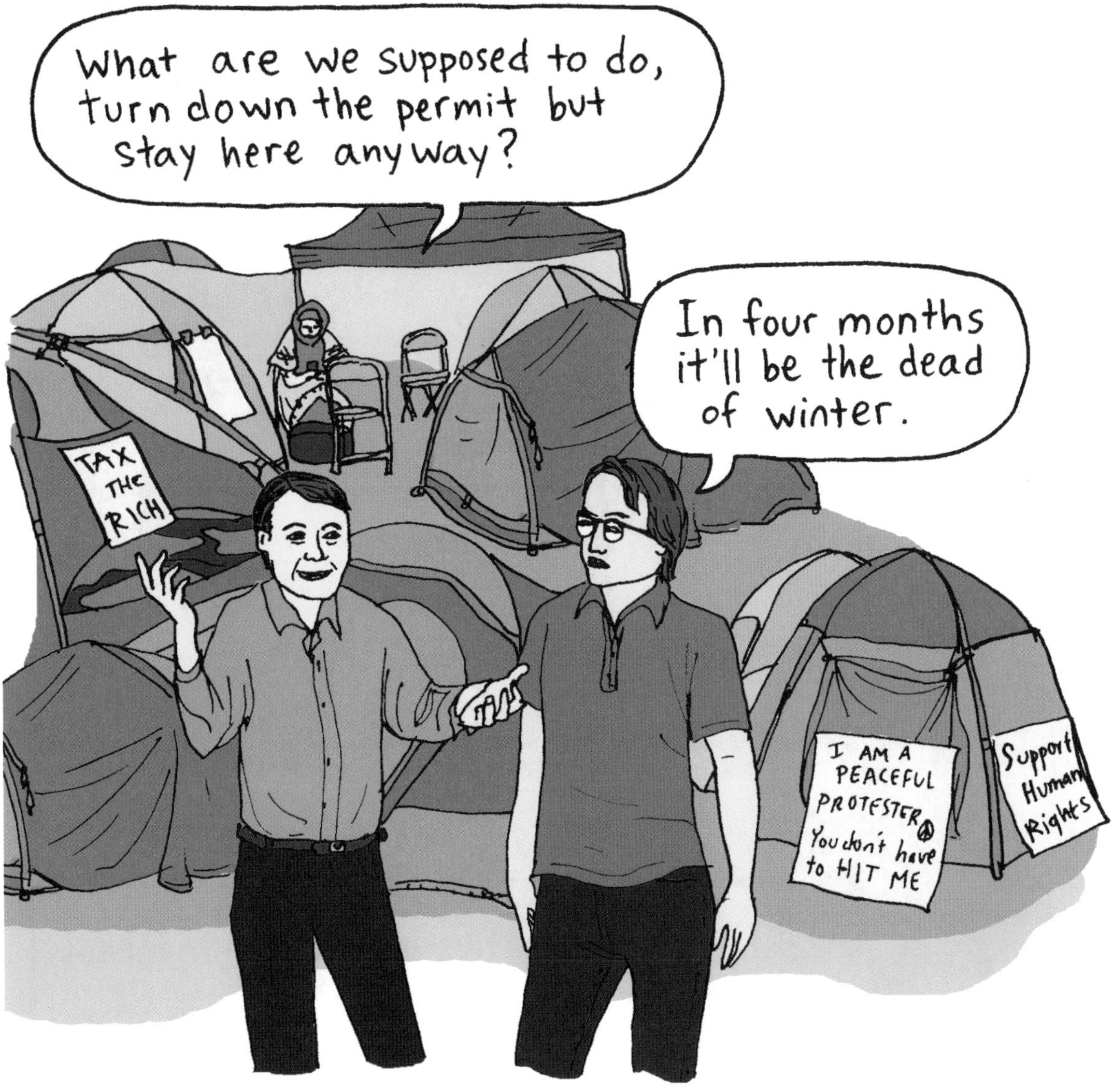
What are we supposed to do, turn down the permit but stay here anyway?
In four months it'll be the dead of winter.
TAX THE RICH
I AM A PEACEFUL PROTESTER You don't have to HIT ME
Support Human Rights

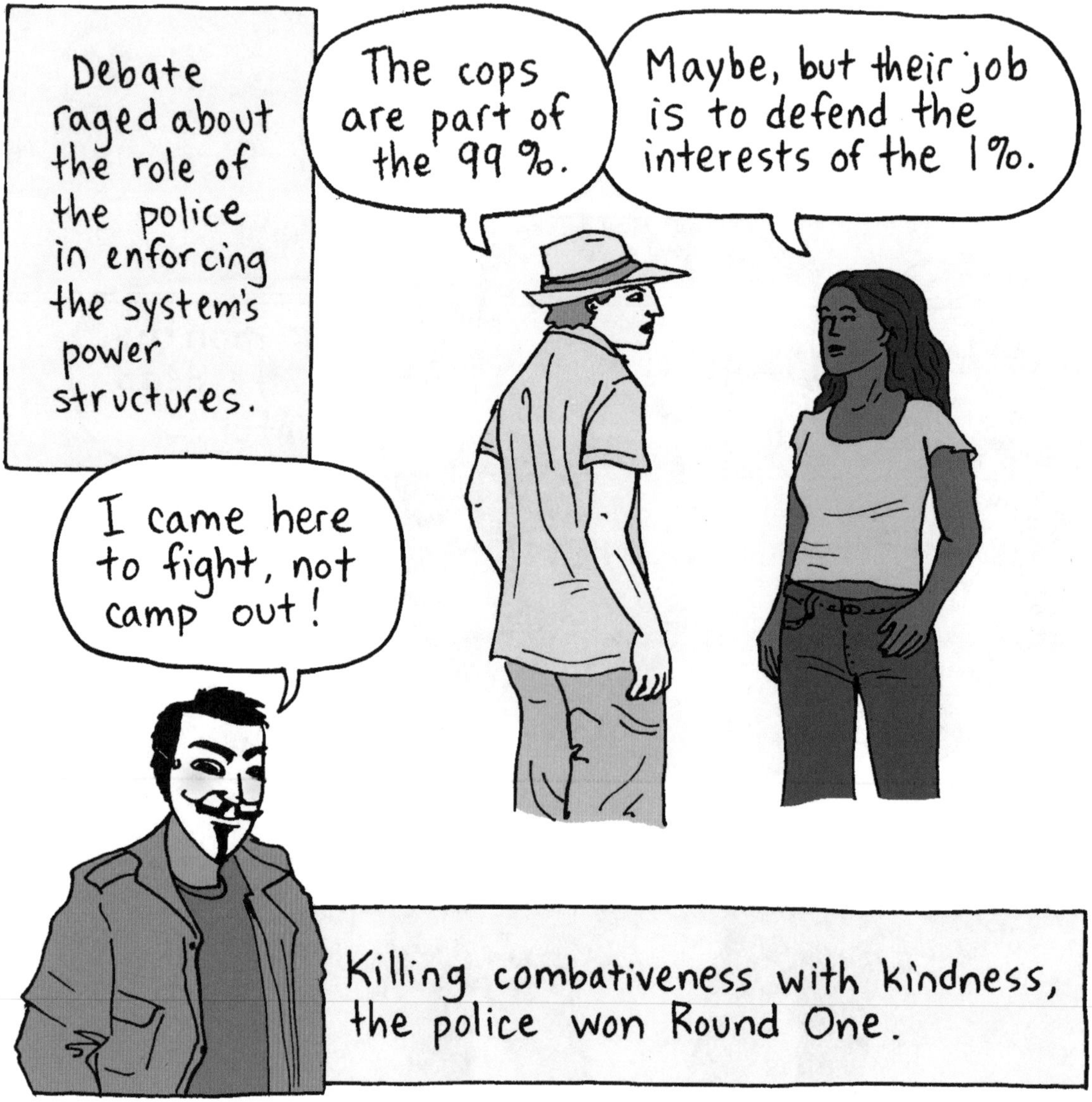
Debate raged about the role of the police in enforcing the system's power structures.
The cops are part of the 99%.
Maybe, but their job is to defend the interests of the 1%.
I came here to fight, not camp out!
Killing combativeness with kindness, the police won Round One.

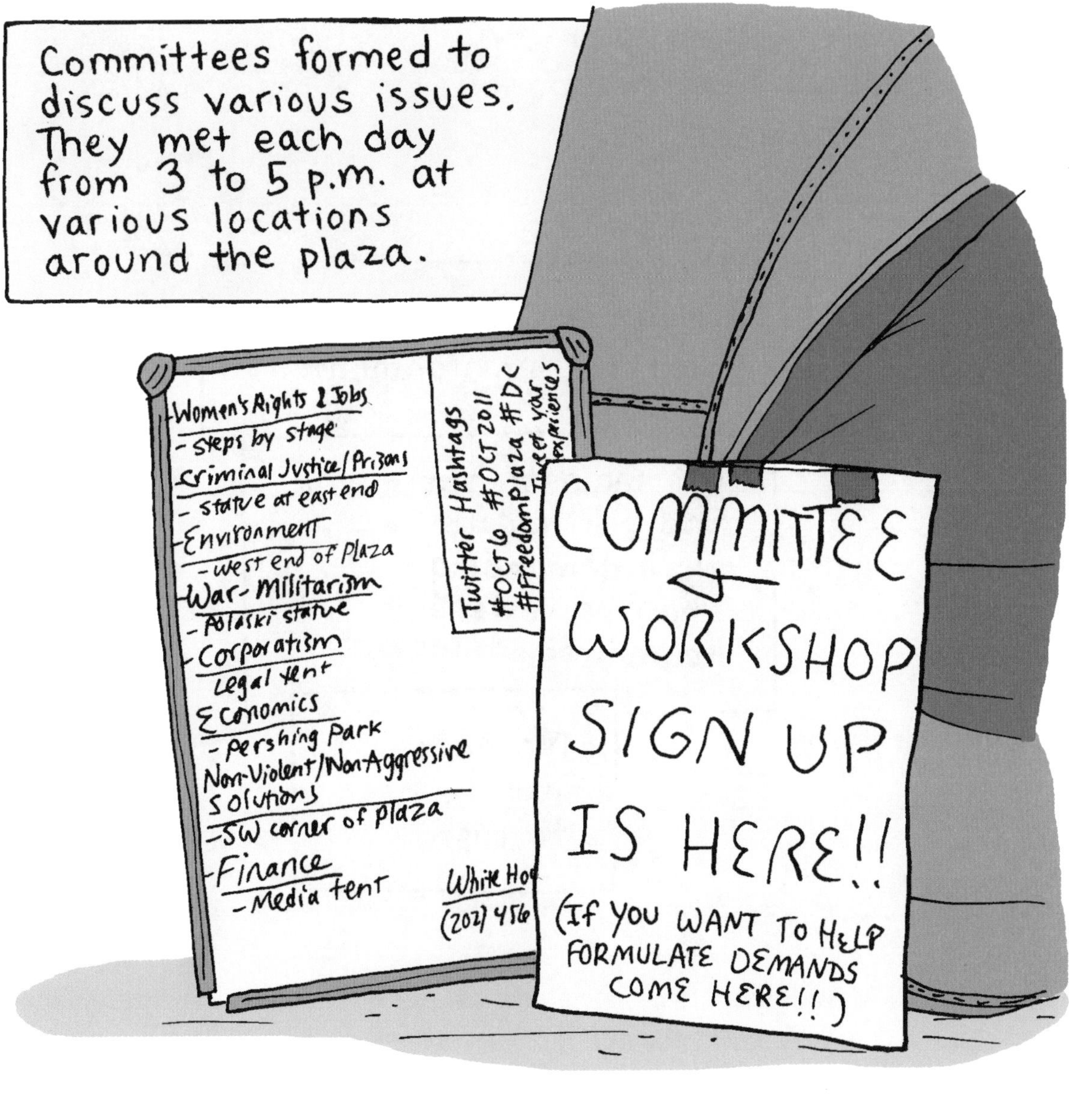
Committees formed to discuss various issues. They met each day from 3 to 5 p.m. at various locations around the plaza.
Women's Rights & Jobs
- steps by stage
Criminal Justice/Prisons
- statue at east end
Environment
- west end of Plaza
War-Militarism
- Polaski statue
Corporatism
Legal tent
Economics
- Pershing Park
Non-Violent/Non Aggressive Solutions
- SW corner of plaza
Finance
- Media tent
Twitter Hashtags
#OCT6 #OCT2011
#FreedomPlaza #DC
Tweet your experiences
COMMITTEE WORKSHOP SIGN UP IS HERE!!
(IF YOU WANT TO HELP FORMULATE DEMANDS COME HERE!!)

I joined a committee about the environment.

The mainstream media and politicians were demanding that protesters formulate demands.

No one saw the need to rush.

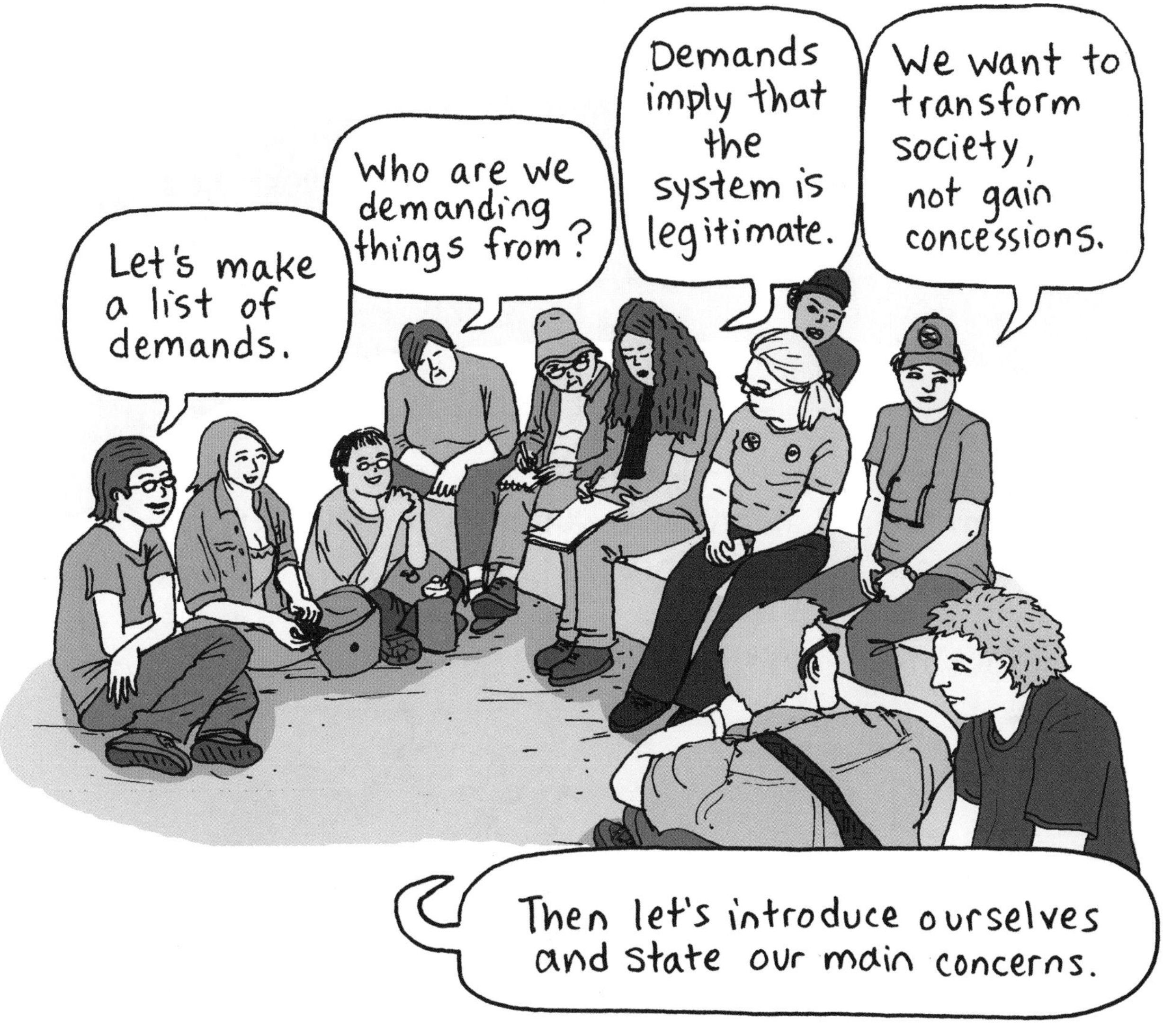
Let's make a list of demands.
Who are we demanding things from?
Demands imply that the system is legitimate.
We want to transform society, not gain concessions.
Then let's introduce ourselves and state our main concerns.

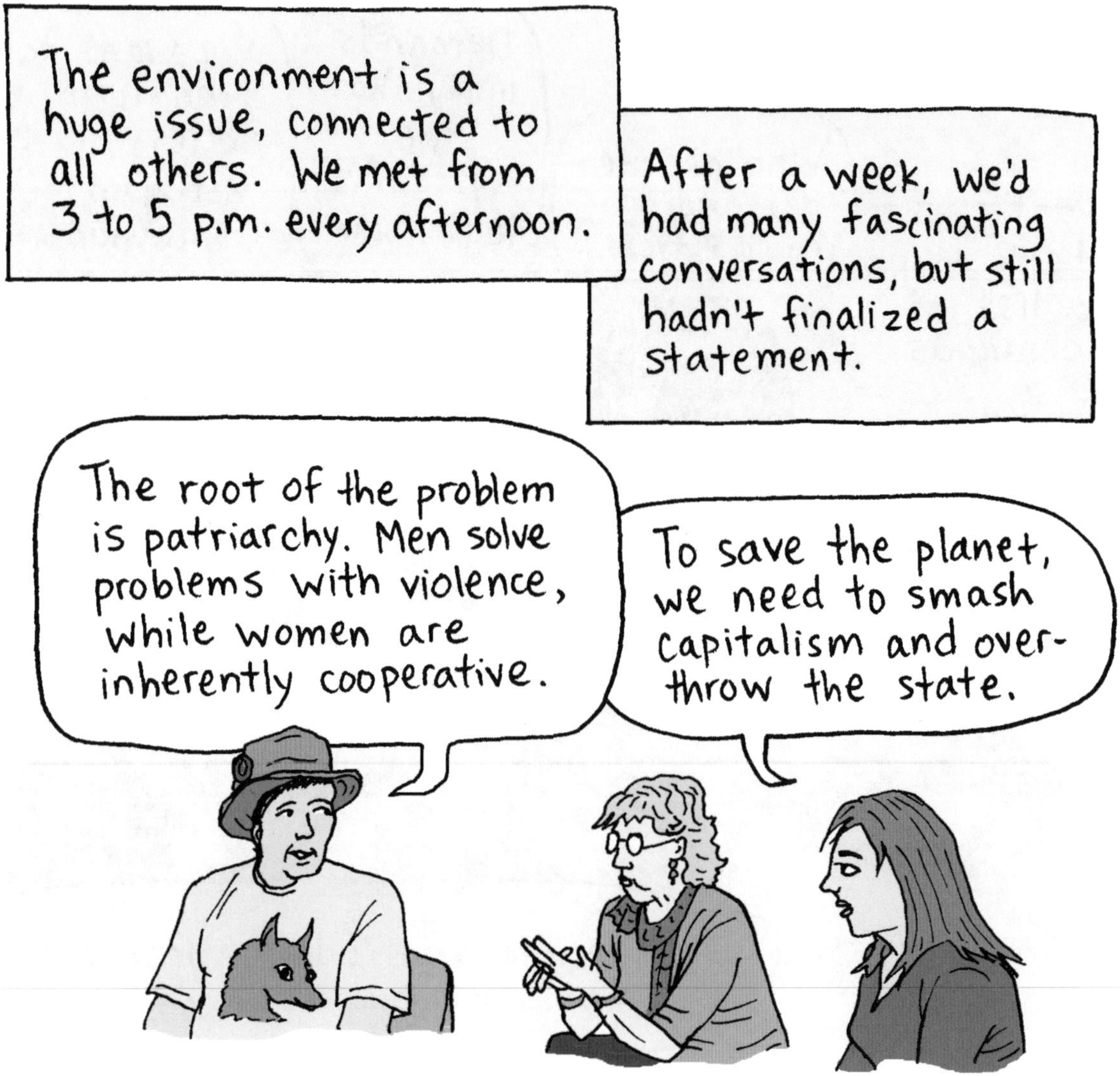
The environment is a huge issue, connected to all others. We met from 3 to 5 p.m. every afternoon.
After a week, we'd had many fascinating conversations, but still hadn't finalized a statement.
The root of the problem is patriarchy. Men solve problems with violence, while women are inherently cooperative.
To save the planet, we need to smash capitalism and overthrow the state.

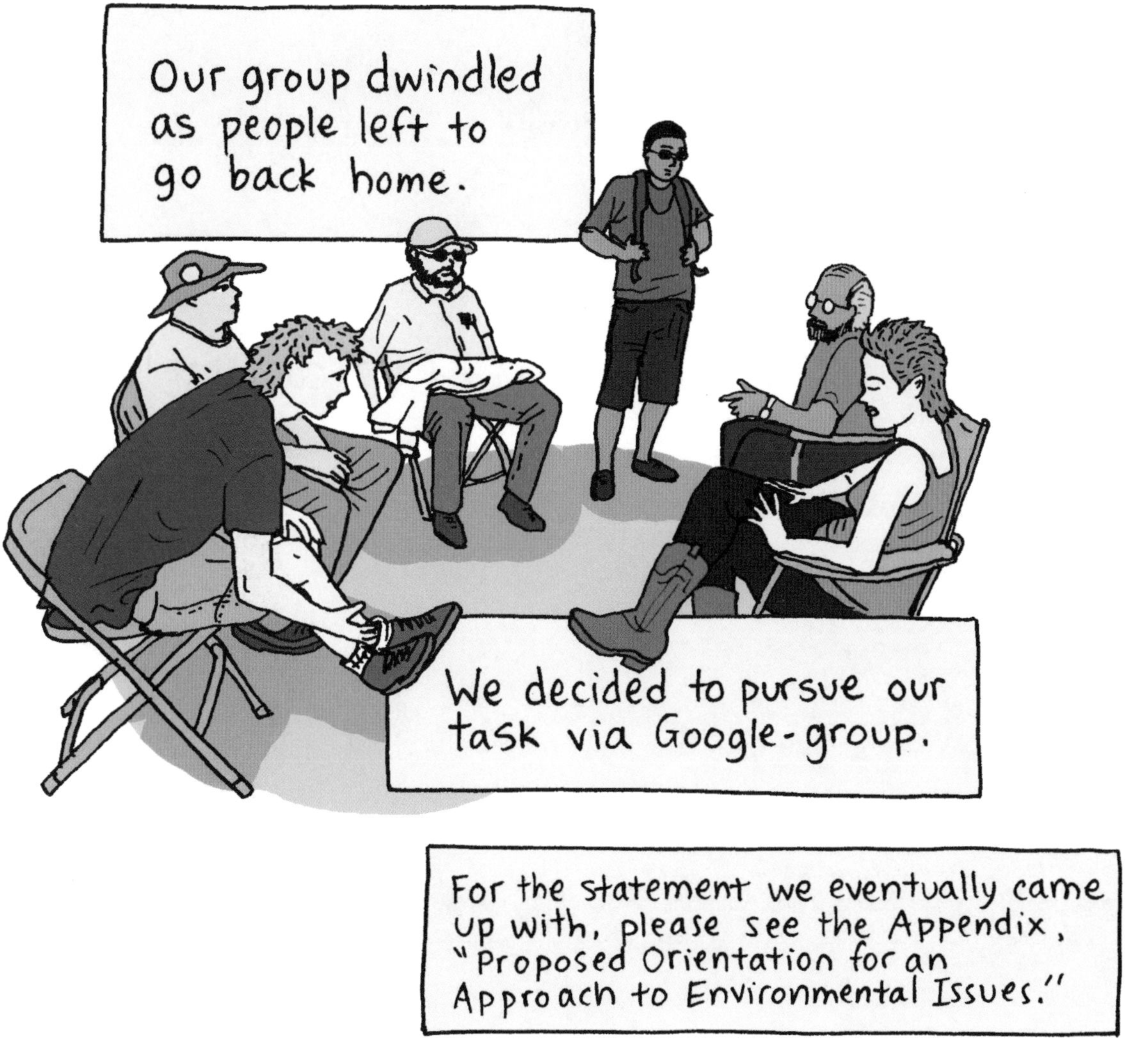
Our group dwindled as people left to go back home.
We decided to pursue our task via Google-group.
For the statement we eventually came up with, please see the Appendix, "Proposed Orientation for an Approach to Environmental Issues."

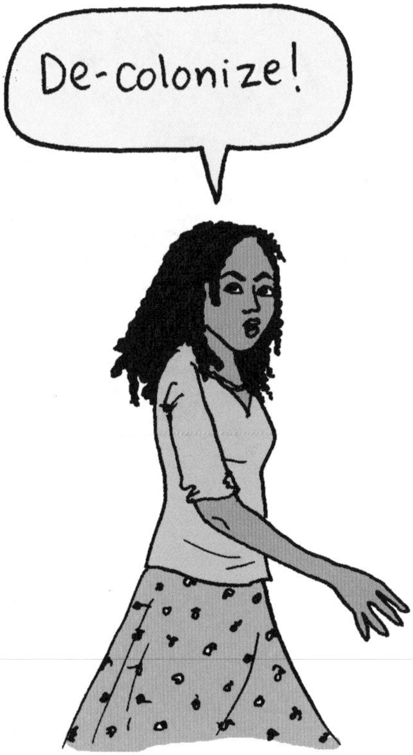
De-colonize!

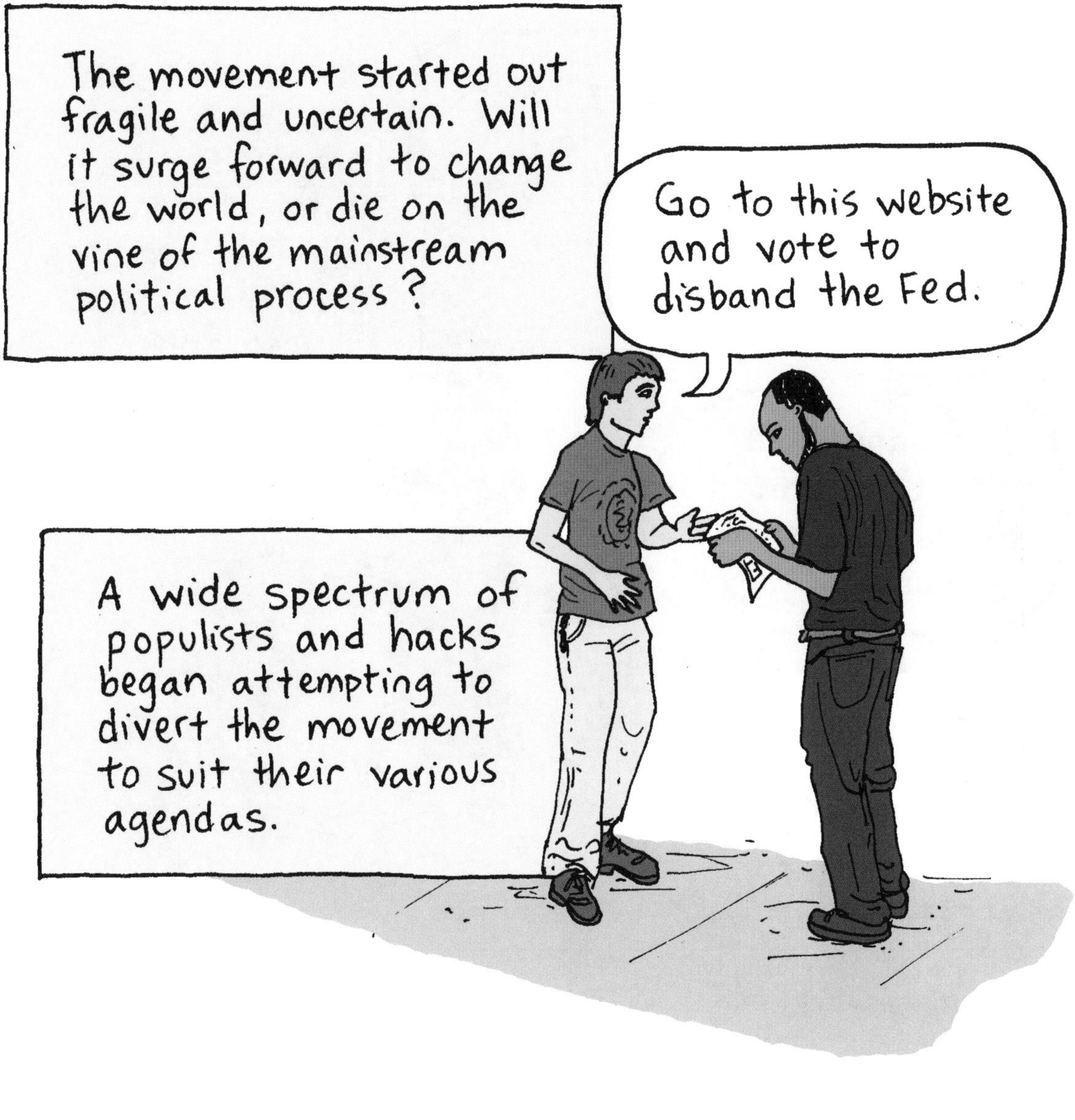
The movement started out fragile and uncertain. Will it surge forward to change the world, or die on the vine of the mainstream political process?
Go to this website and vote to disband the Fed.
A wide spectrum of populists and hacks began attempting to divert the movement to suit their various agendas.

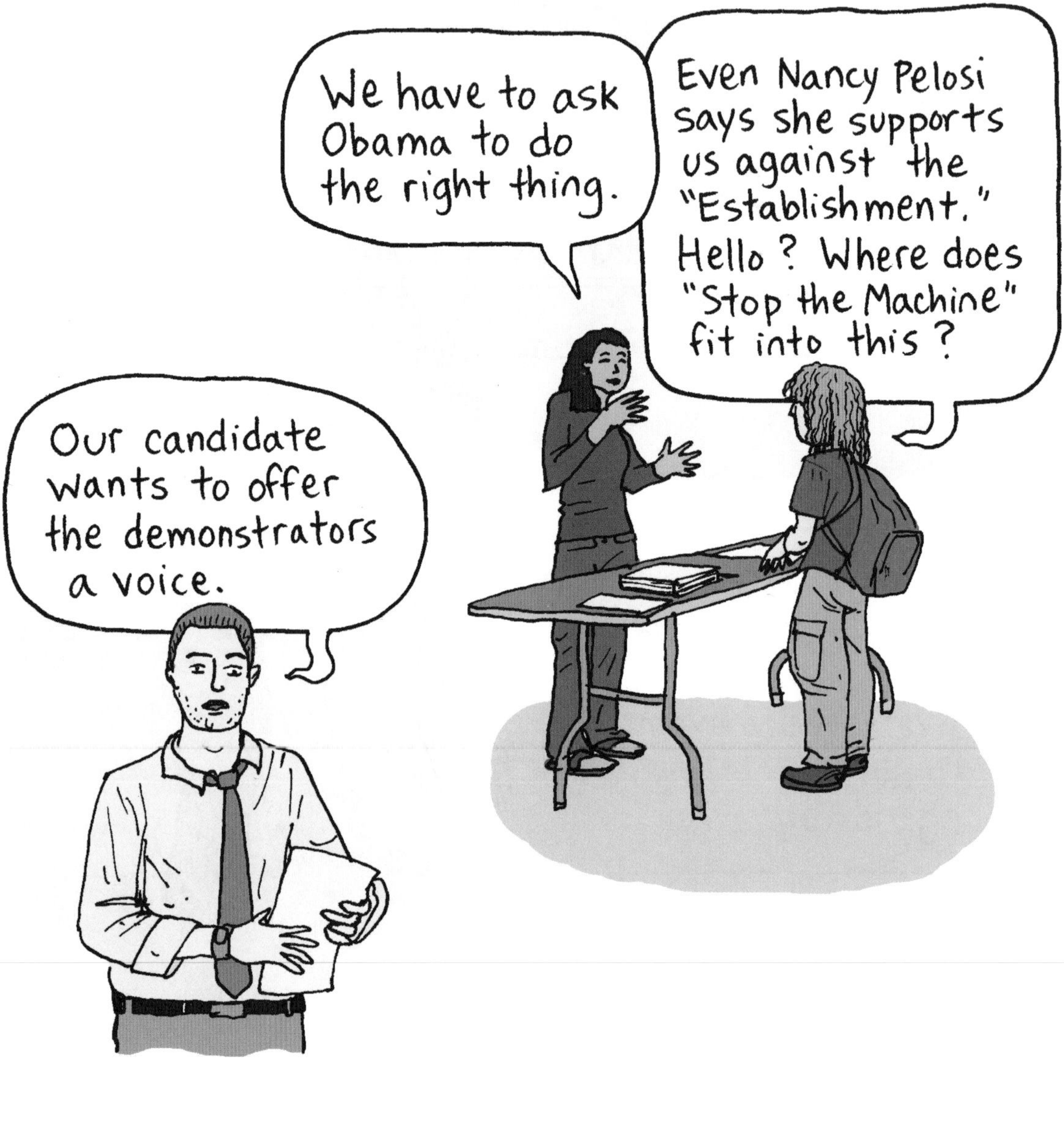
We have to ask Obama to do the right thing.
Even Nancy Pelosi says she supports us against the "Establishment." Hello? Where does "Stop the Machine" fit into this?
Our candidate wants to offer the demonstrators a voice.

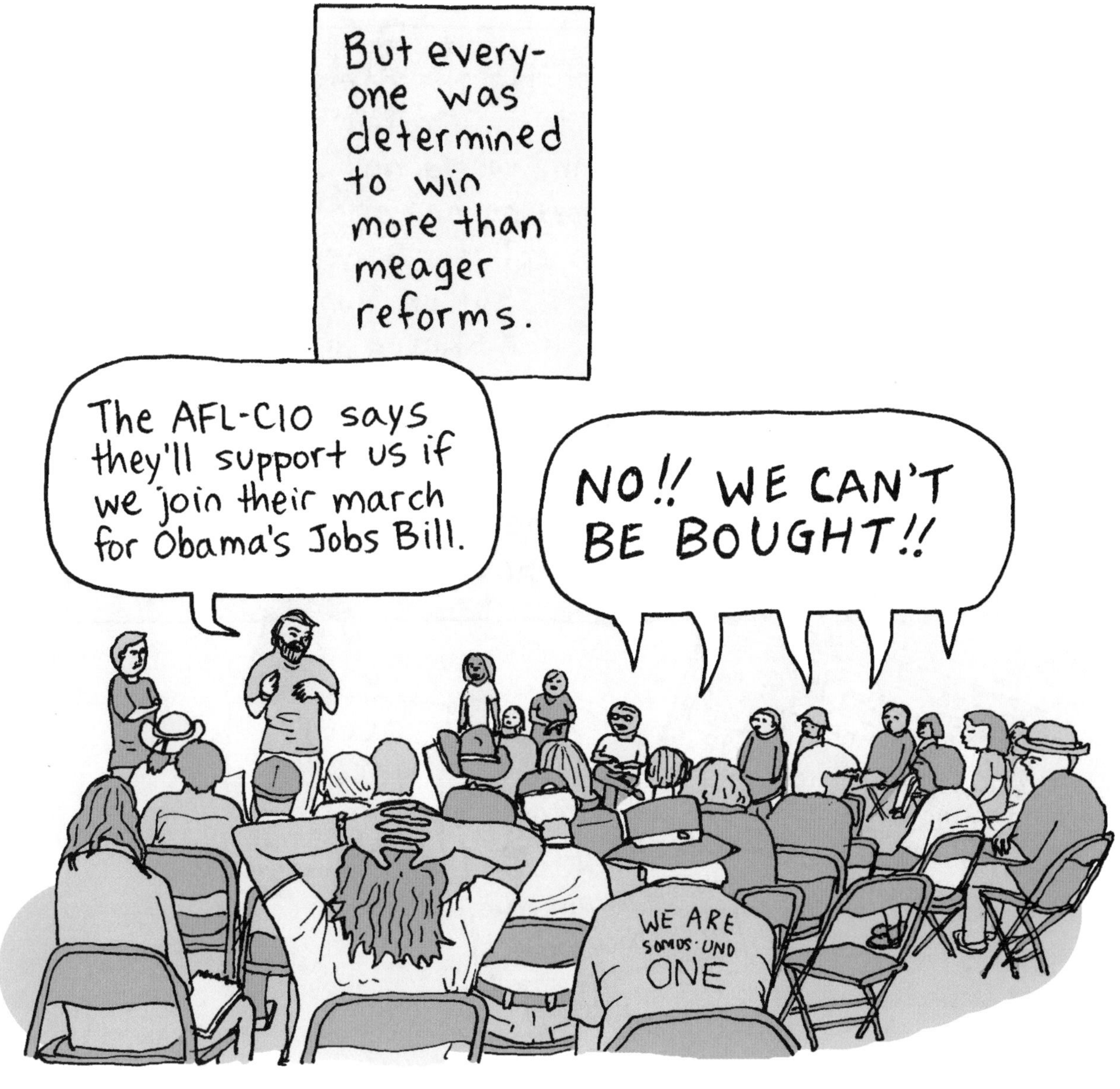
But every-one was determined to win more than meager reforms.
The AFL-CIO says they'll support us if we join their march for Obama's Jobs Bill.
NO!! WE CAN'T BE BOUGHT!!
WE ARE SOMOS UNO ONE

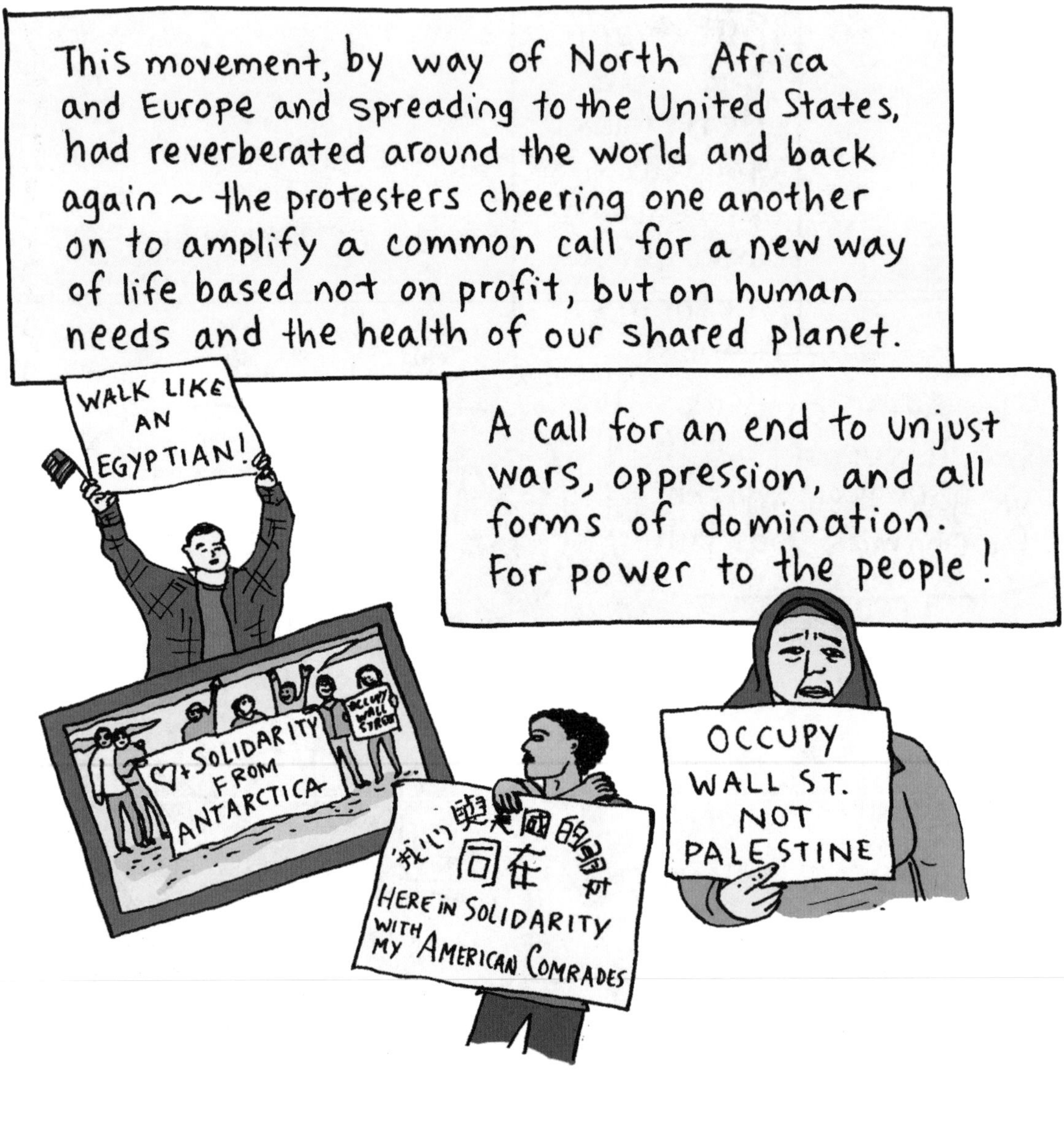
This movement, by way of North Africa and Europe and spreading to the United States, had reverberated around the world and back again ~ the protesters cheering one another on to amplify a common call for a new way of life based not on profit, but on human needs and the health of our shared planet.
WALK LIKE AN EGYPTIAN!
A call for an end to unjust wars, oppression, and all forms of domination. For power to the people!
OCCUPY WALL STREET
♡ + SOLIDARITY FROM ANTARCTICA
我心與美國的朋友
同在
HERE IN SOLIDARITY WITH MY AMERICAN COMRADES
OCCUPY WALL ST. NOT PALESTINE

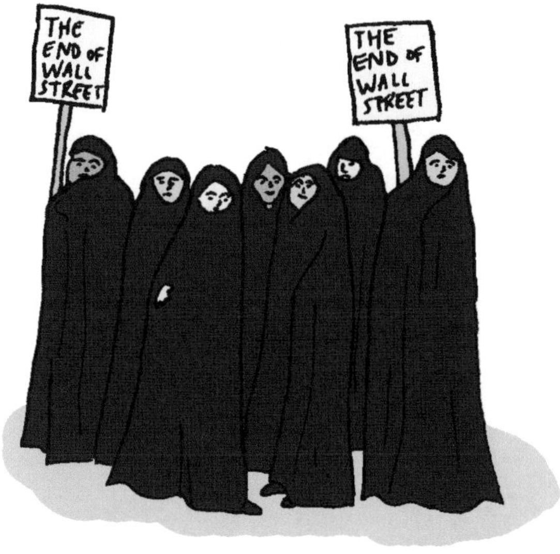
THE END OF WALL STREET
THE END OF WALL STREET

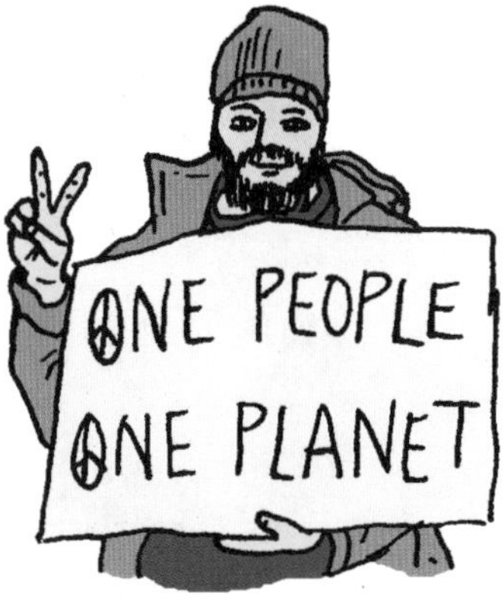
ONE PEOPLE
ONE PLANET

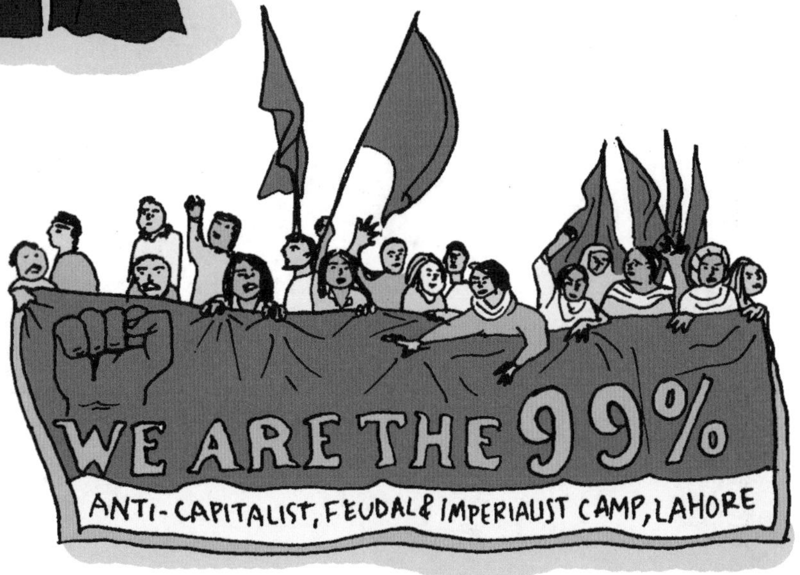
WE ARE THE 99%
ANTI-CAPITALIST, FEUDAL & IMPERIALIST CAMP, LAHORE

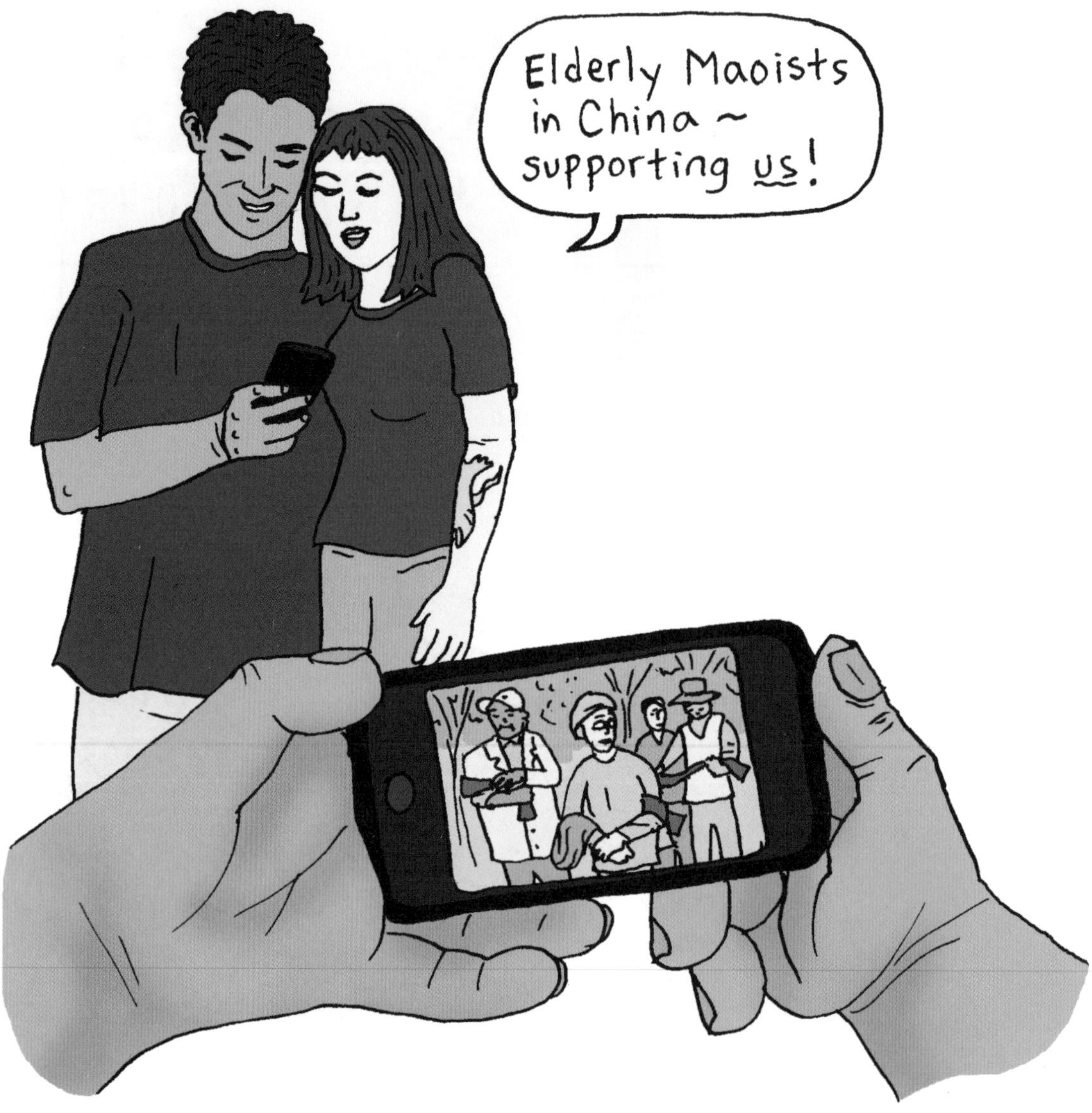
Elderly Maoists in China ~ supporting us!

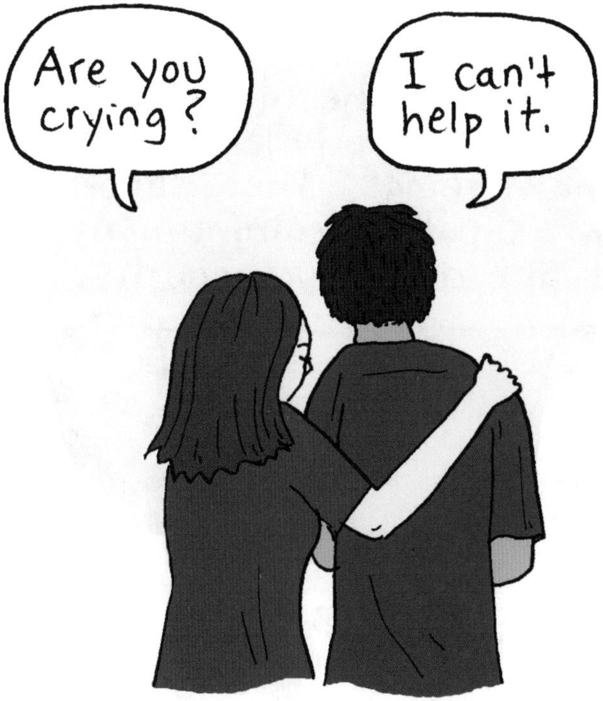
Are you crying?
I can't help it.

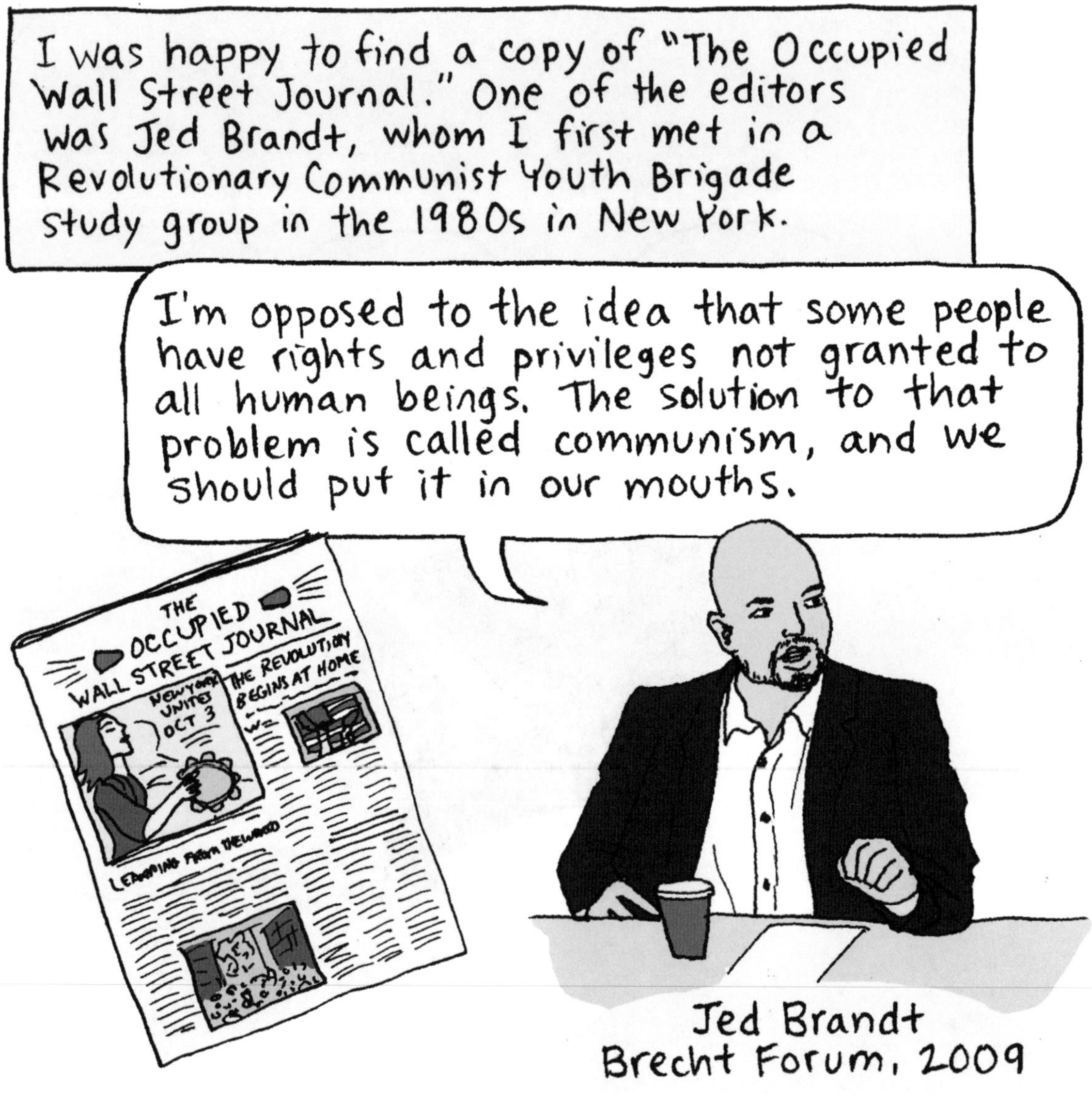
I was happy to find a copy of "The Occupied Wall Street Journal." One of the editors was Jed Brandt, whom I first met in a Revolutionary Communist Youth Brigade study group in the 1980s in New York.
I'm opposed to the idea that some people have rights and privileges not granted to all human beings. The solution to that problem is called communism, and we should put it in our mouths.
THE OCCUPIED WALL STREET JOURNAL
NEW YORK UNITES OCT 3
THE REVOLUTION BEGINS AT HOME
Jed Brandt
Brecht Forum, 2009

Eventually it became clear that the encampment would continue for the long haul as protests spread across the country.

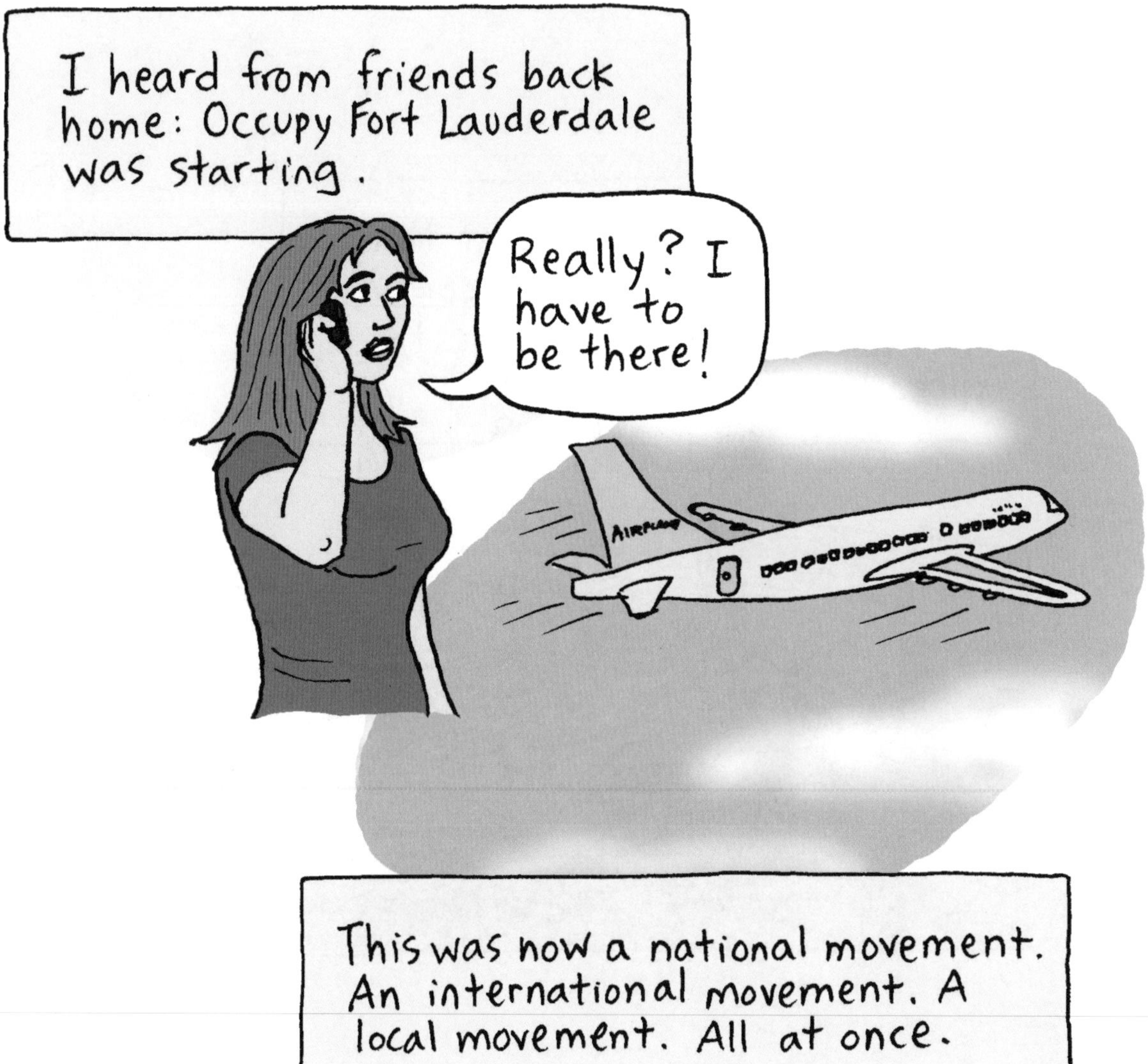
I heard from friends back home: Occupy Fort Lauderdale was starting.
Really? I have to be there!
AIRPLANE
This was now a national movement. An international movement. A local movement. All at once.

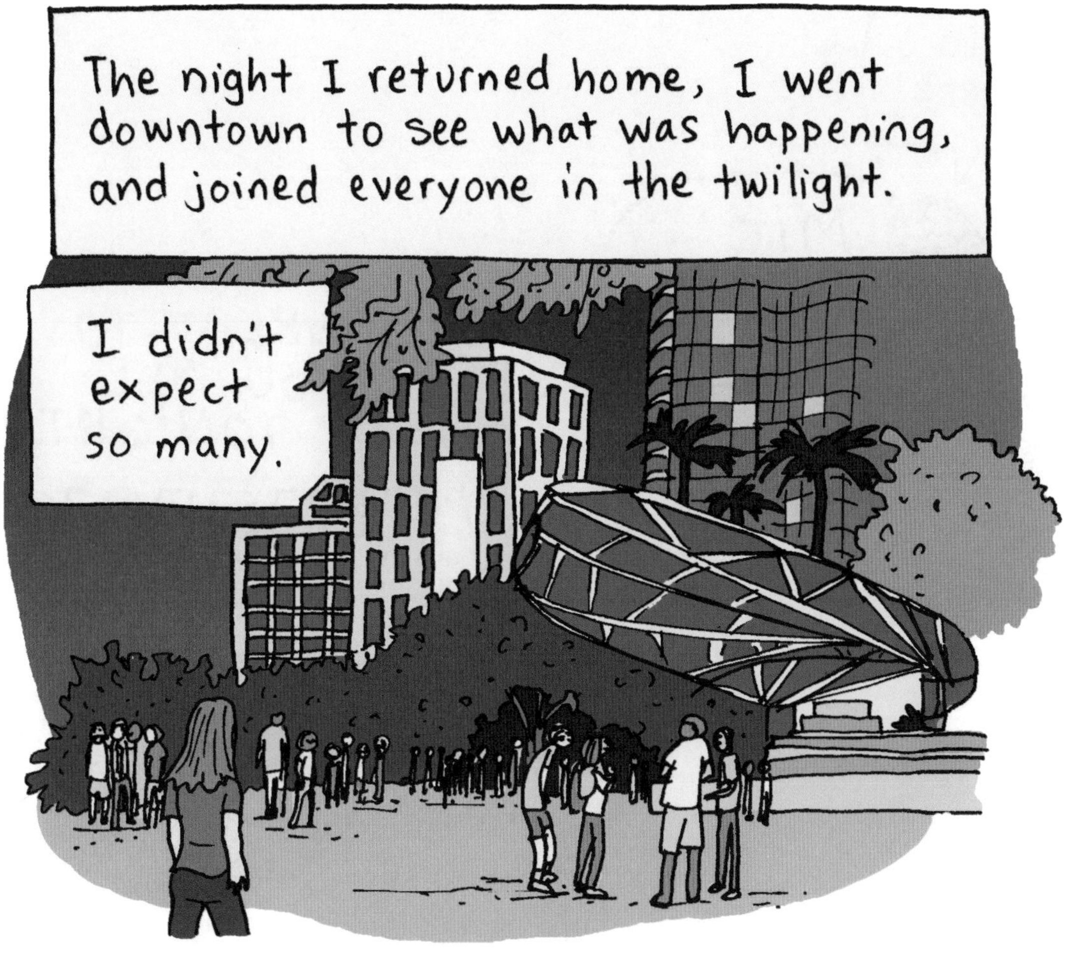
The night I returned home, I went downtown to see what was happening, and joined everyone in the twilight.
I didn't expect so many.

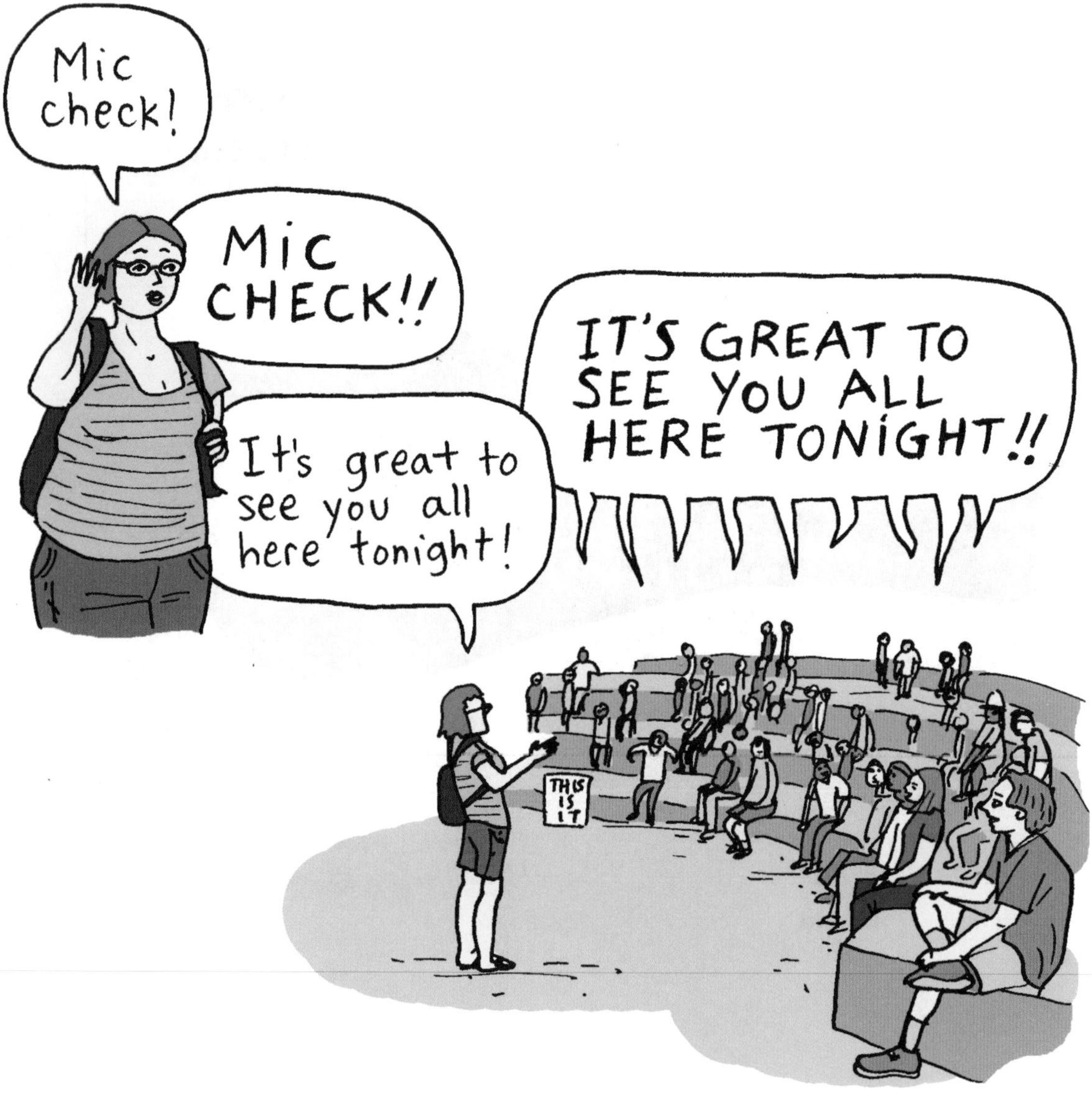

Mic check!
Mic CHECK!!
It's great to see you all here tonight!
IT'S GREAT TO SEE YOU ALL HERE TONIGHT!!
THIS IS IT

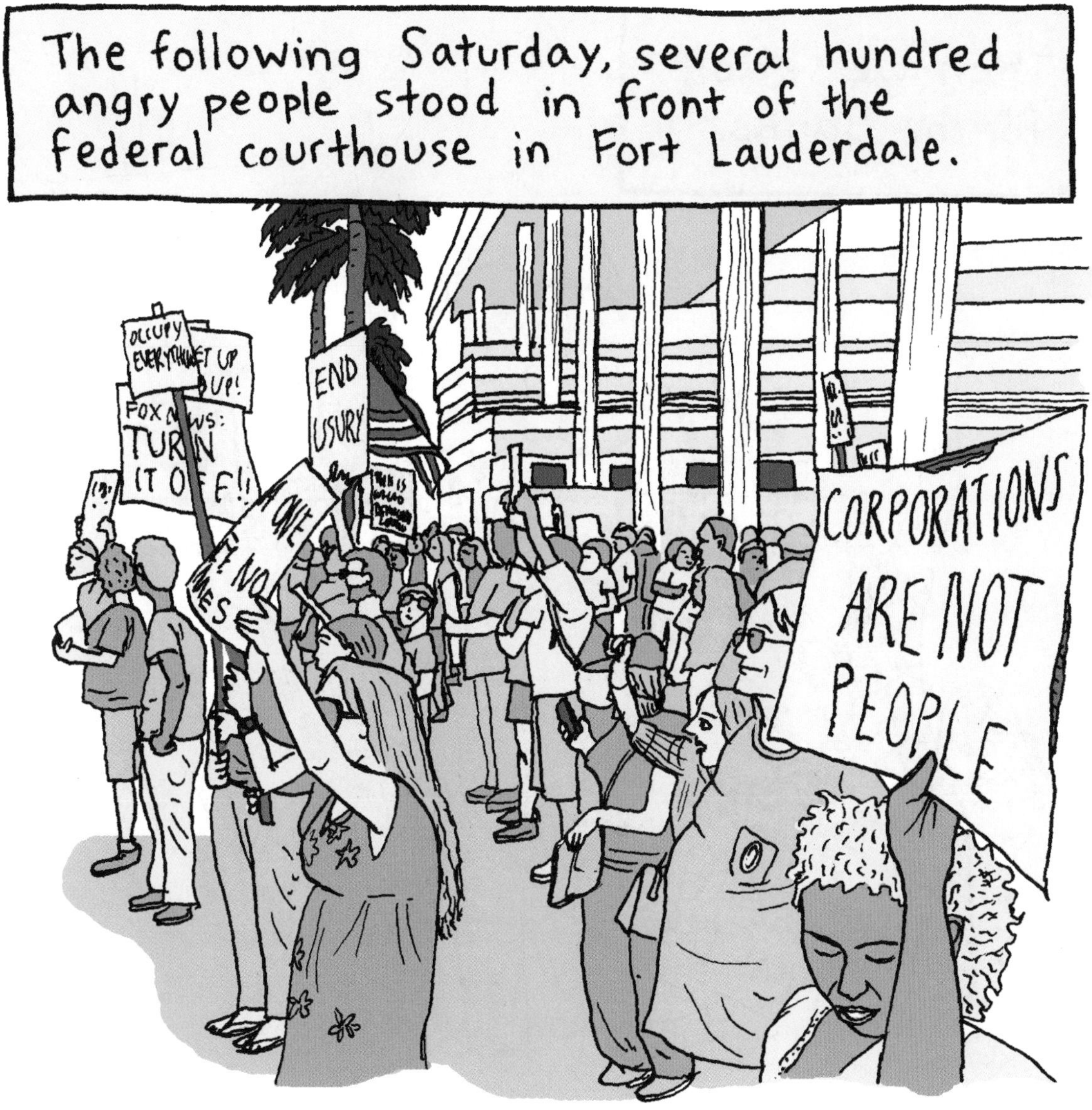
The following Saturday, several hundred angry people stood in front of the federal courthouse in Fort Lauderdale.
OCCUPY
END USURY
CORPORATIONS ARE NOT PEOPLE

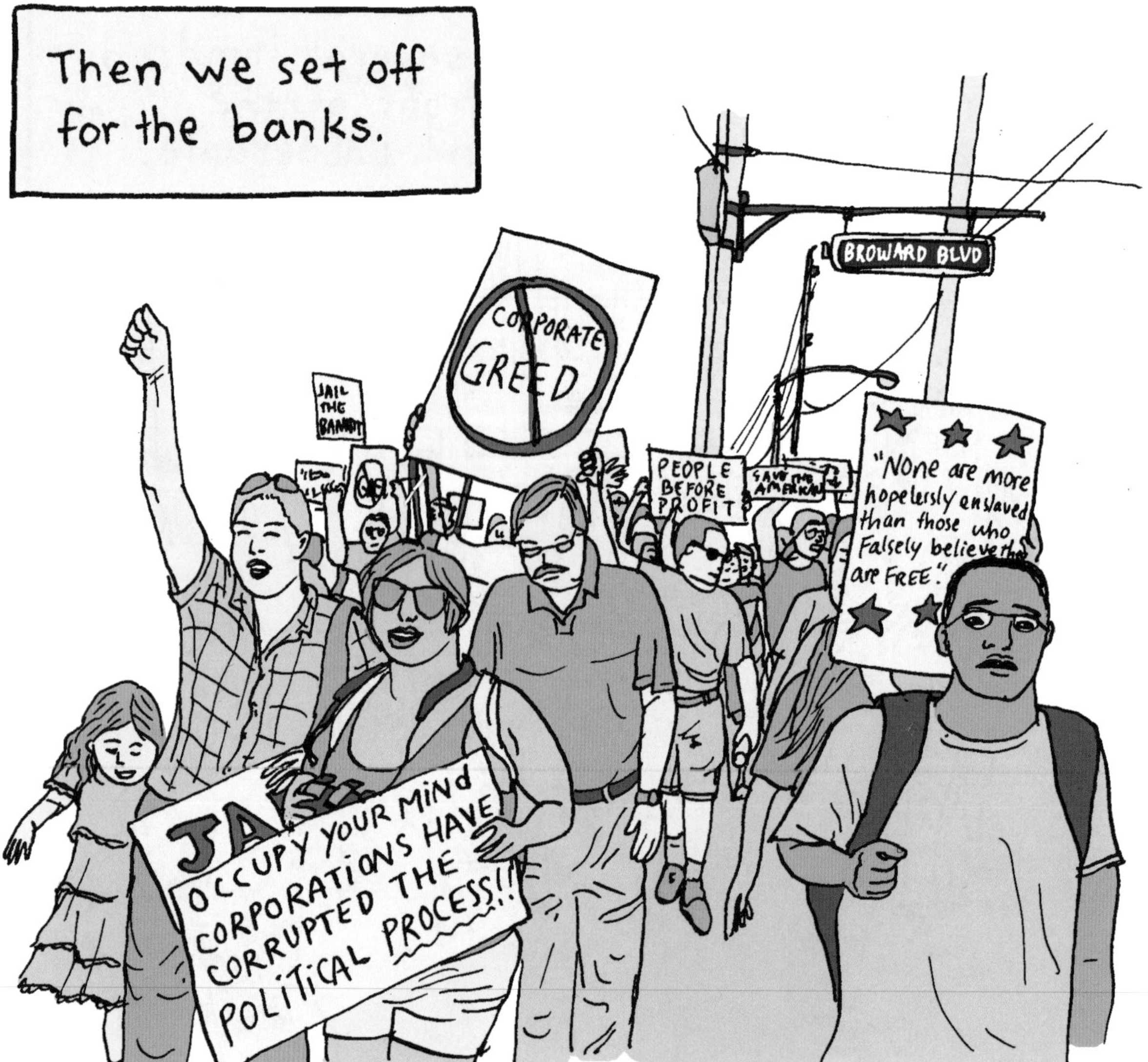
Then we set off for the banks.
CORPORATE GREED
BROWARD BLVD
PEOPLE BEFORE PROFIT
"None are more hopelessly enslaved than those who Falsely believe th
are FREE."
OCCUPY YOUR MIND
CORPORATIONS HAVE CORRUPTED THE POLITICAL PROCESS!!

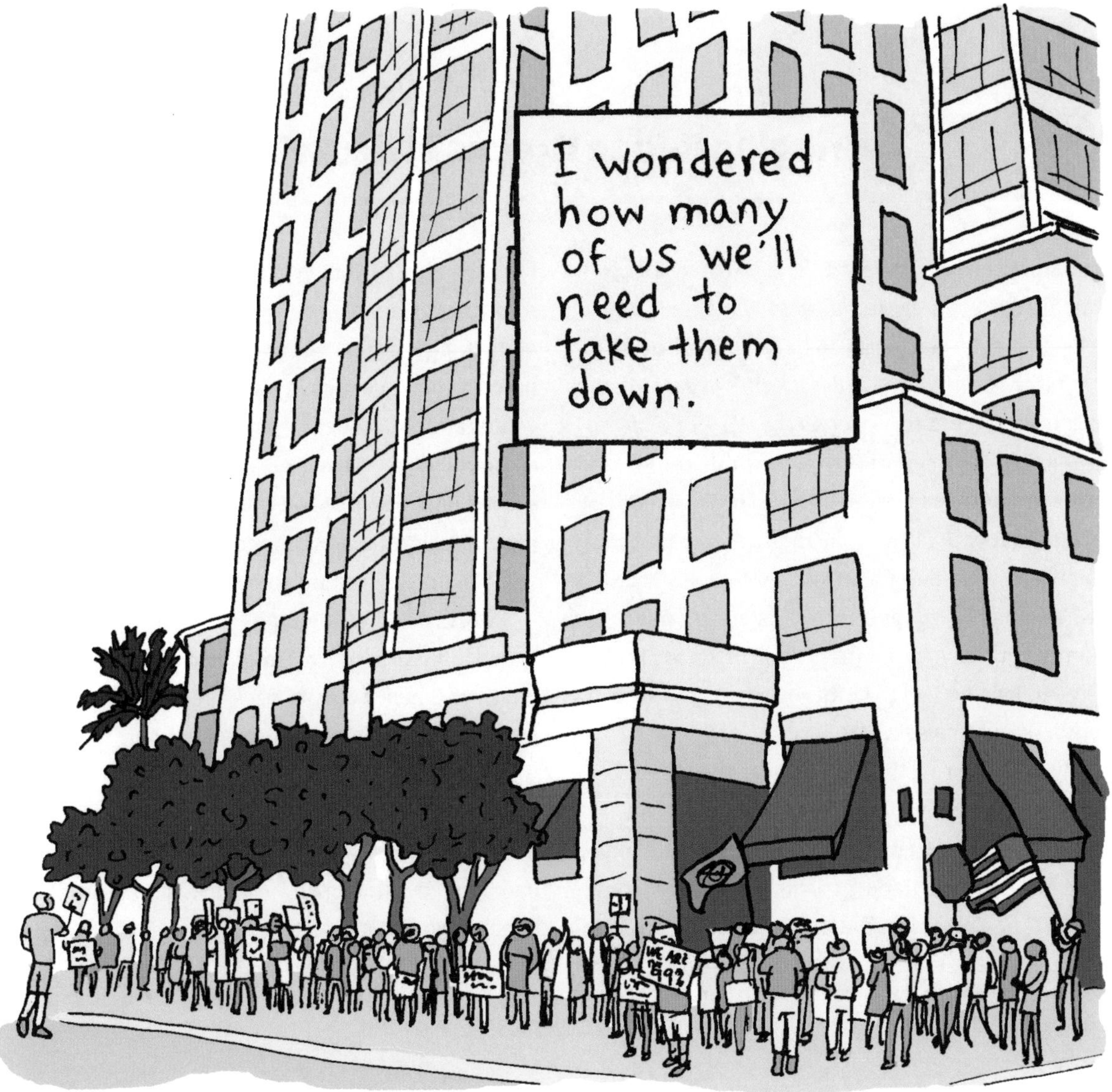
I wondered how many of us we'll need to take them down.

Bringing Red to Greens in Berkeley

I WAS invited to present a talk at Earth at Risk, an all-day event in Berkeley on November 13. Derrick Jensen (author of 16 books including *Endgame*, *A Language Older Than Words*, and our co-authored graphic novel *As the World Burns: 50 Simple Things You Can Do to Stay in Denial*) would interview six speakers: Arundhati Roy (author of, most recently, *Broken Republic: Three Essays*), Waziyatawin (a Dakota writer, teacher, and activist), Thomas Linzy (public interest attorney at Community Environmental Legal Defense Fund), Aric McBay and Lierre Keith (both authors and activists), and myself.

My desire during the last few years has been to build the "red-green bridge"—to bring class consciousness into the environmental movement, and eco-consciousness (biocentrism) to socialists, communists, and others on the left. Earth at Risk would likely be a great chance to reach many radical environmentalists, so I decided that my talk would focus on making these links. For the first part, I described how capitalism works as a system, intertwining the exploitation of labor and extraction of resources in an omnicidal process that can't stop growing. In the second part, I focused on the importance of making strategic alliances between various struggles, in order to destroy capitalism.

I worked on my talk for about three months, and tested it out four or five times on patient friends and relatives. Then, a couple weeks before going to Berkeley, I presented the first part—about how capitalism works—at Occupy Miami.

I was directed to a paved area under a building overhang. At first the place seemed deserted. So much for advertising on Facebook. But eventually people began to arrive.

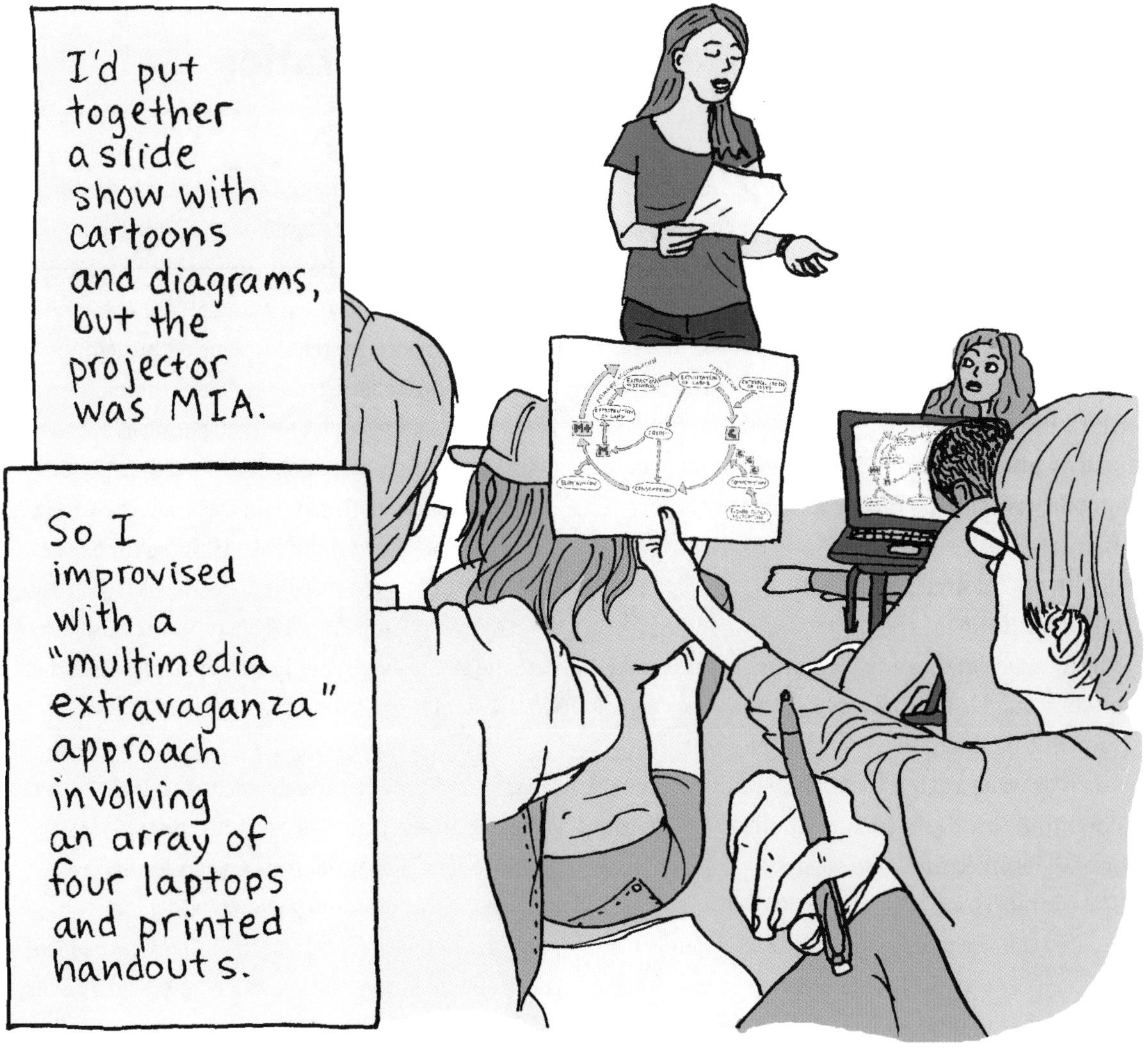
I'd put together a slide show with cartoons and diagrams, but the projector was MIA.
So I improvised with a "multimedia extravaganza" approach involving an array of four laptops and printed handouts.

An Edited Excerpt of My Presentation

CAPITALISM is an economic system characterized by commodity production and private appropriation, in which one section of people monopolizes the means of subsistence and production, and most people are forced to sell their labor to survive.

Capitalism is, on the one hand, a social relation, whereby one class dominates all others. On the other hand it's a process—the endless flow of money to commodity production for the generation of more money.

But it's not linear; it's both cyclical and progressive, like a spiral.

The first part of the process is primary accumulation, where land is expropriated and resources are extracted. A bank or a queen or anyone who already has surplus wealth extends a line of credit to some explorer to gather a group of armed thugs, go out into the world, locate wealth, and steal it.

The expropriation of land does a few things. The conqueror can use that land and extract whatever is in and on it. And as the people are dispossessed—no longer able to live on the land—they're forced into cities and become dependent on jobs. This is how the working class is created and continuously resupplied. It also creates the consumer: without land, we have to pay for food, shelter, and all our other needs.

The next part is production. One of the defining features of capitalist production is the exploitation of labor. Exploitation has a precise meaning in economics, which isn't simply using someone for material gain.

It means the worker is paid less than the exchange value of what they produce. During the time that they're paid $10, they might make items worth $100. That extra $90, minus fixed costs, is surplus value that the capitalist privately appropriates—in other words, steals.

Externalization of costs is another way the capitalist commits theft, and murder as well. Pollution from the production process is discharged into the environment. The numerous and serious consequences, never mind the cleanup which never happens, are not paid for by the capitalist who caused the problem, but by society as a whole, and by every living being on Earth.

PRIMARY ACCUMULATION
PRODUCTION
EXTRACTION OF RESOURCES
EXPLOITATION OF LABOR
EXTERNALIZATION OF COSTS
EXPROPRIATION OF LAND
M+
M
CREDIT
C
C
C
C
COMPETITION
TECHNOLOGICAL ESCALATION
ELIMINATION
CONSUMPTION

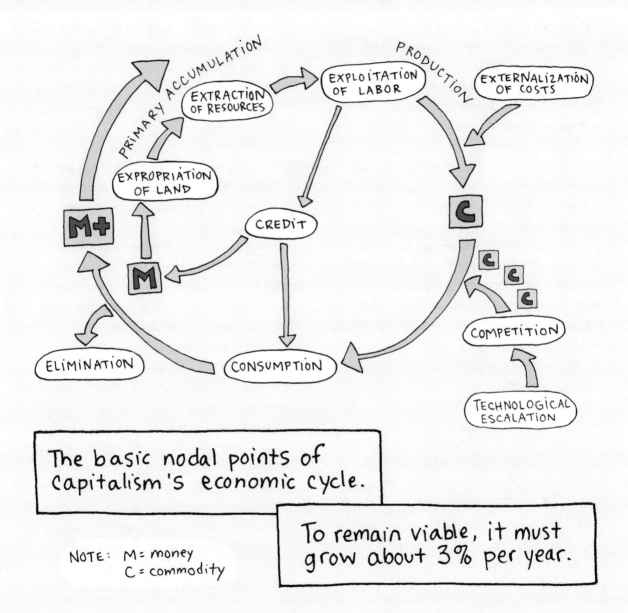

The basic nodal points of capitalism's economic cycle.

To remain viable, it must grow about 3% per year.

NOTE: M = money
C = commodity

Other capitalists are running this same cycle. All their commodities flow into the marketplace. Competition is the major economic driving force of capitalism. Capitalists compete against each other for the sale—by out-marketing each other or by undercutting each other in price. Usually both. This puts pressure on the rate of profit to fall. To remain competitive, the capitalists are forced to continuously cut the costs of production.

Wages are the largest variable cost in most businesses, so there's tremendous pressure on capitalists to keep them as low as possible. To accomplish this, they manipulate the economy to keep the unemployment rate at about 5 percent or higher, so there are always plenty of desperate people competing for jobs. They move their factories to countries where wages are even lower and where repressive governments prevent workers from organizing. They pressure laborers to work longer days, and they escalate productivity so that each worker produces ever more surplus value per hour.

Competition also drives technological development as each capitalist pursues ever-increasing efficiency and speed. They mechanize their factories to minimize the number of workers.

Smaller companies that can't keep up are driven out of business or bought up by larger ones, forming monopolies in certain sectors. Four companies control 90 percent of the world's grain production.

Only ten to twelve produce most semi-conductors. Ten produce most pharmaceuticals. These monopolies can control prices to counteract the falling rate of profit. So while the local hardware store is failing, large oil companies are making more money than ever.

The surplus value, or profit, created in production is locked inside the commodity until the moment of consumption. When you plunk your dollars down to buy the hair dryer or the box of frozen waffles, the capitalist's goal is realized.

Now we run into capitalism's major contradiction. Because the workers are collectively paid less than the total worth of commodities that they produce, there will always be more on the market than what can be consumed by the domestic population. This causes what's called the crisis of over-production. There's too much stuff, and because profit is created by exploiting labor, the people will never—can never—be paid enough to buy it all.

The goal of each individual capitalist is to maximize profits, in other words, to accumulate as much surplus value as possible. But for the system overall, too much surplus value causes problems. It can't all be absorbed back into the economy.

What do they do with it? They can't just leave it lying around to depreciate; they have to get rid of it somehow. A portion is siphoned off for personal use by capitalists, to furnish extravagant lifestyles with

PRIMARY ACCUMULATION
PRODUCTION
EXTRACTION OF RESOURCES
EXPLOITATION OF LABOR
EXTERNALIZATION OF COSTS
EXPROPRIATION OF LAND
M+
C
CREDIT
M
C
C
C
COMPETITION
ELIMINATION
CONSUMPTION
TECHNOLOGICAL ESCALATION

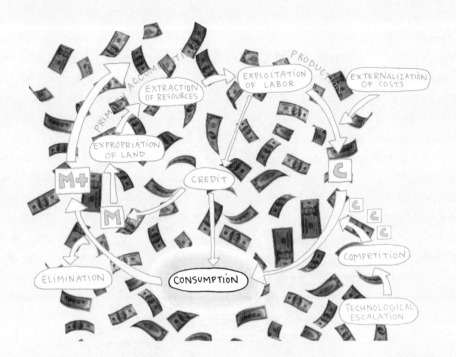

excessive salaries and bonuses. Also, they must force open and seize control of more markets. This is one of the driving forces for imperialism. When more than one country does this, major inter-imperialist conflicts ensue.

Some surplus value is simply thrown away, eliminated through waste, wars, and so-called international "aid." The latter two also function as centers for creating even more profit, which they pursue, but which also exacerbates the overall problem.

They increase the level of consumption with infusions of credit, basing the consumer economy on debt. Of course this creates bubbles and instability, which grow progressively worse.

Back at the start, the surplus value has to be reinvested. It must be more than they started with, because only through expansion can each company gain a competitive edge over all the others. For capitalism as a whole to function, it must grow about 3 percent annually. So the cycle goes around again, but bigger. In the next turn, they must extract more raw materials, exploit more labor, manufacture more products, generate more waste, make more profits.

This isn't easy; as economies become saturated,

there's less opportunity for profitable investment. So they have to invent ways to turn more things into commodities, invading us through privatization and monetizing every aspect of our lives, from our emotions to genetic material.

As we know, you can't have infinite growth on a finite planet. Today the crisis of overproduction has become acute and the system is maxed out. It's reaching the end of all physical limits.

• • •

You may wonder why anyone would put up with this miserable nightmare for even one second. They do because of the superstructure—ideas and institutions that we can picture as a shell around the economic structure, both supporting it and shaped by its needs.

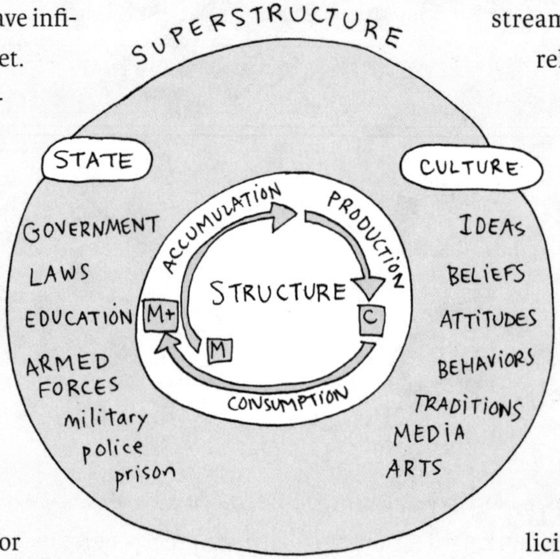
SUPERSTRUCTURE
STATE
GOVERNMENT
LAWS
EDUCATION
ARMED FORCES
military
police
prison
CULTURE
IDEAS
BELIEFS
ATTITUDES
BEHAVIORS
TRADITIONS
MEDIA
ARTS
STRUCTURE
ACCUMULATION
PRODUCTION
CONSUMPTION
M+
M
C

The sole purpose of the state is to keep the flow of capital running smoothly. It administers and regulates the process with its government and legal system. It enforces it with its military, police, prison complex, and security apparatus.

The culture also serves capitalist interests. The only ideas allowed to participate in the market are pro-system; any others are starved of support. The dominant culture tells us how to think and behave through the stories and myths of mainstream media, entertainment, and religion. It indoctrinates us in its schools. Its traditions train us in habits of individualism, competition, and subservience to authority. Its ideologies reinforce structural oppression such as misogyny, racism, homophobia, xenophobia, and nationalism. The nuclear family is a self-policing social unit enforcing the domination of children and women.

We need to break through this superstructure to choke off the flow of capital.

The conversion of nature into commodities is intertwined with the exploitation of human labor; one can't happen without the other. Similarly, the fight to defend the land and traditional land-based ways of life is also connected to the fight for an end to exploitation, a classless society. One can't be won without the other. When we understand this, liberating ourselves and saving the planet become the same act.

Capitalists have been very good at dividing the interests of the workers from the environment. This is, of course, intentional. After the Gulf oil spill, workers demanded that oil rigs open back up because they needed jobs to survive. Yet these are the very same people being poisoned by the externalization of costs.

This is a bind that workers have been placed in. It can only be resolved by the overthrow of capitalism and taking back our means of subsistence. We don't need jobs at all—in fact that just helps the capitalists. What we need is a sustainable way of life.

Two ideological elements are essential at the revolutionary core: biocentrism and class consciousness. The major flaw of the class struggle has been anthropocentrism, a total focus on human needs and a utilitarian view of nature. The major flaw of environmentalists and, frankly, the labor movement as well (which has been mostly destroyed, or co-opted by sold-out unions) has been a lack of class analysis and understanding of capitalism as a system that we need to defeat. Instead, many fall victim to illusions of reformism, bourgeois democracy, technotopianism, lifestylism and other bogus schemes.

As the revolutionary project gains common experience, these movements will cross-pollinate, come closer together in their struggles against their common enemy.

RAISING CONSCIOUSNESS
BUILDING ORGANIZATIONS
EXERCISING POWER

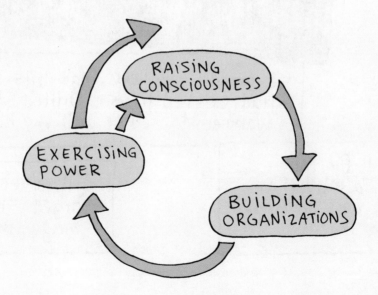

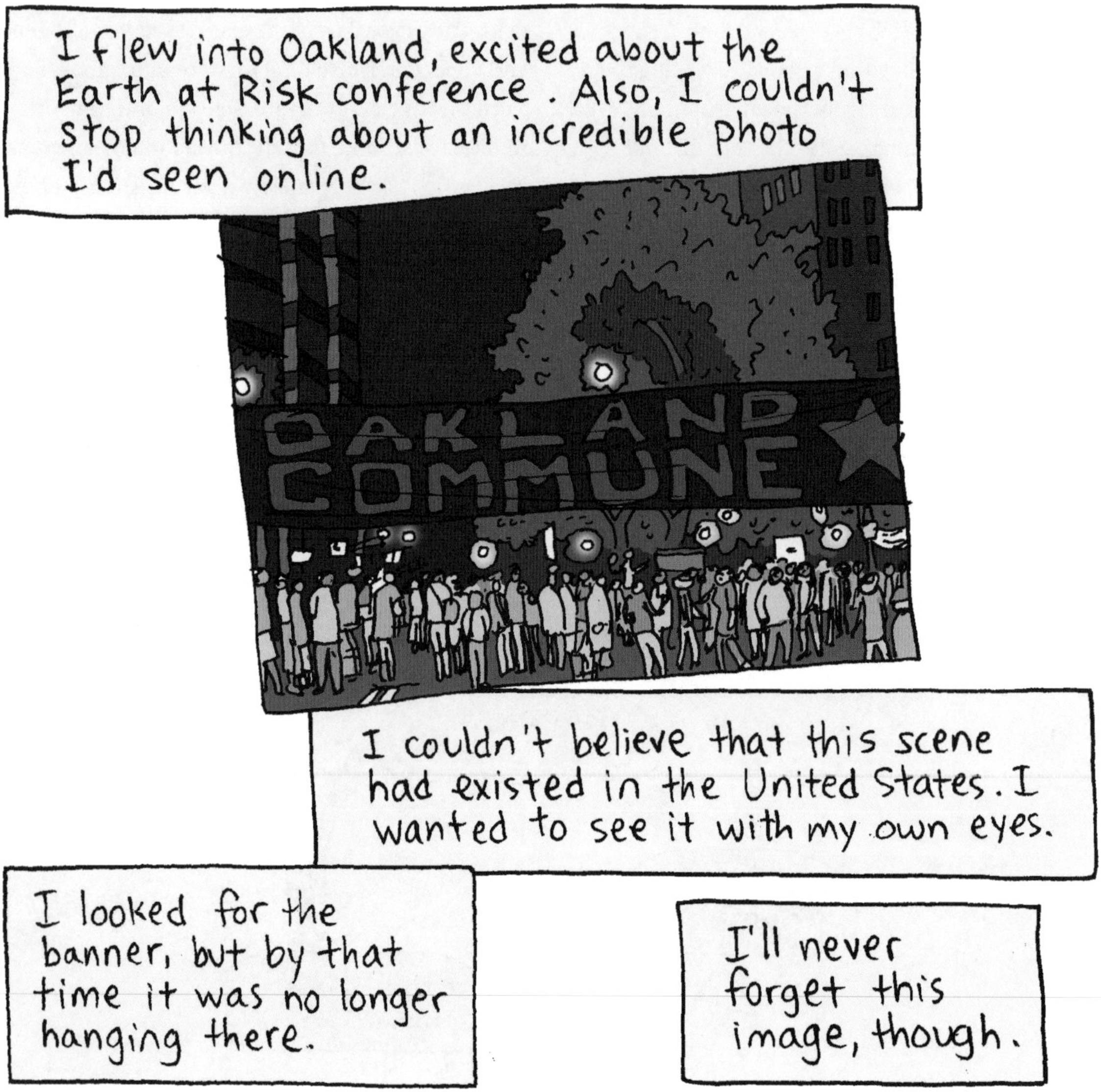
I flew into Oakland, excited about the Earth at Risk conference. Also, I couldn't stop thinking about an incredible photo I'd seen online.
OAKLAND COMMUNE
I couldn't believe that this scene had existed in the United States. I wanted to see it with my own eyes.
I looked for the banner, but by that time it was no longer hanging there.
I'll never forget this image, though.

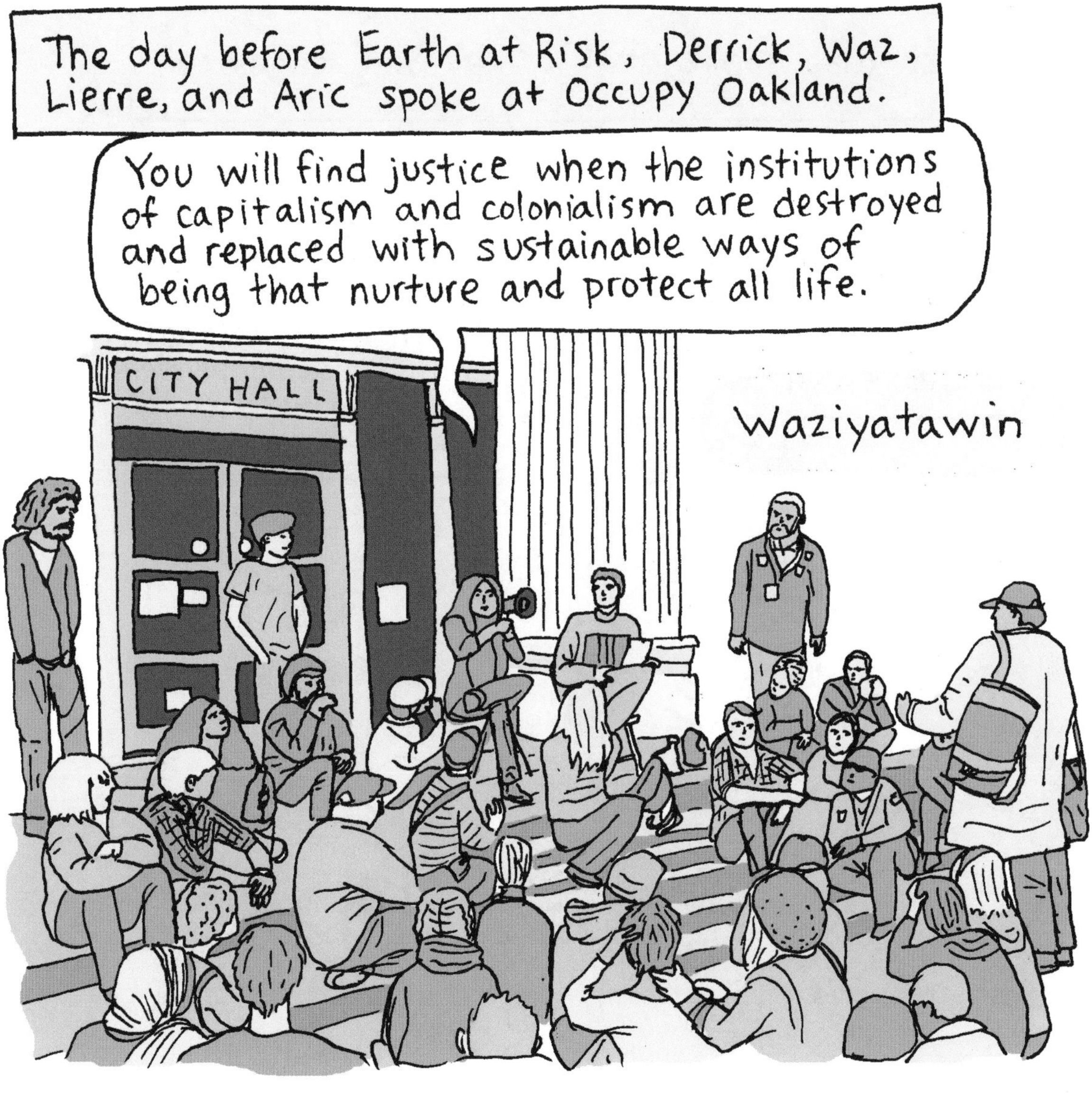

The day before Earth at Risk, Derrick, Waz, Lierre, and Aric spoke at Occupy Oakland.
You will find justice when the institutions of capitalism and colonialism are destroyed and replaced with sustainable ways of being that nurture and protect all life.
CITY HALL
Waziyatawin

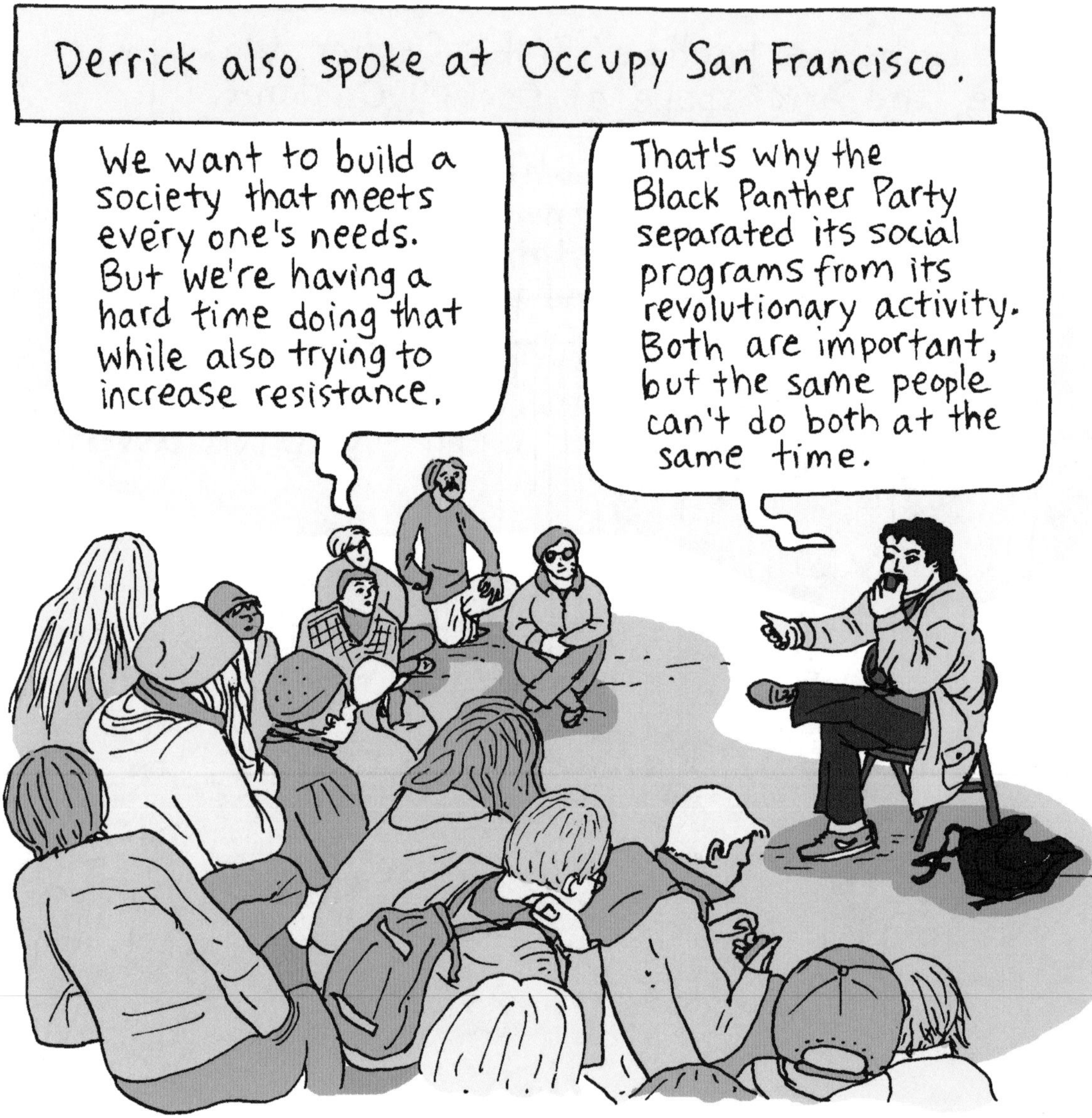

Derrick also spoke at Occupy San Francisco.
We want to build a society that meets every one's needs. But we're having a hard time doing that while also trying to increase resistance.
That's why the Black Panther Party separated its social programs from its revolutionary activity. Both are important, but the same people can't do both at the same time.

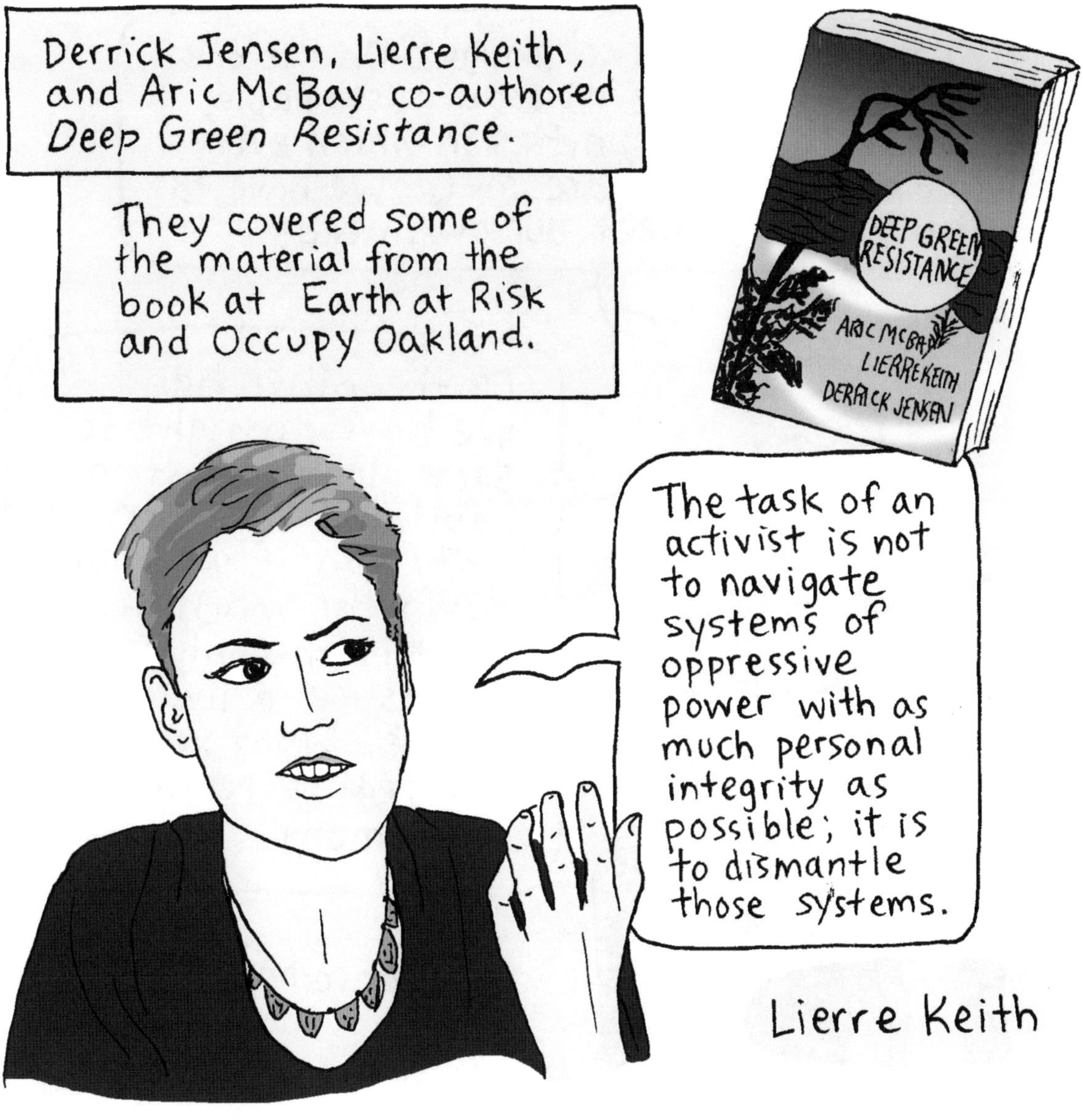

Derrick Jensen, Lierre Keith, and Aric McBay co-authored Deep Green Resistance.
They covered some of the material from the book at Earth at Risk and Occupy Oakland.
DEEP GREEN RESISTANCE
ARIC MCBAY
LIERRE KEITH
DERRICK JENSEN
The task of an activist is not to navigate systems of oppressive power with as much personal integrity as possible; it is to dismantle those systems.
Lierre Keith

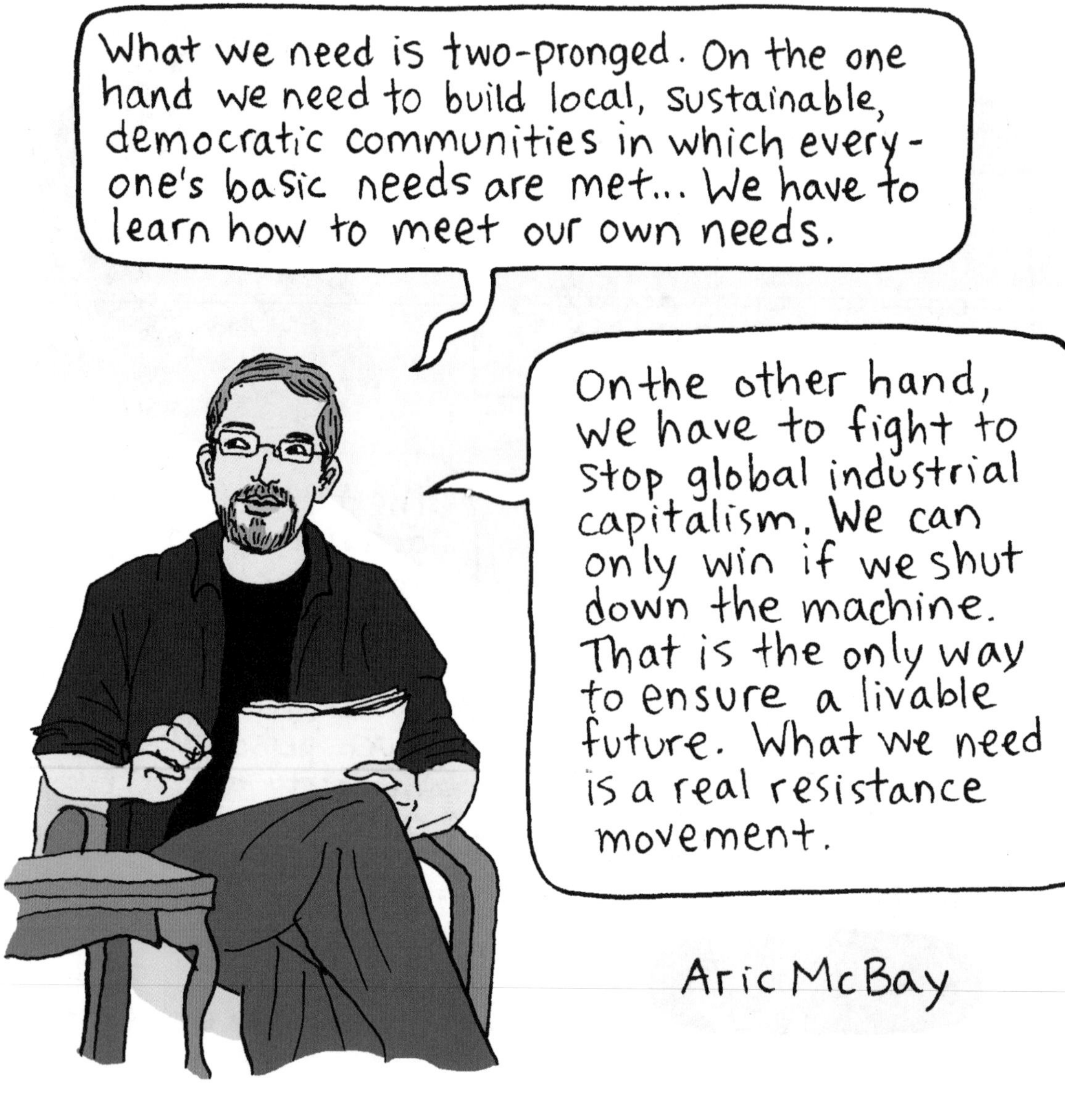
What we need is two-pronged. On the one hand we need to build local, sustainable, democratic communities in which every-one's basic needs are met... We have to learn how to meet our own needs.
On the other hand, we have to fight to stop global industrial capitalism. We can only win if we shut down the machine. That is the only way to ensure a livable future. What we need is a real resistance movement.
Aric McBay

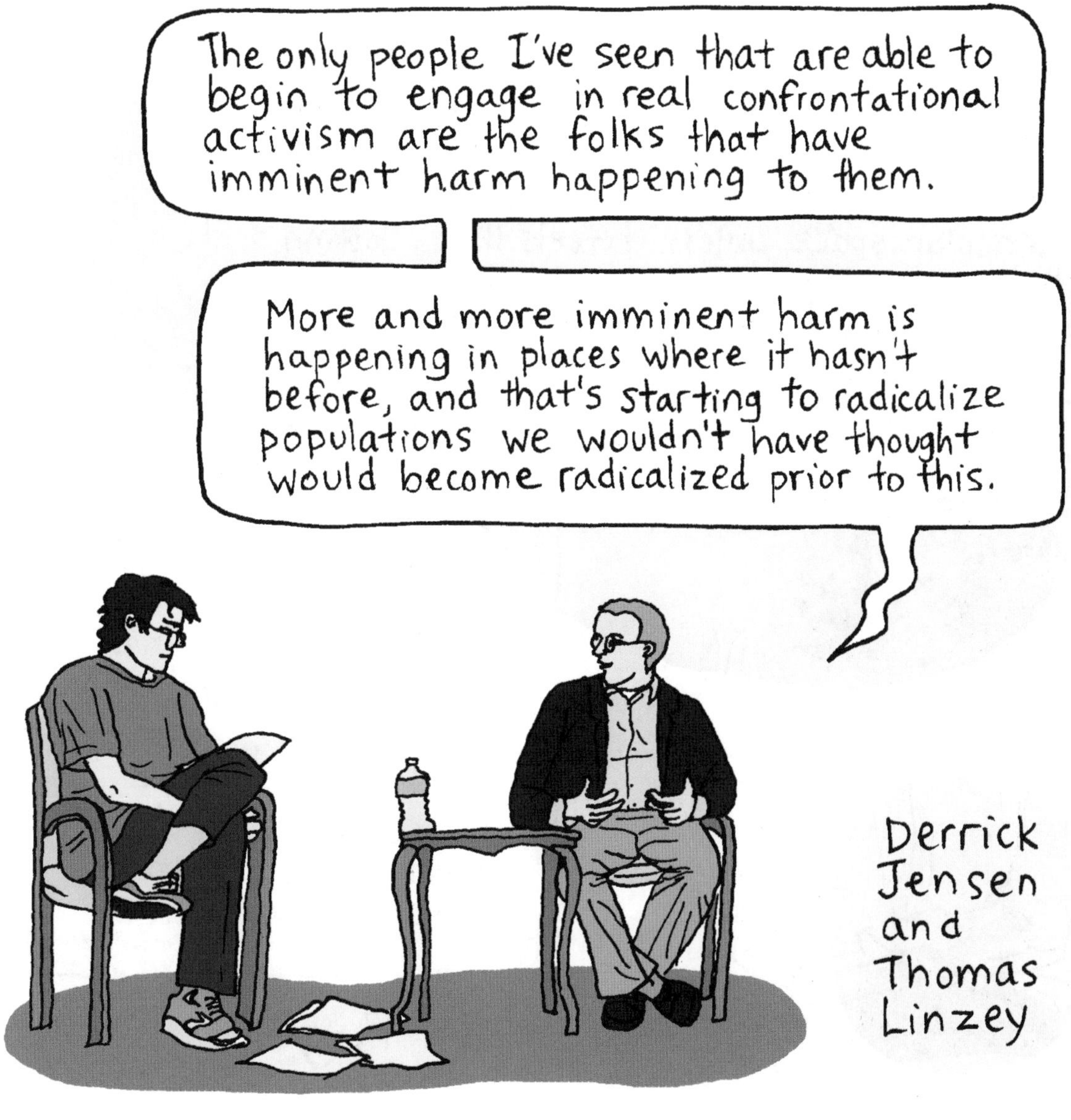
The only people I've seen that are able to begin to engage in real confrontational activism are the folks that have imminent harm happening to them.
More and more imminent harm is happening in places where it hasn't before, and that's starting to radicalize populations we wouldn't have thought would become radicalized prior to this.
Derrick Jensen and Thomas Linzey

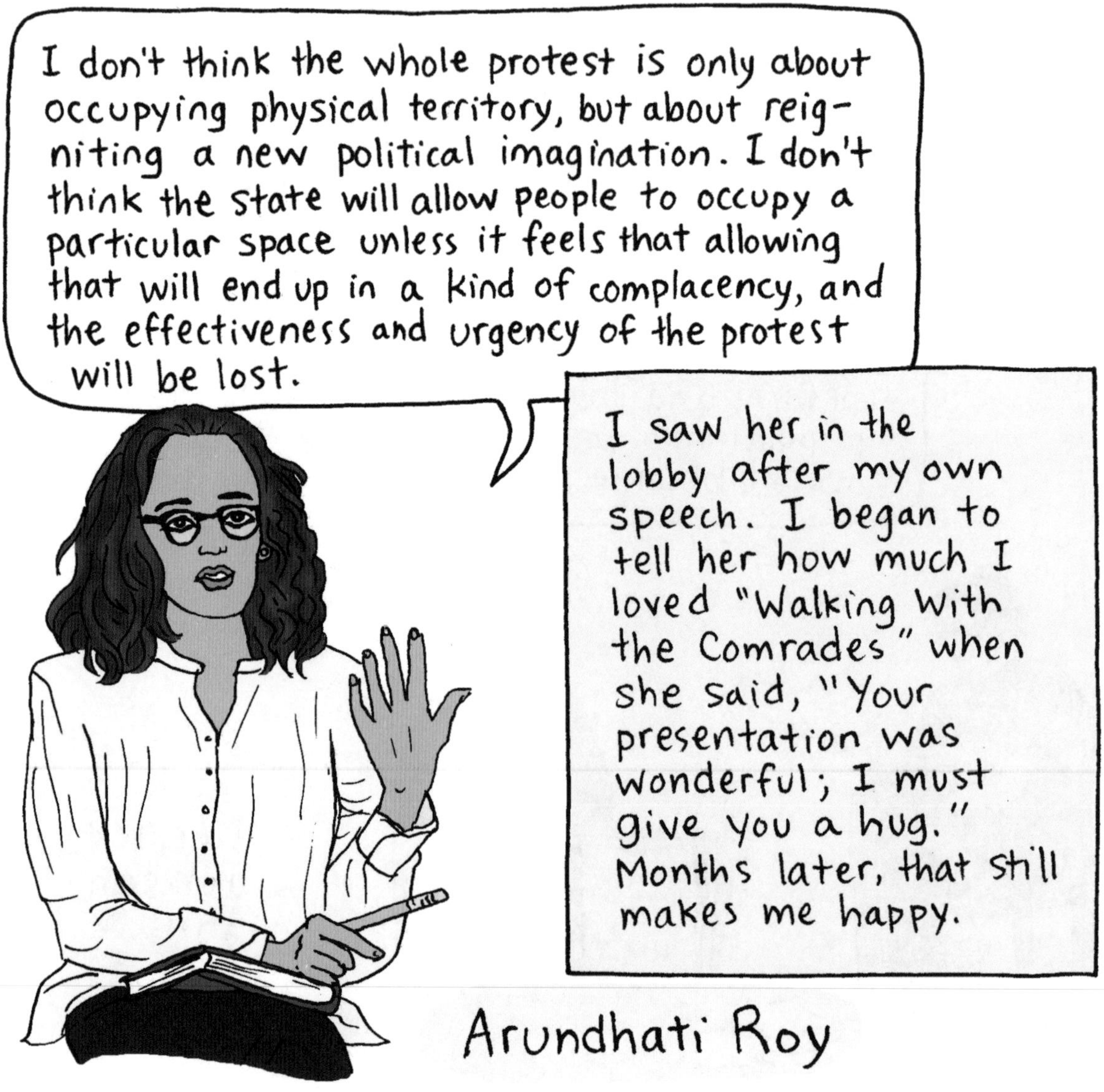
I don't think the whole protest is only about occupying physical territory, but about reigniting a new political imagination. I don't think the state will allow people to occupy a particular space unless it feels that allowing that will end up in a kind of complacency, and the effectiveness and urgency of the protest will be lost.
I saw her in the lobby after my own speech. I began to tell her how much I loved "Walking With the Comrades" when she said, "Your presentation was wonderful; I must give you a hug." Months later, that still makes me happy.
Arundhati Roy

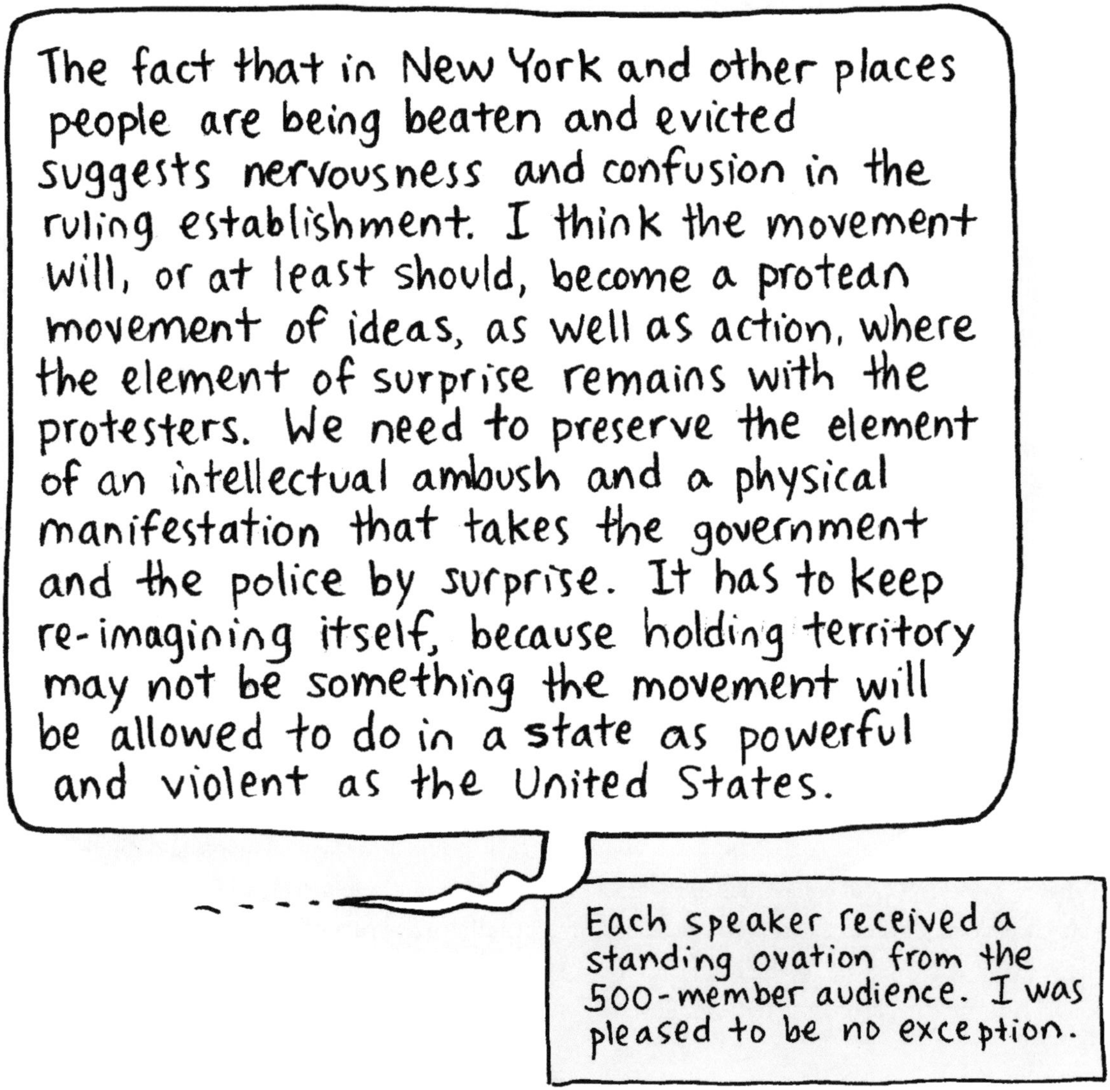
The fact that in New York and other places people are being beaten and evicted suggests nervousness and confusion in the ruling establishment. I think the movement will, or at least should, become a protean movement of ideas, as well as action, where the element of surprise remains with the protesters. We need to preserve the element of an intellectual ambush and a physical manifestation that takes the government and the police by surprise. It has to keep re-imagining itself, because holding territory may not be something the movement will be allowed to do in a state as powerful and violent as the United States.
Each speaker received a standing ovation from the 500-member audience. I was pleased to be no exception.

Separate Paths Reconverge

PREMADASI, at the time the main national organizer for Deep Green Resistance, walked next to me along Telegraph Avenue as I dragged my suitcase from one hotel (cold) to a better room (warm) in another one. (Chris Hedges had cancelled his appearance but the room remained paid for, so I took it).

The work Premadasi had done in a few short months was remarkable, and I told her how impressed I was. "You've pulled together 13 DGR chapters so far since the book came out—that's amazing!" I hadn't seen that kind of persistence and determination since I'd worked with the Revolutionary Communist Youth Brigade (associated with the Revolutionary Communist Party), many years ago in New York.

Whatever critiques I might have had of them, being lazy wasn't one of them. There were no excuses with the RCYB. Are you tired? Well, the masses are probably tired of being oppressed too. Would you rather take the day off? The millions of children being exploited in sweatshops would probably like to take the day off too. The work must be done, and failure wasn't an option. No excuses.

"Waaaaait a minute," she said, peering into my face. "We've met before." I looked more closely at her too. A different name came to mind. "Luna!"

"Robin!" she responded. That had been the nom de guerre I'd used long ago: Robin Banks. *The New York Times* actually printed it, not noticing the pun, under a photo of me at a protest against the KKK in Atlanta back in 1988.

We figured out how long it had been since we'd worked together in New York: twenty-six years. It seemed fitting that my path, which had split off from the RCYB/RCP in the mid-1990s, had converged here with that of a long-ago comrade. The system was grinding forward with an intensity of violence that couldn't have been imagined by our young selves, and here we were again, confronting it still.

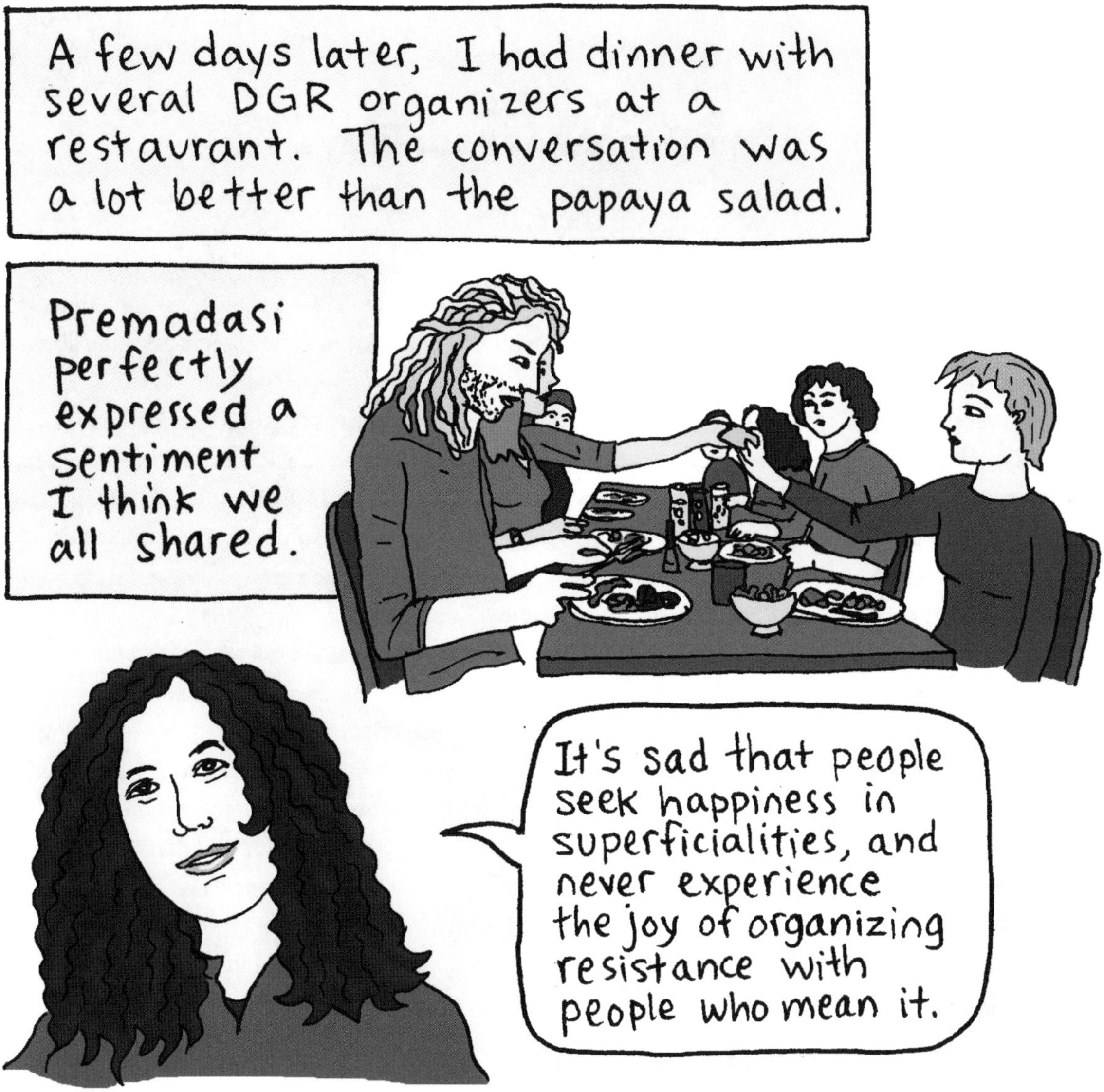
A few days later, I had dinner with several DGR organizers at a restaurant. The conversation was a lot better than the papaya salad.
Premadasi perfectly expressed a sentiment I think we all shared.
It's sad that people seek happiness in superficialities, and never experience the joy of organizing resistance with people who mean it.

The Danger of Populism

BARELY into Occupy's second month, Daniel raised a warning about populism. "This, along with opportunism, is the biggest danger. It could set the movement back decades, and the American left is totally unprepared," he said.

Most of the rest of us didn't have a clear conception of what populism was. I had some vague notion that it referred to ideas that were prevalent while not explicitly working-class-oriented, but I didn't understand what the problem was. Public wrath at "the elite" or "the 1 percent" was basically good, wasn't it? We were so excited that something—anything—was finally happening that this wasn't on the top of our worry list (inactivity was). But Daniel, who had seen populism wipe out years of revolutionary work in Haiti, insisted that we talk about it.

He proposed a document on the topic for us to discuss within One Struggle, and worked with two others to produce it. "Too much jargon," was the verdict of one young member. "Our conception of popular movements needs to be more fluid," said another.

With so much going on in the first months of Occupy's rapid growth, we couldn't collectively focus on it long enough to refine it to a point where we could all agree on it, so it wasn't publicly released. (I include excerpts as an Appendix with the group's permission.)

Daniel set the topic aside for the time being. He'd tried. "One Struggle itself is separated by only a thin hairline from populism," he said. "It's the nature of this moment. At least we raised the question among ourselves."

Later I was reading Slavoj Žižek's *Living in the End Times*. He also warned: "The key question now is: who will articulate this [social] discontent? Will it be left to nationalist populists to exploit? Therein resides the big task for the Left."

Most of us in the US don't understand populism or many other concepts relevant to political struggle. Even those of us who are active lag far behind much of the world in our grasp of theory—we don't recognize views as coherent lines, and therefore we're incapable of calling them by name, much less foreseeing their far-ranging implications.

But we can't keep blithely disdaining the use of "jargon." These words may feel cumbersome and persnickety in our casual, 140-characters-or-less, news-o-tainment culture, but their precision allows us to conceptualize, identify, and decide to accept or reject ideological and political phenomena that could make all the difference to our eventual success or failure.

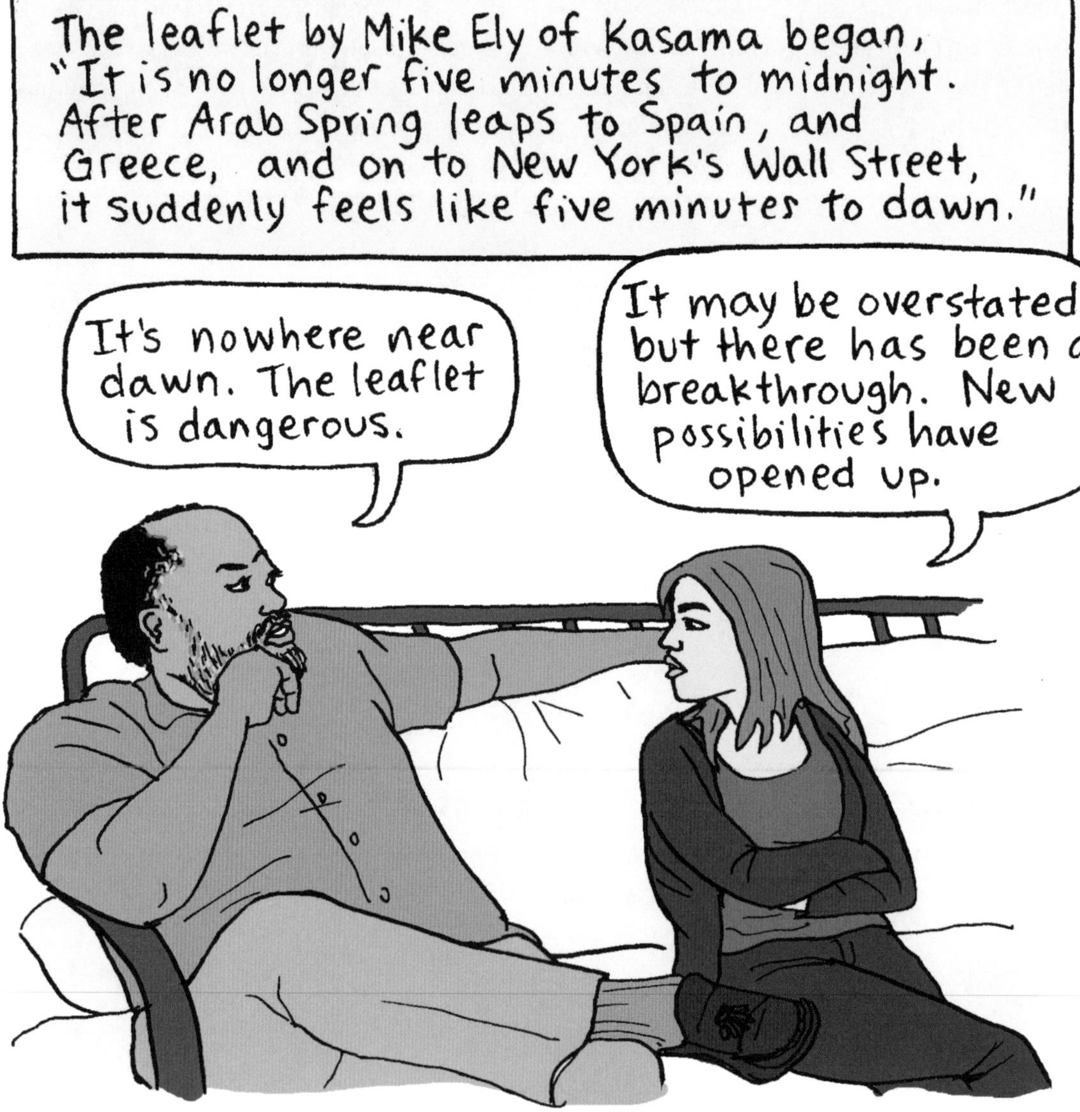
The leaflet by Mike Ely of Kasama began, "It is no longer five minutes to midnight. After Arab Spring leaps to Spain, and Greece, and on to New York's Wall Street, it suddenly feels like five minutes to dawn."
It's nowhere near dawn. The leaflet is dangerous.
It may be overstated, but there has been a breakthrough. New possibilities have opened up.

Had the revolution begun?
Pfft. This is not a revolution. It's not even a movement. Unless we organize, we'll end up with nothing.
It's a qualitatively new development. The revolution has to start somewhere. It can't appear fully formed. For the first time in decades, people are questioning the structure of society.
We're so far behind where we need to be.

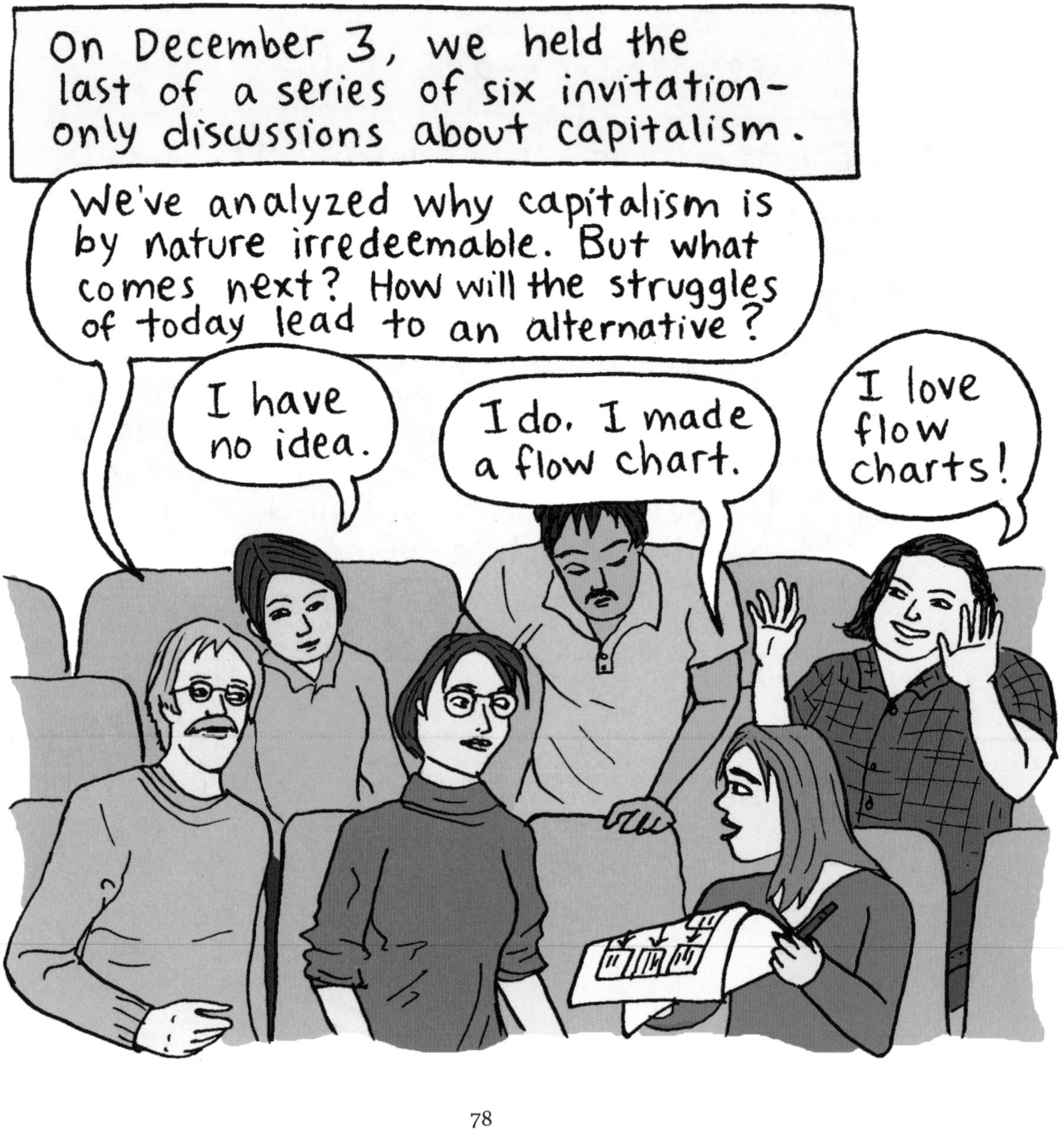
On December 3, we held the last of a series of six invitation-only discussions about capitalism.
We've analyzed why capitalism is by nature irredeemable. But what comes next? How will the struggles of today lead to an alternative?
I have no idea.
I do. I made a flow chart.
I love flow charts!

state power

WE ARE HERE	→	Stop the horrors	→	Positive steps	→	GOALS
Economic exploitation	Universal equal income	Cancel debts. End inheritance	Dispossess capitalists of capital	De-incentivize competition	Collective meeting of needs	Collective
Monopolization of means of subsistence	Free food, medical care, housing, education, etc.	Shut down unnecessary production	Shift to cooperative local production			
Imperialism	Shut down military bases	Stop exports of waste, weapons. Stop unnecessary imports	Withdraw from global economy	End international commerce	Local gift economies	
Ecocide	Shut down extreme extraction	Conservation/ Less energy use	Shift to sustainable farming methods	Clean up and repair damage	Transition to non-extractive way of life	Sustainable
Repression	Open up political process	Free flow of information	Facilitate universal participation		Collective decision-making	Egalitarian
Oppression	End institutional oppression (death penalty, prisons, unequal pay, etc.)	Combat ideological support for oppression	Autonomy/ self-determination	Oppressed define path to liberation	End oppressive social forms (nuclear families, states, etc.)	Voluntary

Draft 12/3/11

Meanwhile, Oakland, CA, with a long history of struggle, experienced harsh repression and became a center of advanced resistance.

On October 24, Iraq War veteran Scott Olsen was severely injured by a police projectile.

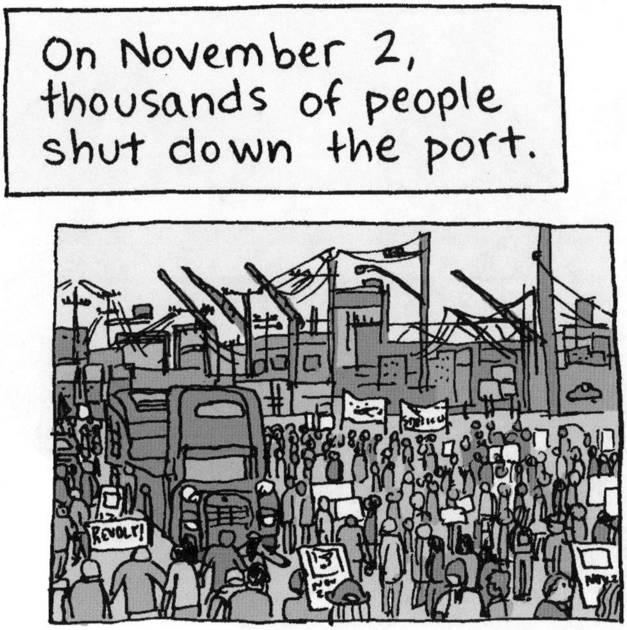
On November 2, thousands of people shut down the port.
REVOLT!

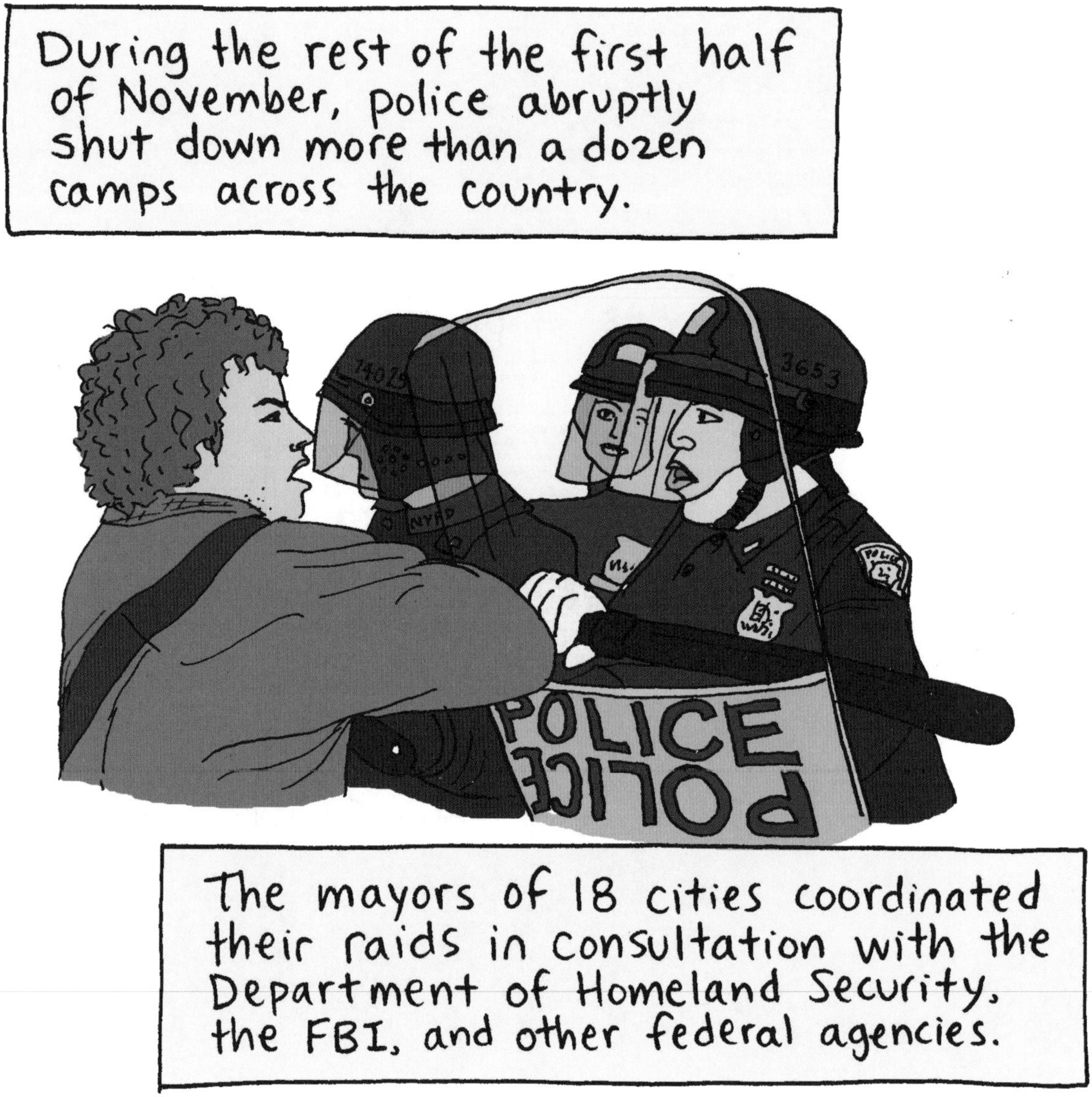
During the rest of the first half of November, police abruptly shut down more than a dozen camps across the country.
14025
3653
NYPD
POLICE
POLICE
The mayors of 18 cities coordinated their raids in consultation with the Department of Homeland Security, the FBI, and other federal agencies.

UC-DAVIS. NOVEMBER 18.

University police pepper sprayed students sitting peacefully in the quad. Video of the incident was shared around the world.

"A lot of the students who were on the fence or weren't following the movement closely are getting very involved now."
~Thomas Fowler, student

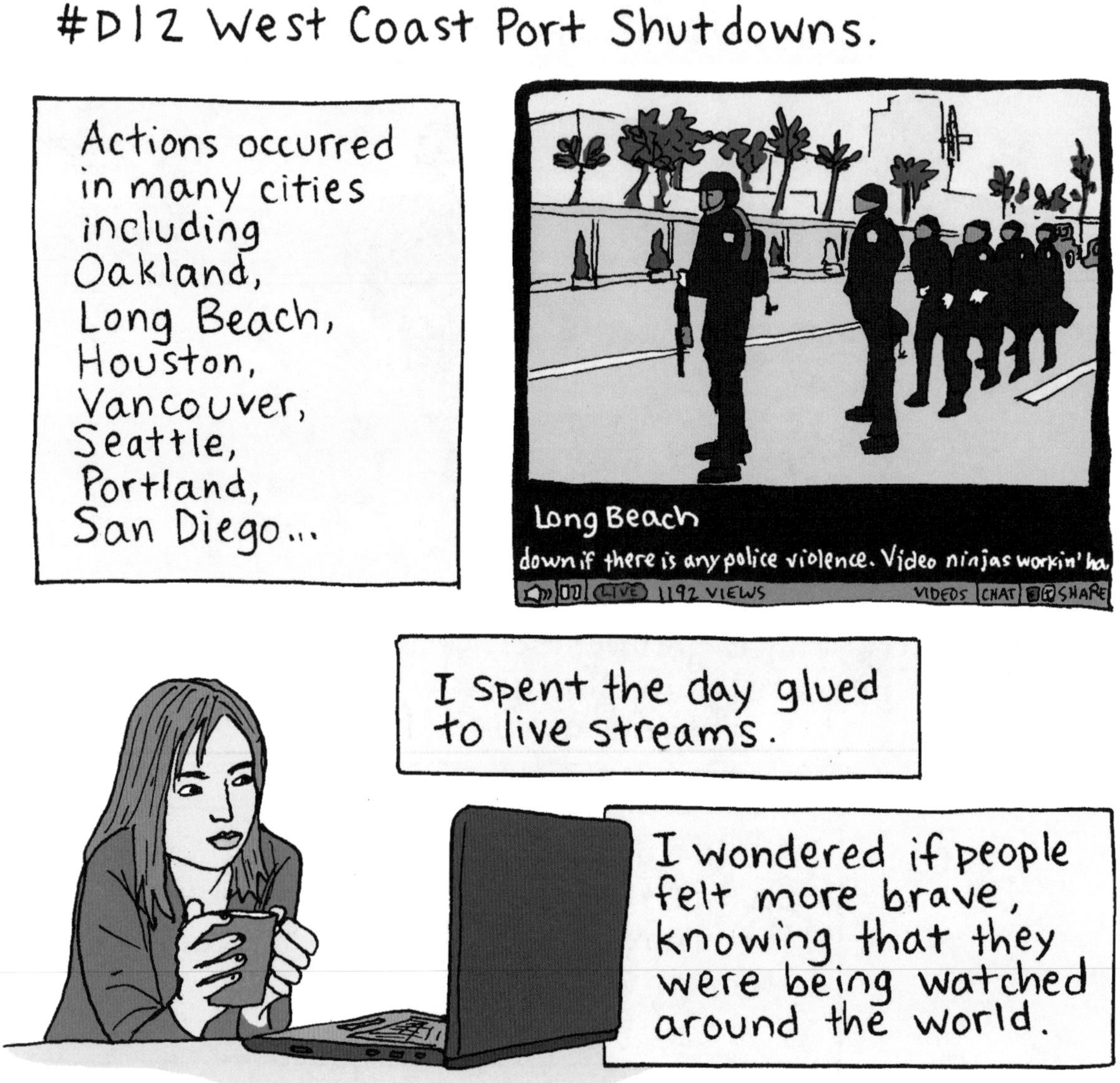
#D12 West Coast Port Shutdowns.
Actions occurred in many cities including Oakland, Long Beach, Houston, Vancouver, Seattle, Portland, San Diego...
Long Beach
down if there is any police violence. Video ninjas workin' ha
LIVE 1192 VIEWS
VIDEOS CHAT SHARE
I spent the day glued to live streams.
I wondered if people felt more brave, knowing that they were being watched around the world.

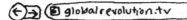

#OCCUPYWALLSTREET– LIVE STREAMING SINCE SEPTEMBER 17TH

LIVE San Diego
Threatened with dispersal

Shut down! Long Beach: Longshoremen not coming to work today! The people

◁)) OD LIVE 1027 VIEWS   VIDEOS CHAT SHARE

I teared up when military vets filed into the space in front of the police to protect the protesters...

...a much nobler act than fighting wars for U.S. imperialism.

These events spilled over into my daily comic strip, "Minimum Security." I had to revise the entire story I had planned, after real life surpassed my predictions.

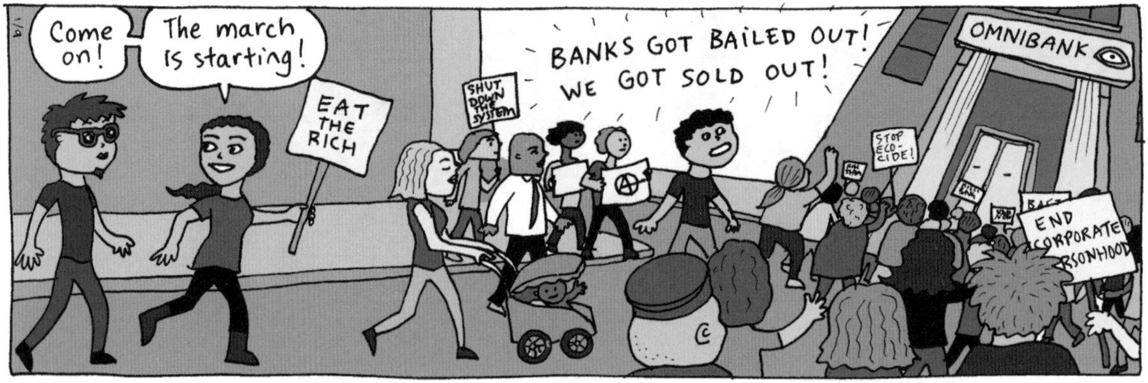
1/9
Come on!
The march is starting!
EAT THE RICH
SHUT DOWN THE SYSTEM
BANKS GOT BAILED OUT! WE GOT SOLD OUT!
OMNIBANK
STOP ECO-CIDE!
END CORPORATE

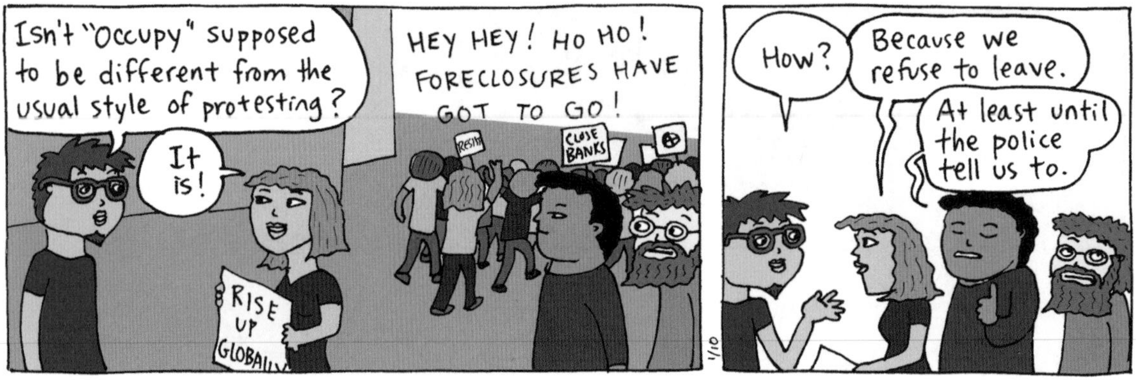
Isn't "Occupy" supposed to be different from the usual style of protesting?
It is!
RISE UP
HEY HEY! HO HO! FORECLOSURES HAVE GOT TO GO!
CLOSE BANKS
1/10
How?
Because we refuse to leave.
At least until the police tell us to.

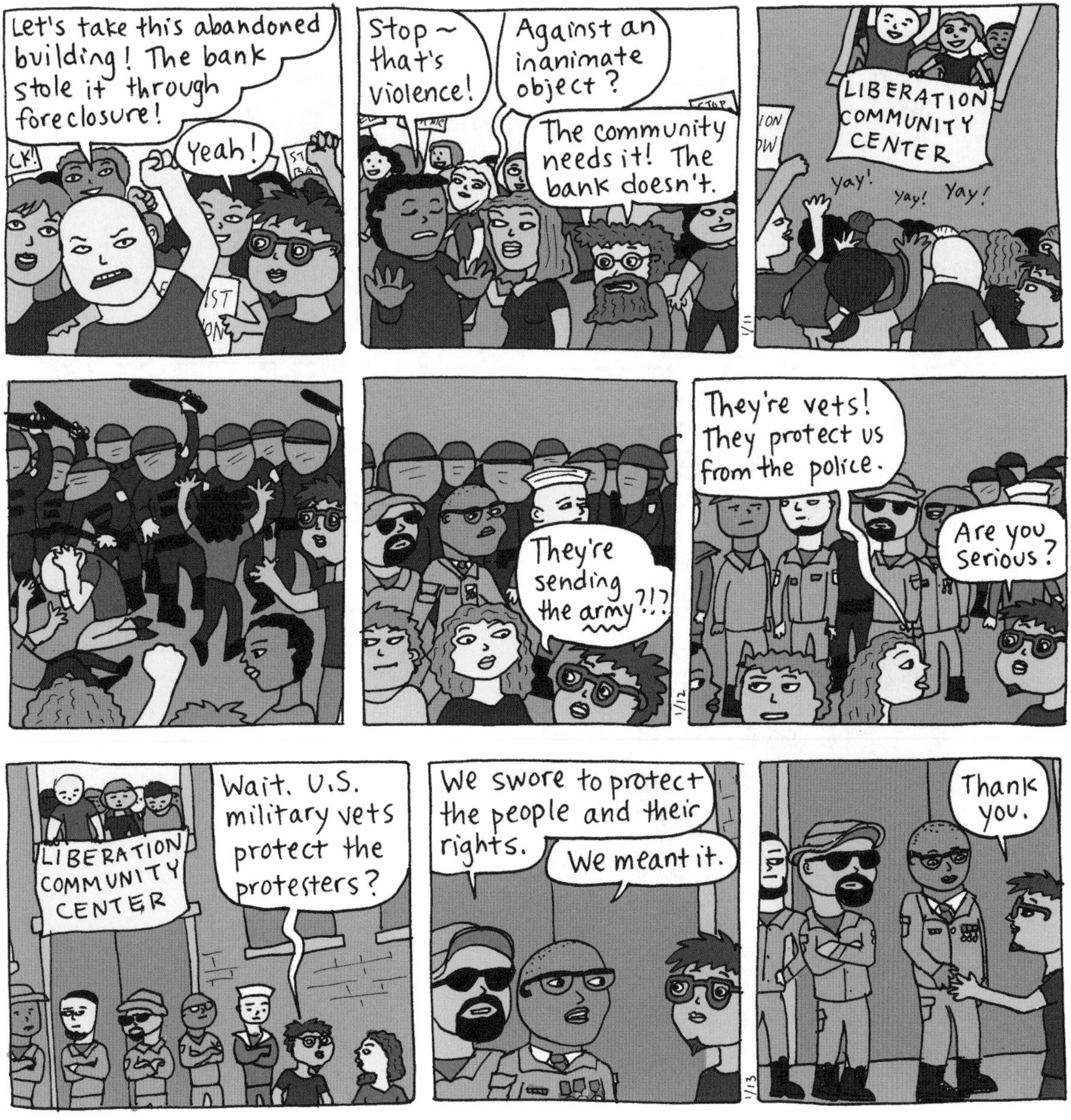
Let's take this abandoned building! The bank stole it through foreclosure!
Yeah!
Stop ~ that's violence!
Against an inanimate object?
The community needs it! The bank doesn't.
1/11
LIBERATION COMMUNITY CENTER
Yay!
Yay!
Yay!
They're sending the army?!?
1/12
They're vets! They protect us from the police.
Are you serious?
LIBERATION COMMUNITY CENTER
Wait. U.S. military vets protect the protesters?
We swore to protect the people and their rights.
We meant it.
1/13
Thank you.

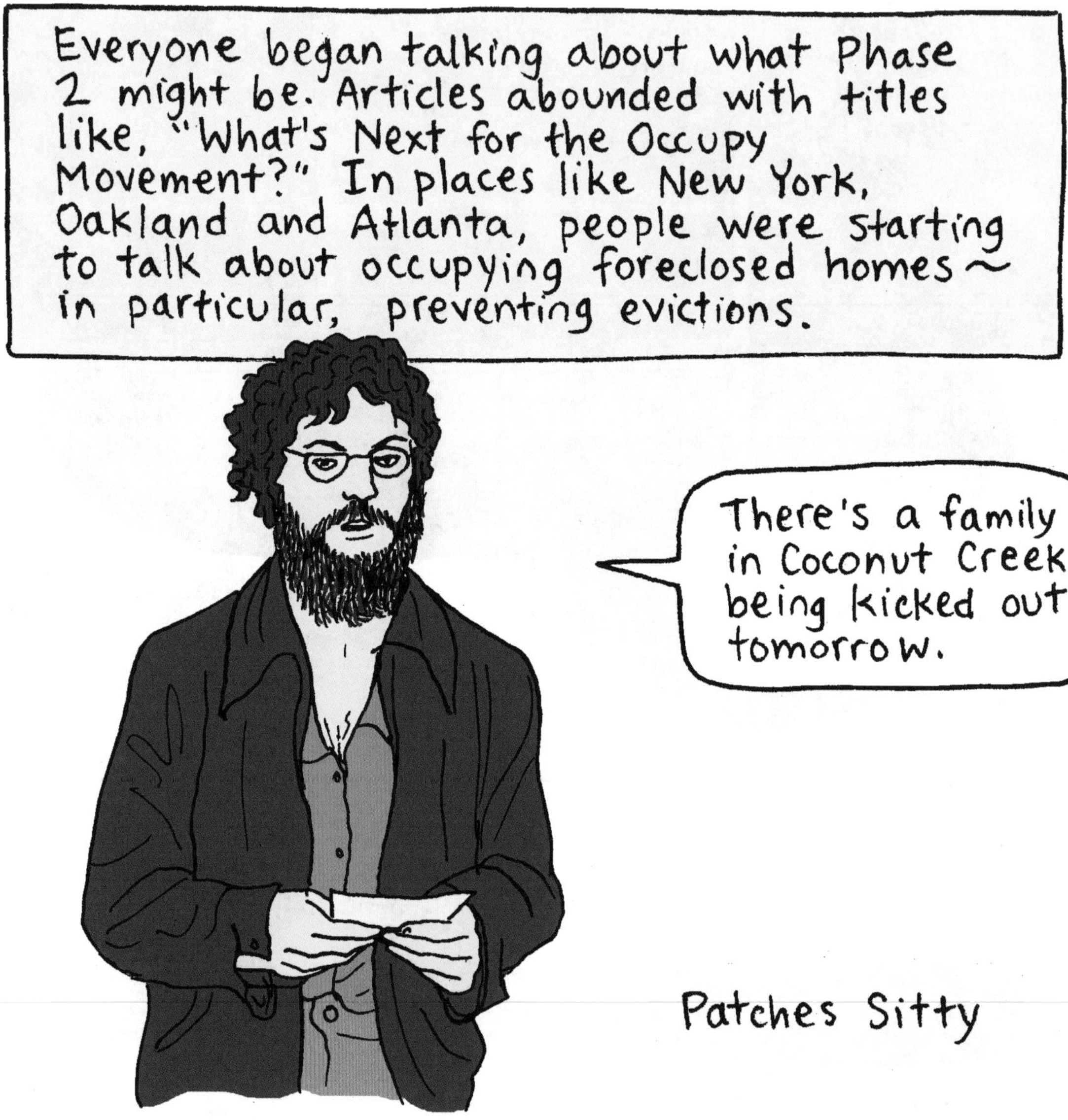
Everyone began talking about what Phase 2 might be. Articles abounded with titles like, "What's Next for the Occupy Movement?" In places like New York, Oakland and Atlanta, people were starting to talk about occupying foreclosed homes ~ in particular, preventing evictions.
There's a family in Coconut Creek being kicked out tomorrow.
Patches Sitty

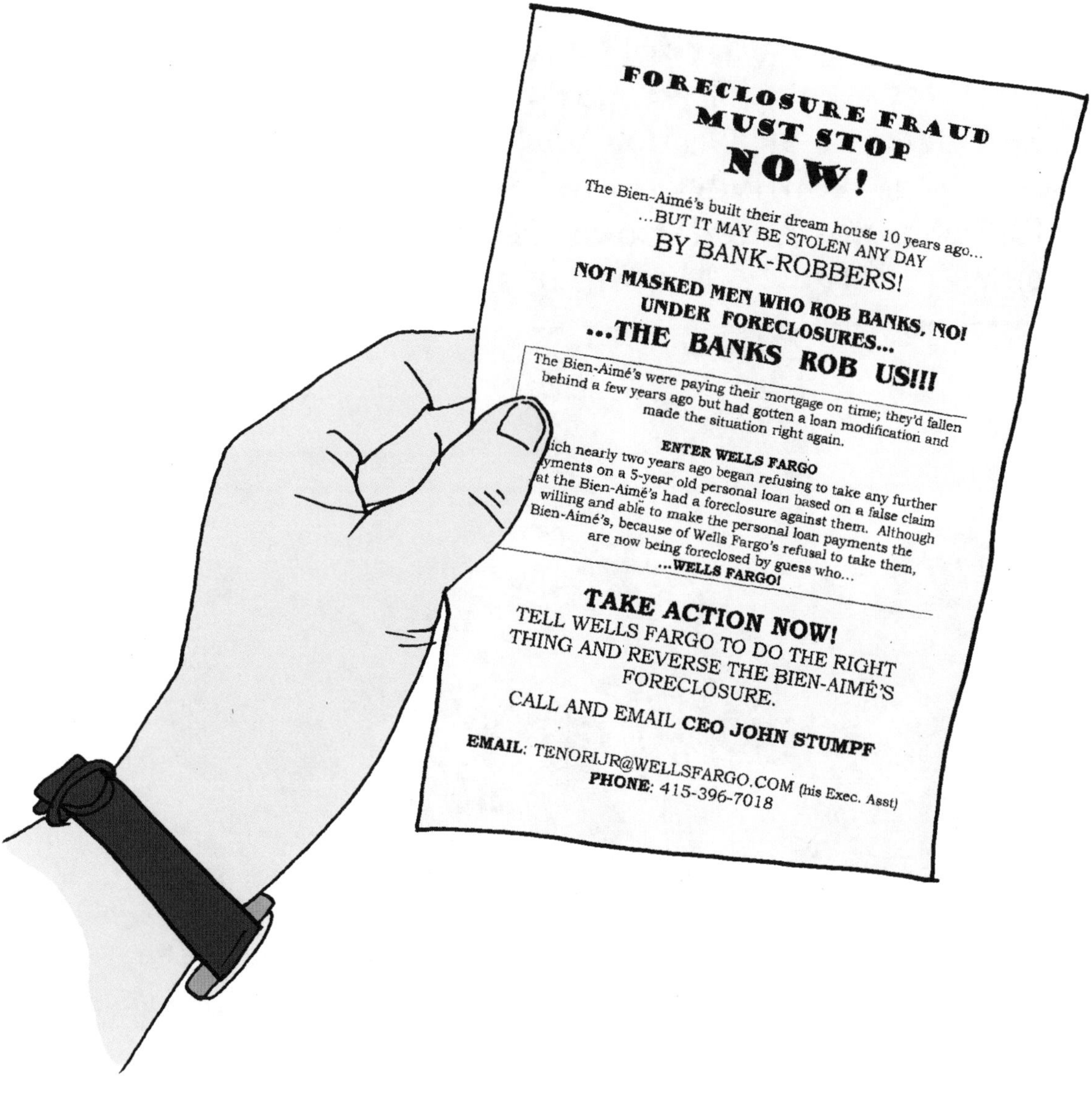
FORECLOSURE FRAUD
MUST STOP
NOW!
The Bien-Aimé's built their dream house 10 years ago...
...BUT IT MAY BE STOLEN ANY DAY
BY BANK-ROBBERS!
NOT MASKED MEN WHO ROB BANKS, NO!
UNDER FORECLOSURES...
...THE BANKS ROB US!!!
The Bien-Aimé's were paying their mortgage on time; they'd fallen behind a few years ago but had gotten a loan modification and made the situation right again.
ENTER WELLS FARGO
ich nearly two years ago began refusing to take any further yments on a 5-year old personal loan based on a false claim at the Bien-Aimé's had a foreclosure against them. Although willing and able to make the personal loan payments the Bien-Aimé's, because of Wells Fargo's refusal to take them, are now being foreclosed by guess who...
...WELLS FARGO!
TAKE ACTION NOW!
TELL WELLS FARGO TO DO THE RIGHT THING AND REVERSE THE BIEN-AIMÉ'S FORECLOSURE.
CALL AND EMAIL CEO JOHN STUMPF
EMAIL: TENORIJR@WELLSFARGO.COM (his Exec. Asst)
PHONE: 415-396-7018

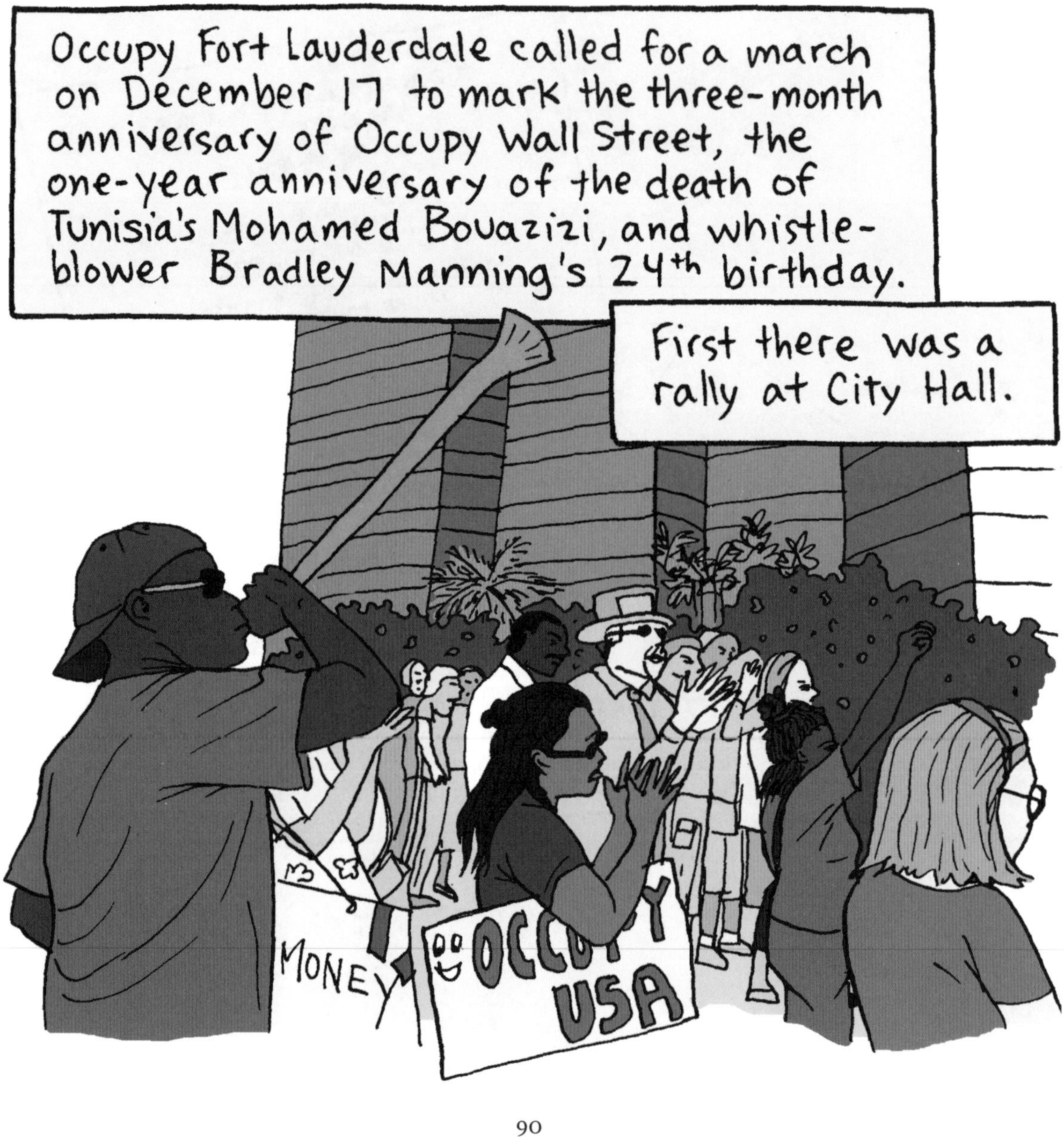
Occupy Fort Lauderdale called for a march on December 17 to mark the three-month anniversary of Occupy Wall Street, the one-year anniversary of the death of Tunisia's Mohamed Bouazizi, and whistle-blower Bradley Manning's 24th birthday.
First there was a rally at City Hall.
MONEY
USA

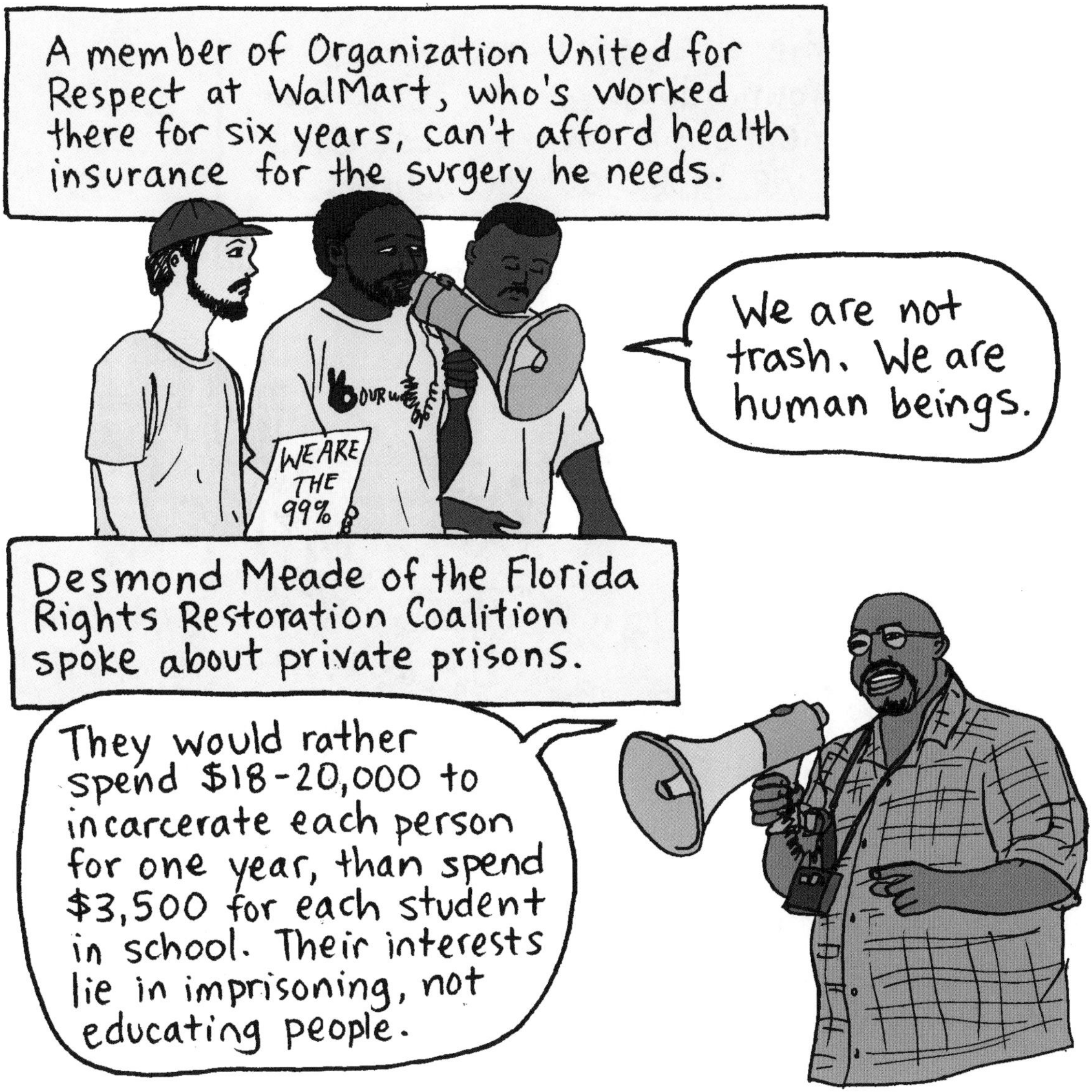
A member of Organization United for Respect at WalMart, who's worked there for six years, can't afford health insurance for the surgery he needs.
WE ARE THE 99%
We are not trash. We are human beings.
Desmond Meade of the Florida Rights Restoration Coalition spoke about private prisons.
They would rather spend $18-20,000 to incarcerate each person for one year, than spend $3,500 for each student in school. Their interests lie in imprisoning, not educating people.

Taking to the sidewalks, protesters marched around downtown. For a few heady moments on swanky Las Olas Boulevard, we broke out of bounds and took the street.

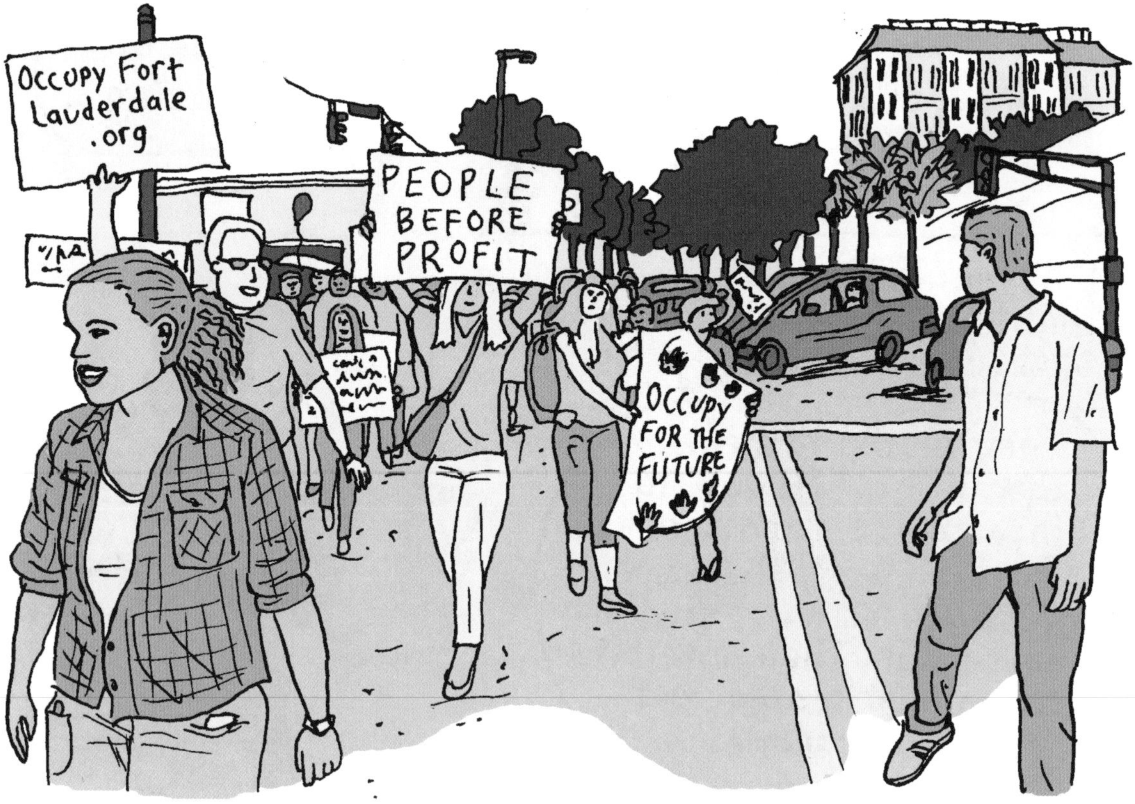
Occupy Fort Lauderdale .org
PEOPLE BEFORE PROFIT
OCCUPY FOR THE FUTURE

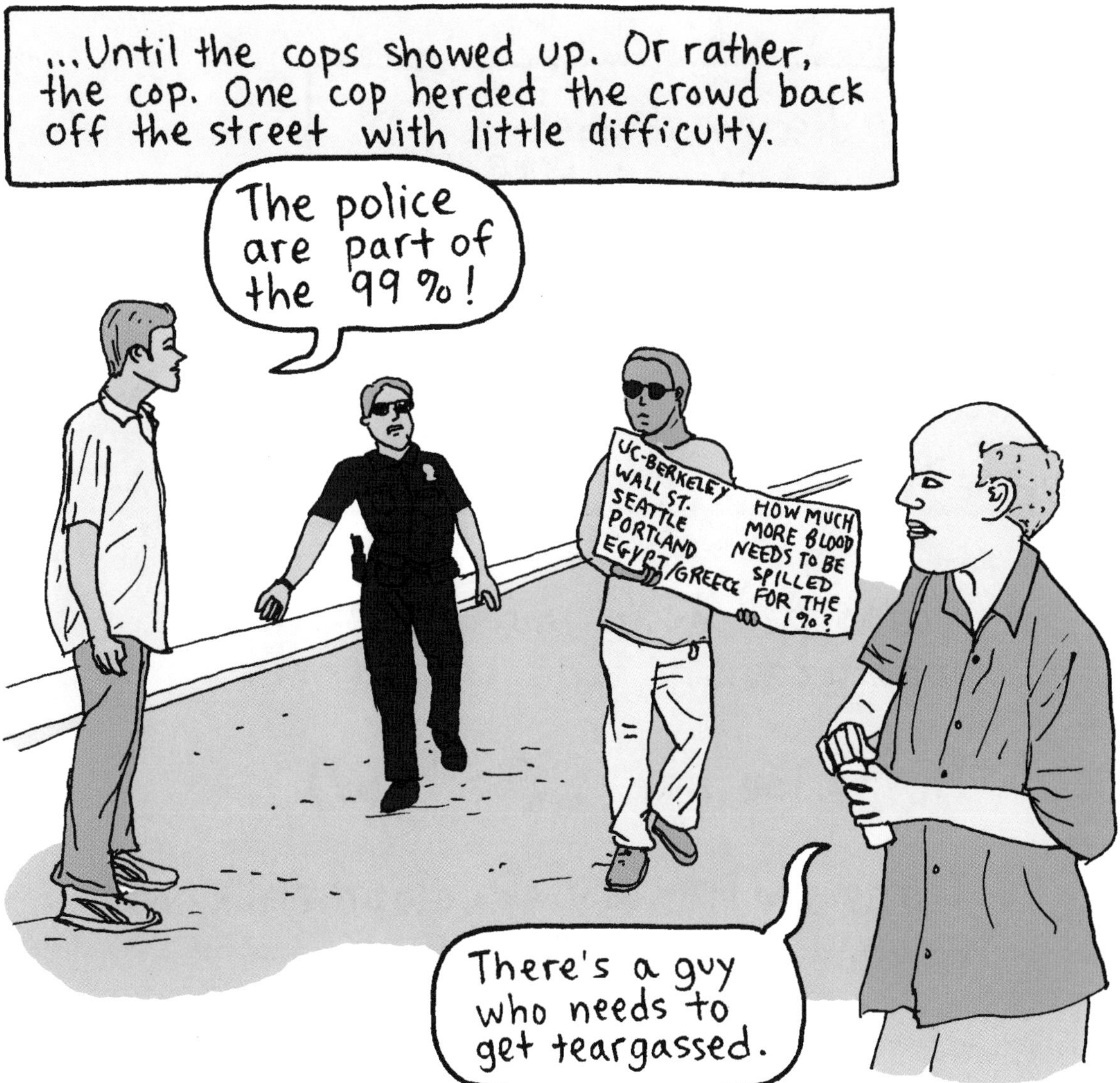
...Until the cops showed up. Or rather, the cop. One cop herded the crowd back off the street with little difficulty.
The police are part of the 99%!
UC-BERKELEY
WALL ST.
SEATTLE
PORTLAND
EGYPT/GREECE
HOW MUCH MORE BLOOD NEEDS TO BE SPILLED FOR THE 1%?
There's a guy who needs to get teargassed.

We discussed the advantages and pitfalls of working on foreclosures.

Pros:

- Trains people in mutual defense, organization, and resistance.

- Hurts the banks (perhaps).

- Turns stationary encampments into nimble, mobile teams.

Cons:

- Danger of getting diverted into social work.

- Encourages the concept of private property.

- If an organization only addresses immediate needs but not in a political context, it will lead to either being taken over by NGOs* or becoming one.

  (What could prevent that is if the people involved are organized to lead the work themselves, instead of activists leading it).

> *NGO: Non-Governmental Organization. NGOs and CBOs (Community-Based Organizations) are non-profit social service organizations that often receive funding from governments and/or business interests.

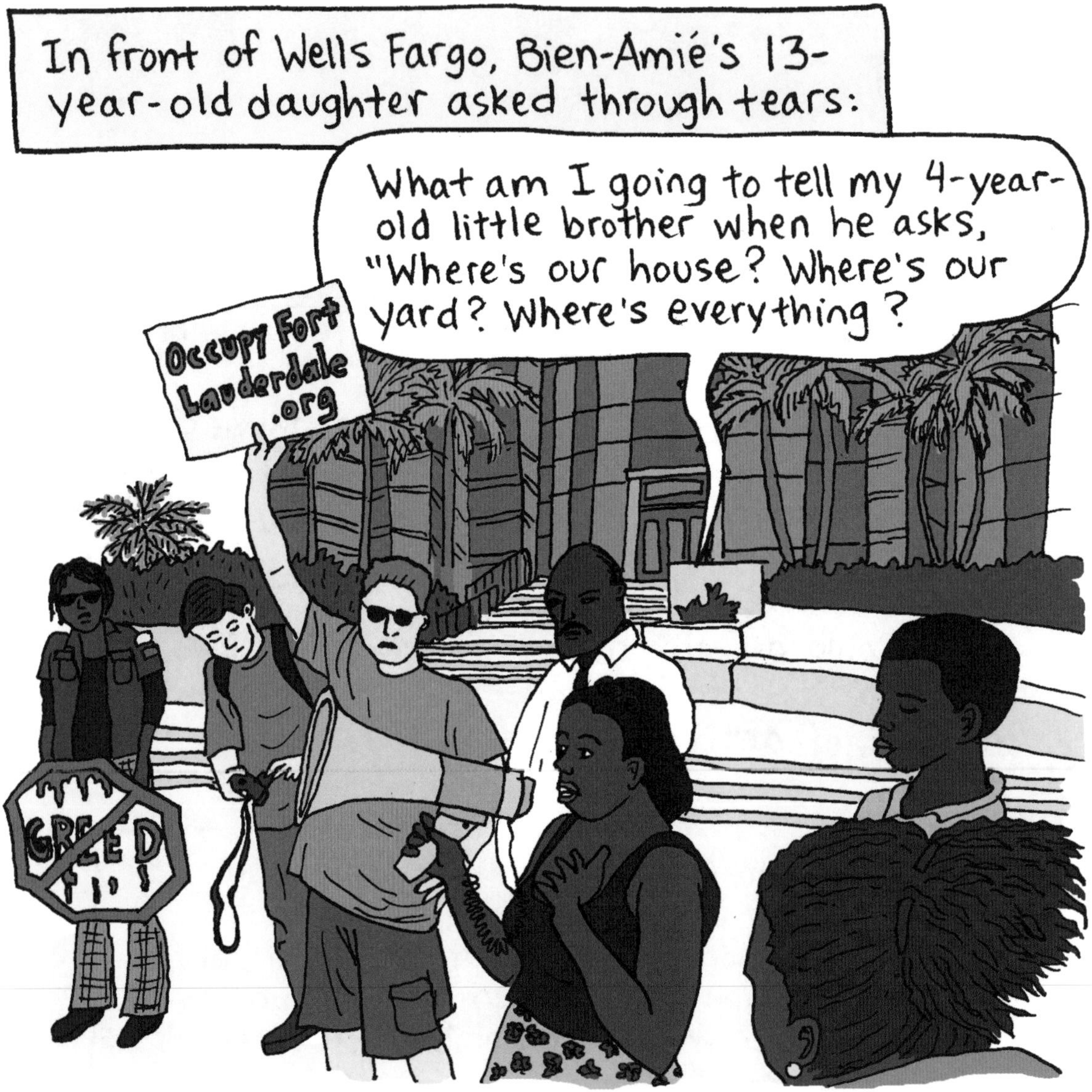
In front of Wells Fargo, Bien-Amié's 13-year-old daughter asked through tears:
What am I going to tell my 4-year-old little brother when he asks, "Where's our house? Where's our yard? Where's everything?
OccupyFortLauderdale.org
GREED

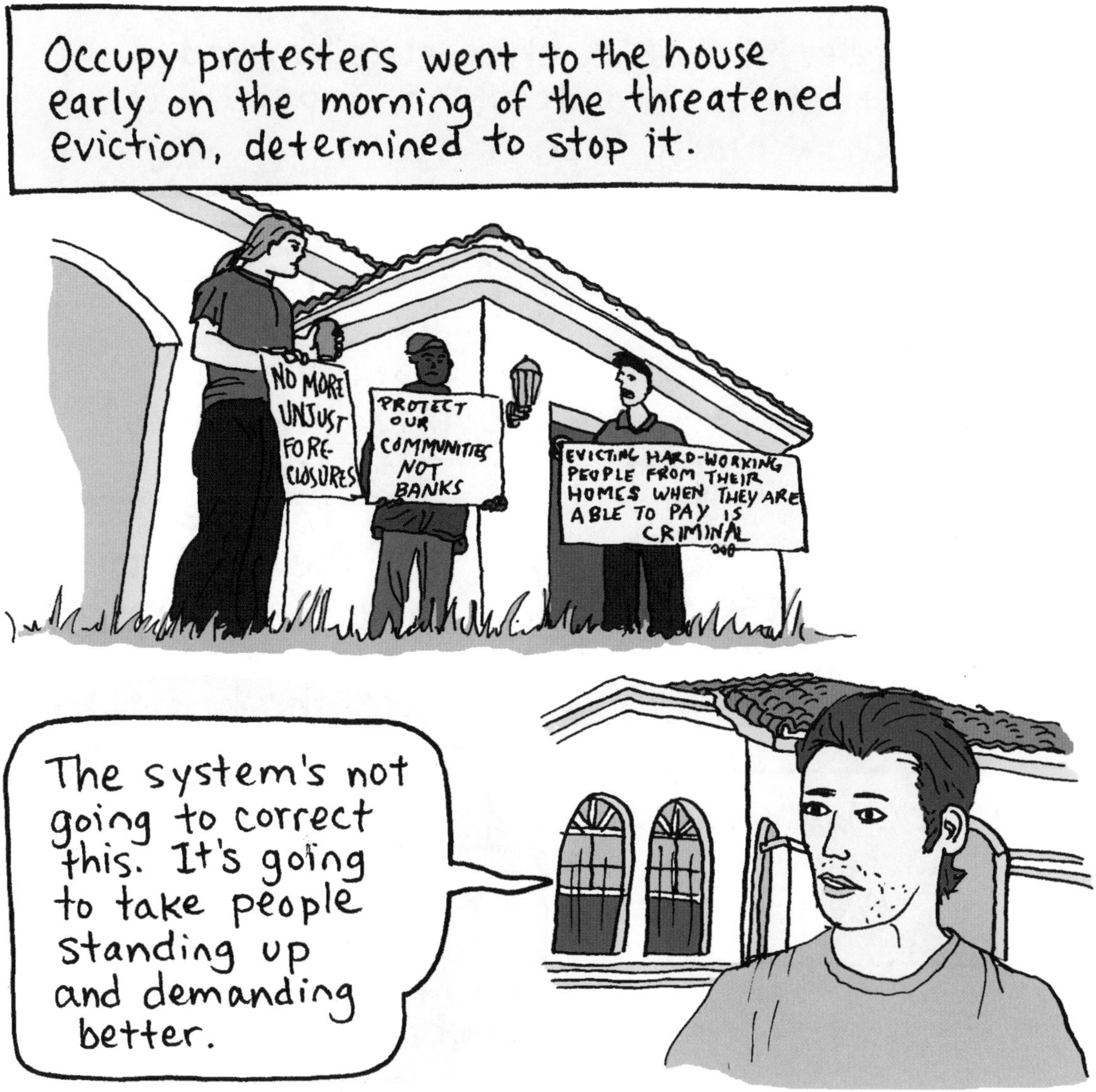
Occupy protesters went to the house early on the morning of the threatened eviction, determined to stop it.
NO MORE UNJUST FORE-CLOSURES
PROTECT OUR COMMUNITIES NOT BANKS
EVICTING HARD-WORKING PEOPLE FROM THEIR HOMES WHEN THEY ARE ABLE TO PAY IS CRIMINAL
The system's not going to correct this. It's going to take people standing up and demanding better.

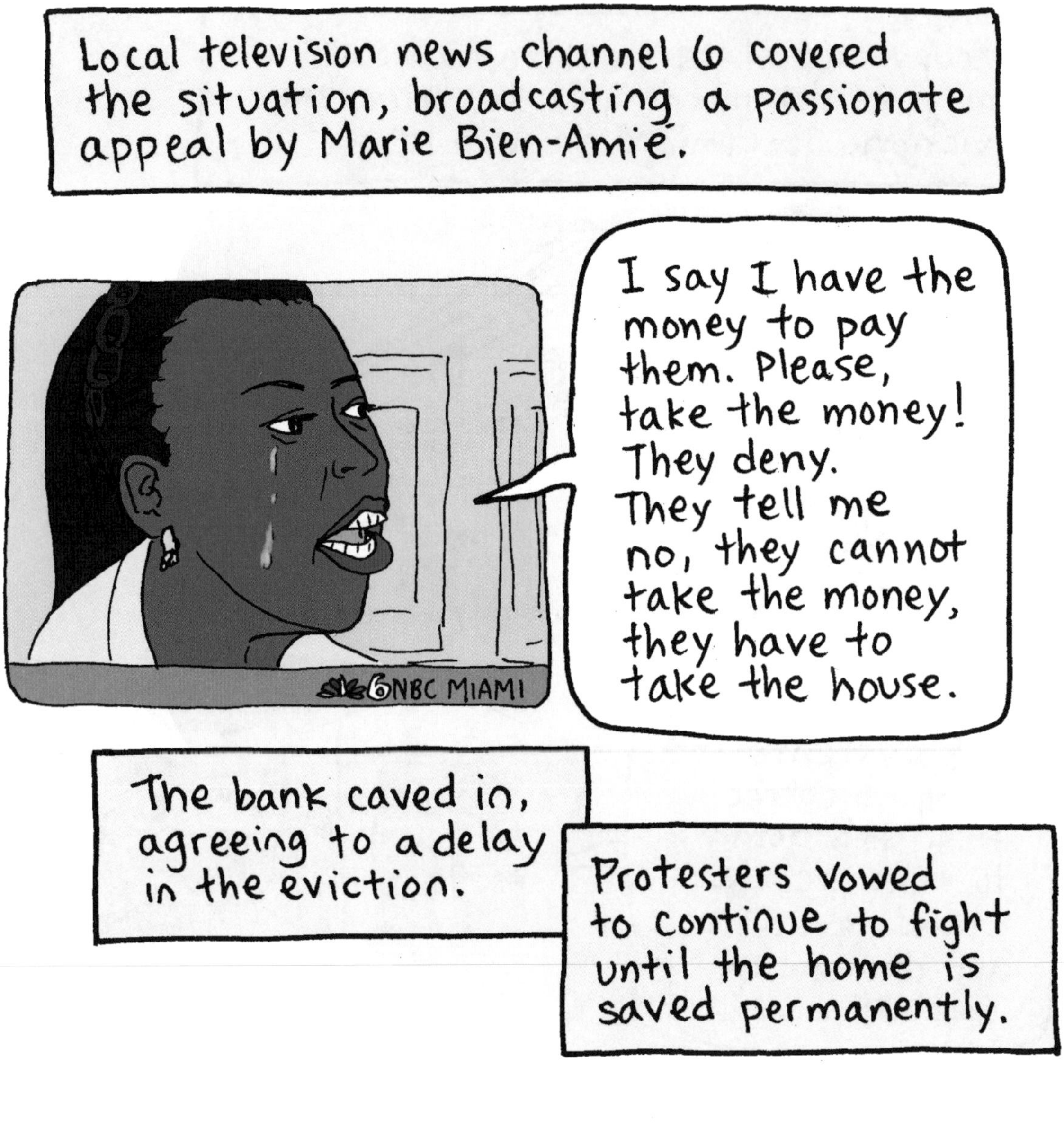
Local television news channel 6 covered the situation, broadcasting a passionate appeal by Marie Bien-Amié.
6NBC MIAMI
I say I have the money to pay them. Please, take the money! They deny. They tell me no, they cannot take the money, they have to take the house.
The bank caved in, agreeing to a delay in the eviction.
Protesters vowed to continue to fight until the home is saved permanently.

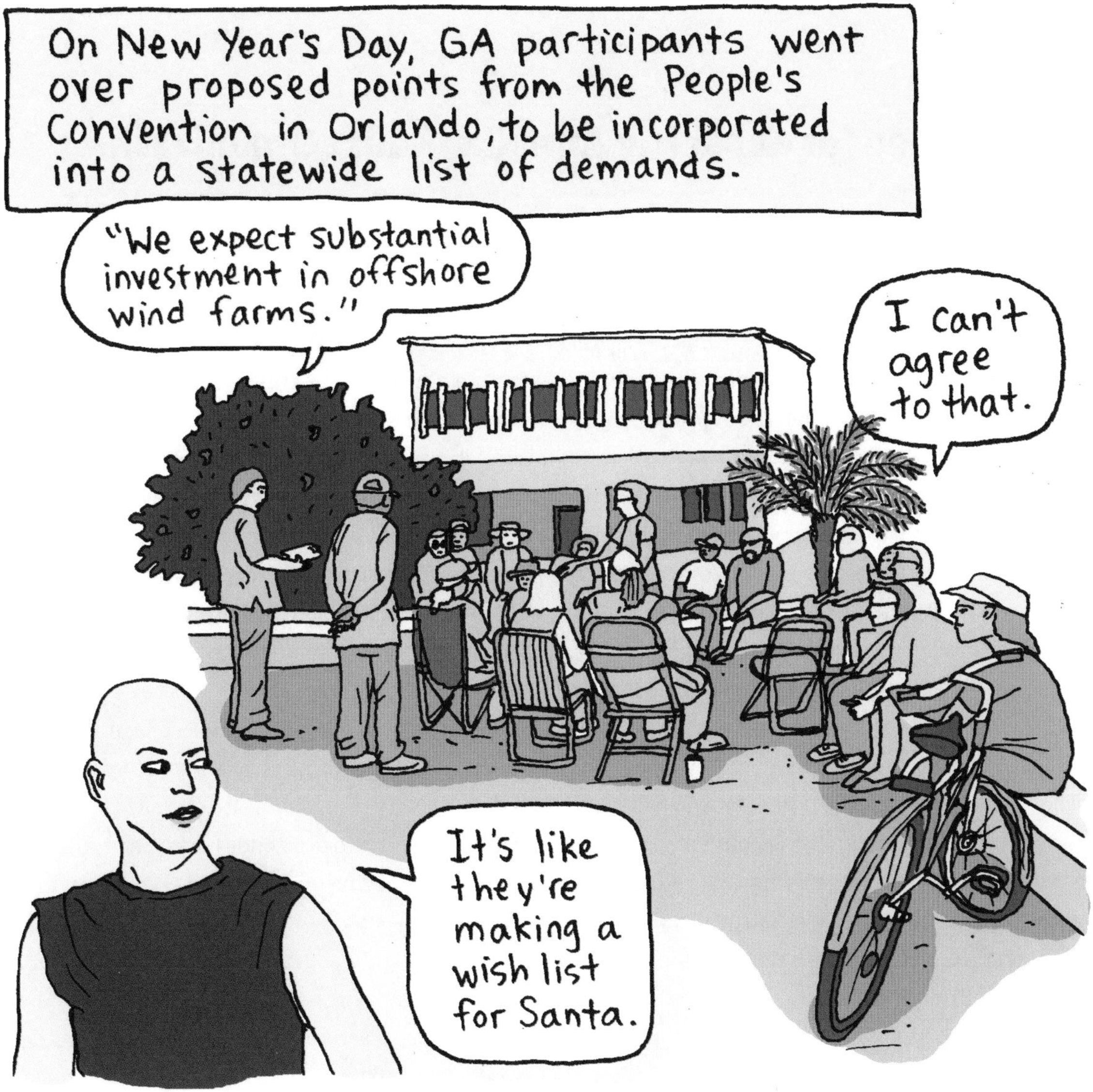
On New Year's Day, GA participants went over proposed points from the People's Convention in Orlando, to be incorporated into a statewide list of demands.
"We expect substantial investment in offshore wind farms."
I can't agree to that.
It's like they're making a wish list for Santa.

The Need for Explicitly Anti-Capitalist Organizations

MANY activists don't know how capitalism actually functions. We have to understand why the system is structurally impossible to reform, so that we can deal with the necessity—and our responsibility—not to fix it (because oppression is built into it from the start) but to do away with it, and figure out all that will entail. We may in fact be the last generation with the opportunity to do this.

Without digging under the surface to understand the system's true nature, it'll defeat us every time. In 2010, the spontaneous response by local activists to the BP oil spill in the Gulf of Mexico convinced me that we needed an organization united on an anti-capitalist basis.

When the spill happened, I had, for various reasons, drifted away from being politically active years before. Instead of organizing, I had shifted to attempting to influence "hearts and minds" by drawing cartoons as a means to expose the system. But the oil spill angered me so profoundly that I felt compelled to join a demonstration in front of a neighborhood BP station, holding a sign in the hot sun—which I got tired of in five minutes. I've done my time holding signs on sidewalks, and it never accomplished anything before, and it wasn't accomplishing anything this time either. BP was still setting oil-covered sea turtles on fire and spraying Corexit into the water.

So I decided to strategize with a few local activists to come up with something more effective. We called for an open meeting to form a coalition to shut down BP and stop offshore oil drilling, and publicized it. That seems like a common-sense approach, but it was a mistake.

The system has many methods of dealing with dissent. One is open repression. But before they resort to that, they try everything else, including co-opting it. They draw it into dead ends it creates for this purpose: pressuring public officials, working with corporate and state funded non-profits, exercising formal civil rights such as free speech—as long as we don't threaten the actual relationship of power, we have all these means of dissent that we're permitted to exercise. And because the system has ideological hegemony (in other words, brainwashing), most people can't conceptualize resistance outside of this framework allowed by the system itself. Spontaneously, they follow the paths that have been laid out for them.

The first meeting had fifty people, which I initially thought was great. About 10 percent was a variety of progressive radicals; the rest were either long-time liberal activists or those who had never done anything political before but were outraged about the spill.

It seemed like a viable ratio. I figured that radicals could function as one trend within a diverse range. The problem was, we hadn't organized as a trend going into it. We didn't know each other very well, or have a plan. So what ended up happening was that radical approaches and proposals were ignored in favor of responses that the majority believed were open to them: to protest at a congressperson's office; to help a liberal commissioner get elected; to invite institutional environmental groups for yet another protest on the sidewalk, with signs reading "Clean Energy Now;" and to present public talks by "green" businesses.

One radical immediately saw where this was going, and walked out in the middle of the first meeting. By the third or fourth meeting, all the rest were gone. The collective demand shifted from stopping BP and all offshore drilling to one more "realistic"—

for safer valves on oil rigs. Finally, the group decided to plant a tree at a church.

There's absolutely nothing wrong with planting a tree at a church. It's a very nice thing to do. But it doesn't stop BP, much less challenge the system that allows entities like BP to destroy the planet.

I learned several lessons.

One: In society overall (and thus any open gathering), the default majority doesn't grasp the system's unreformable structure. They fail to identify it as the enemy, or to oppose it in any fundamental sense. So liberal and reformist ideas will tend to overwhelm the more radical ones.

Two: Individual radicals have little power. We need to be organized autonomously to exert collective influence within larger groups.

Three: There's an essential difference between mobilizations and movement building. Mobilizations aren't that difficult: when some new outrage occurs, issue a call and a bunch of angry people might come out. They don't have to agree on much. But when they go home again, we end up with nothing. We need to build organizations resilient enough to withstand the inevitable ebbs and flows of mass struggles.

This convinced me of the need to re-construct One Struggle (or something like it). Now we can organize on a radical/progressive basis and have a stronger presence when working with other groups and coalitions.

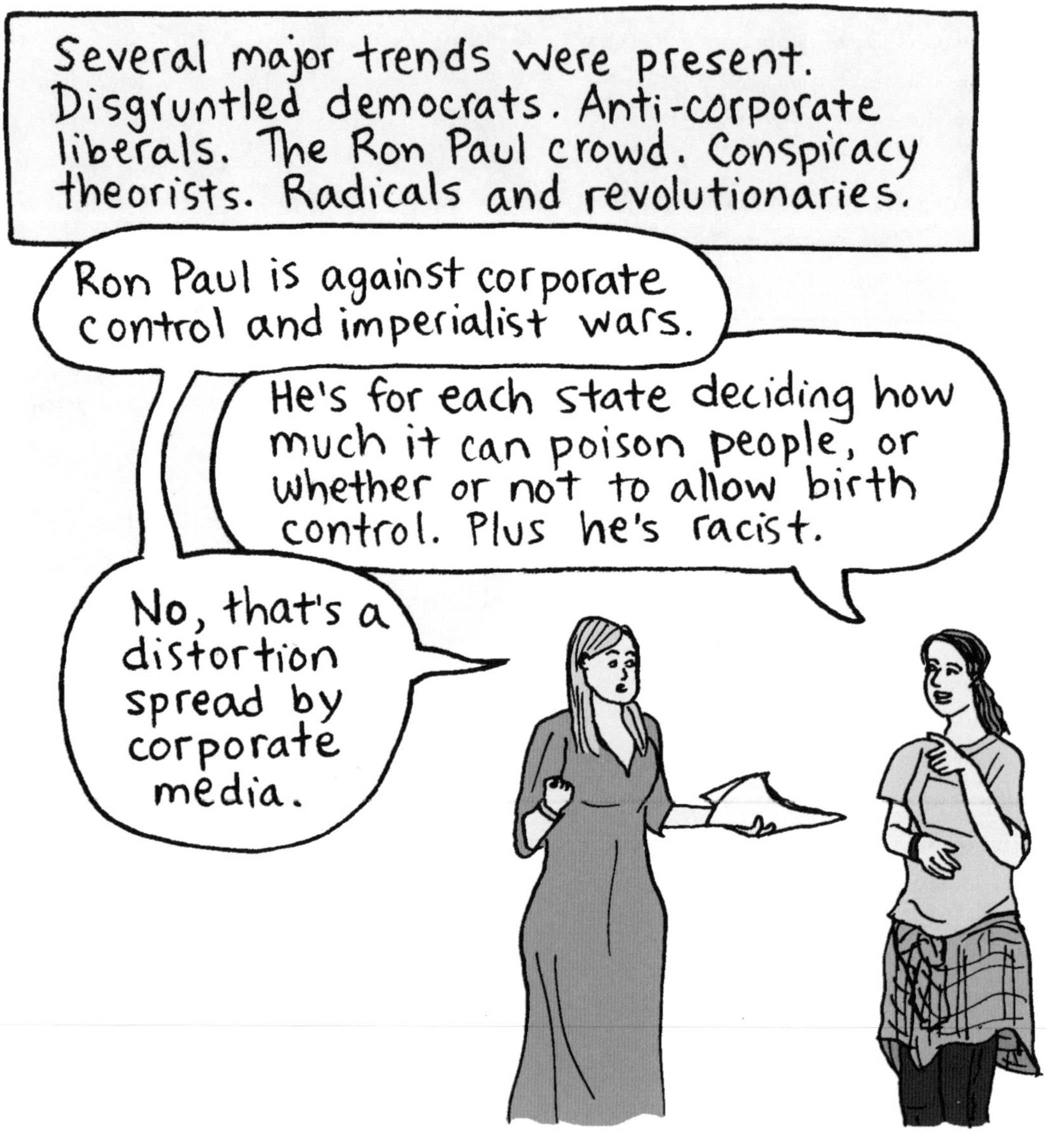

Several major trends were present. Disgruntled democrats. Anti-corporate liberals. The Ron Paul crowd. Conspiracy theorists. Radicals and revolutionaries.
Ron Paul is against corporate control and imperialist wars.
He's for each state deciding how much it can poison people, or whether or not to allow birth control. Plus he's racist.
No, that's a distortion spread by corporate media.

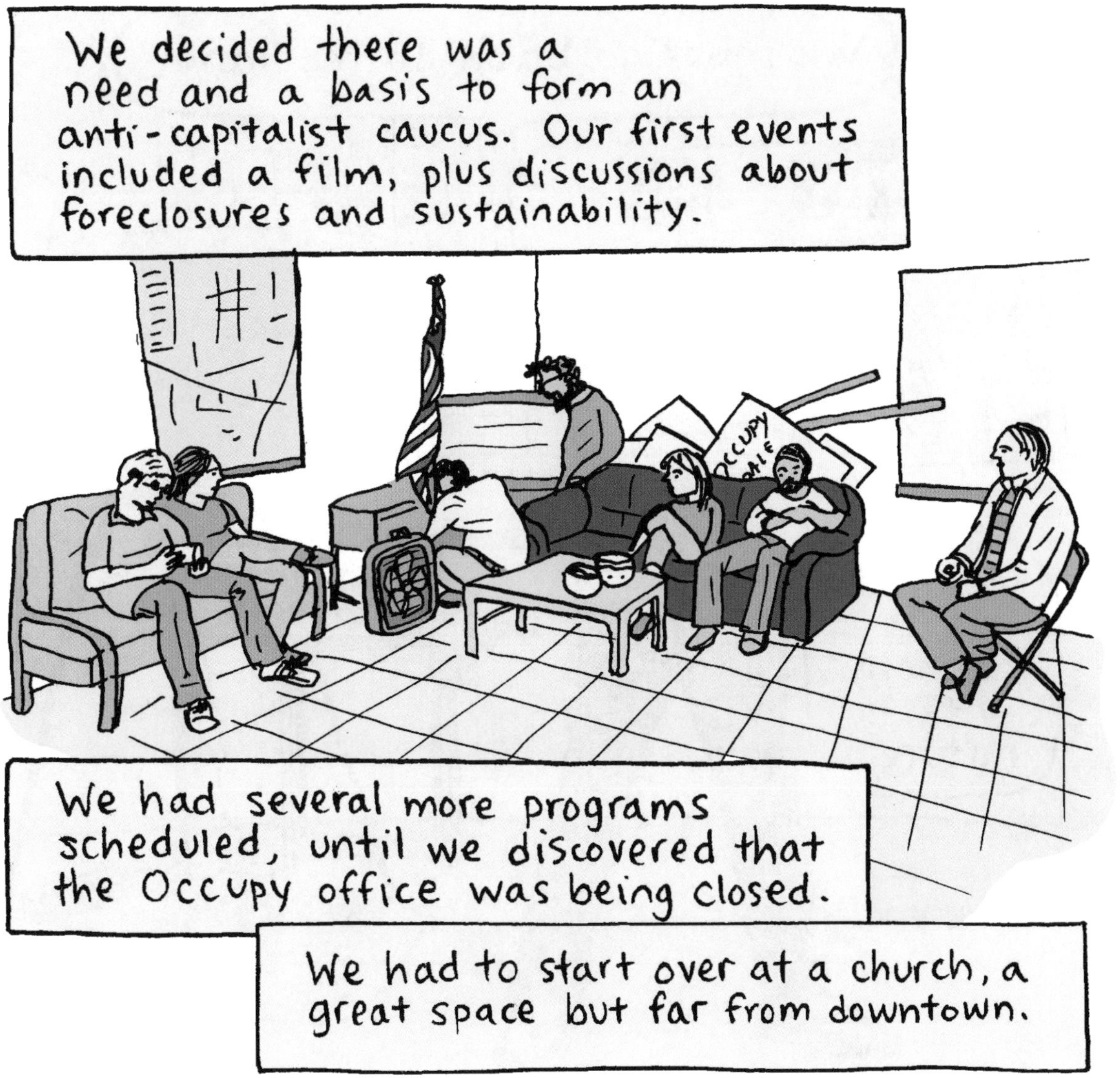
We decided there was a need and a basis to form an anti-capitalist caucus. Our first events included a film, plus discussions about foreclosures and sustainability.
We had several more programs scheduled, until we discovered that the Occupy office was being closed.
We had to start over at a church, a great space but far from downtown.

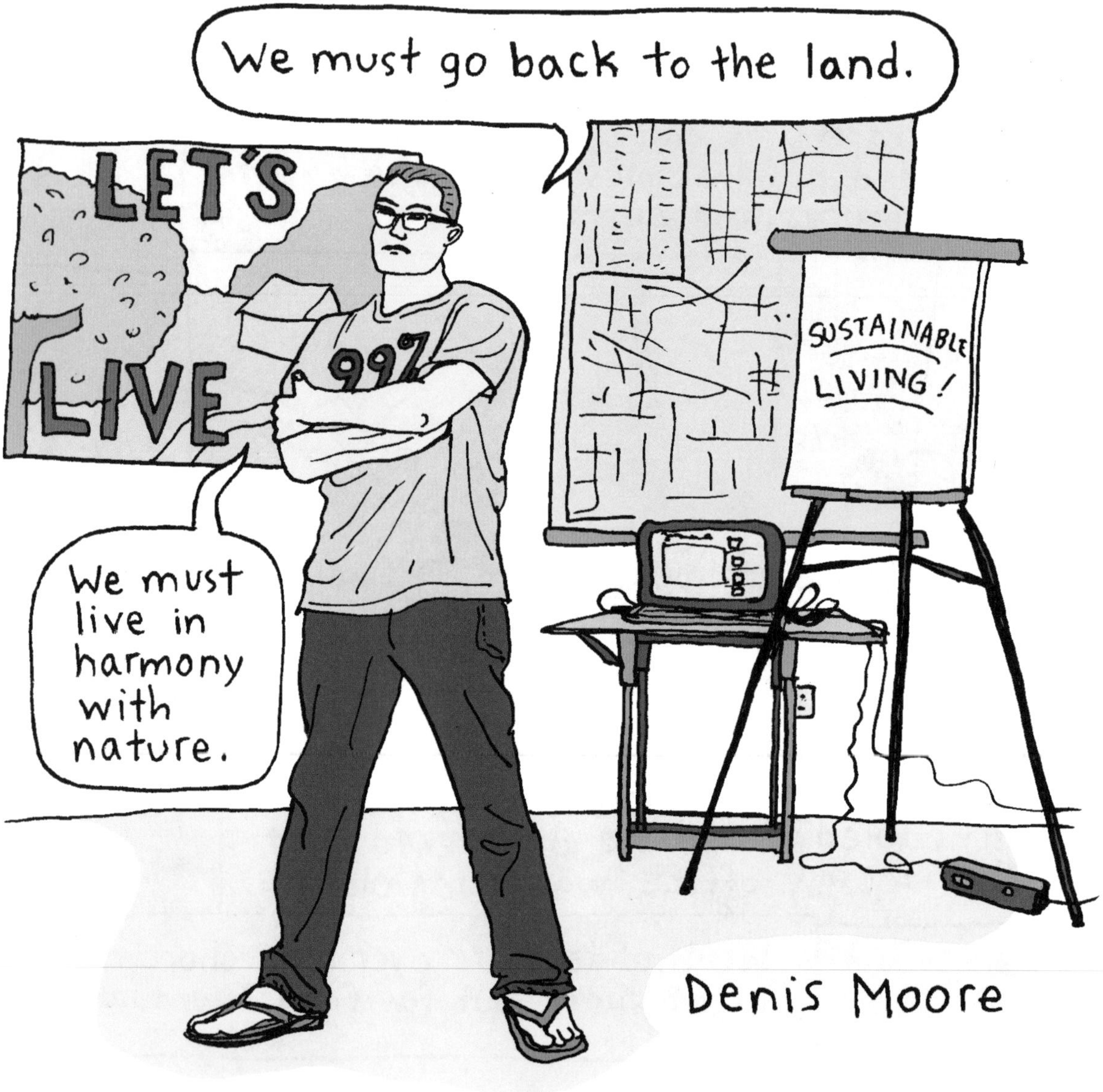
We must go back to the land.
LET'S LIVE
997
SUSTAINABLE LIVING!
We must live in harmony with nature.
Denis Moore

Taking Back Our Means of Subsistence

DENIS advocated building a new society within the old. I agree it needs to be done. We need to take back control of our means of subsistence and build an alternative to capitalism.

But what Denis didn't talk about and for me is an essential point, was that without also smashing the capitalists' state and seizing power, so that we can overturn the social relations that the state protects—so that we can stop them—harmony with nature can never be achieved.

Should we plant community gardens? Of course that's important, but it's not enough.

Monique asks: "How can food justice be anti-capitalist?"

A perfect question.

I don't have a full answer, but I know this:

This needs to be organized within our own communities, rather than be assisted or funded by any kind of non-profit, reformist entities.

We need to make land public, and collectively controlled by the people.

The system wants us to be sick and dysfunctional; we need to take control of our health and not accept toxic food.

We need to grow our food in dispersed locations that we'll be able to defend.

It's essential that we figure this out, since it's only when we can collectively provide for our own needs that we can break our dependency on the capitalist system and create an alternative to it that works. We need to take back the means of subsistence that they tore from us—for most of us, many generations ago. We need access to land, and to reconnect with the living world in mutually beneficial ways, re-learn how to live within (and preserve the health of) our bioregions.

Anti-Capitalism, Sure. But What Kind?

AT another anti-capitalist caucus meeting, I made a passing (and to me, obvious) point about needing to shift to sustainable farming methods like permaculture. The conversation snagged on an objection from a socialist of the "limitless abundance through development of the productive forces" type.

"As long as we don't have to do physical labor."

"Who's going to do it?"

"Robots."

"You want robots to work with plants and raise our food?"

"Right."

"That sounds like a total dystopia."

"You mean utopia."

"No, I mean dystopia."

He still didn't believe I knew what I was saying. "Utopia. A dystopia is— "

I broke in. "It sounds like hell."

Incredulous: "Really?"

Never mind the Democrats and Ron Paul enthusiasts—can we even find enough common ground among the few of us way over here on the far left? I mean, the anti-capitalist caucus meeting only drew about fifteen people, max, as it was. Were we really going to have to split up over the fine points of what kind of anti-capitalism?

We need to build a multi-tendency alliance if we're going to win, that embraces reds, greens, anarchists, anti-oppression activists of all kinds. But how can we achieve that, when even the difference between bright green and deep green is truly fundamental, leading in utterly opposite directions?

"We'll work that out later." I waved away the question of future food production for now. I knew we'd end up doing it by hand. He was equally as certain that robots would be invented and manufactured to do it. Meanwhile, we focused on our immediate concern: inflicting damage on our common enemy.

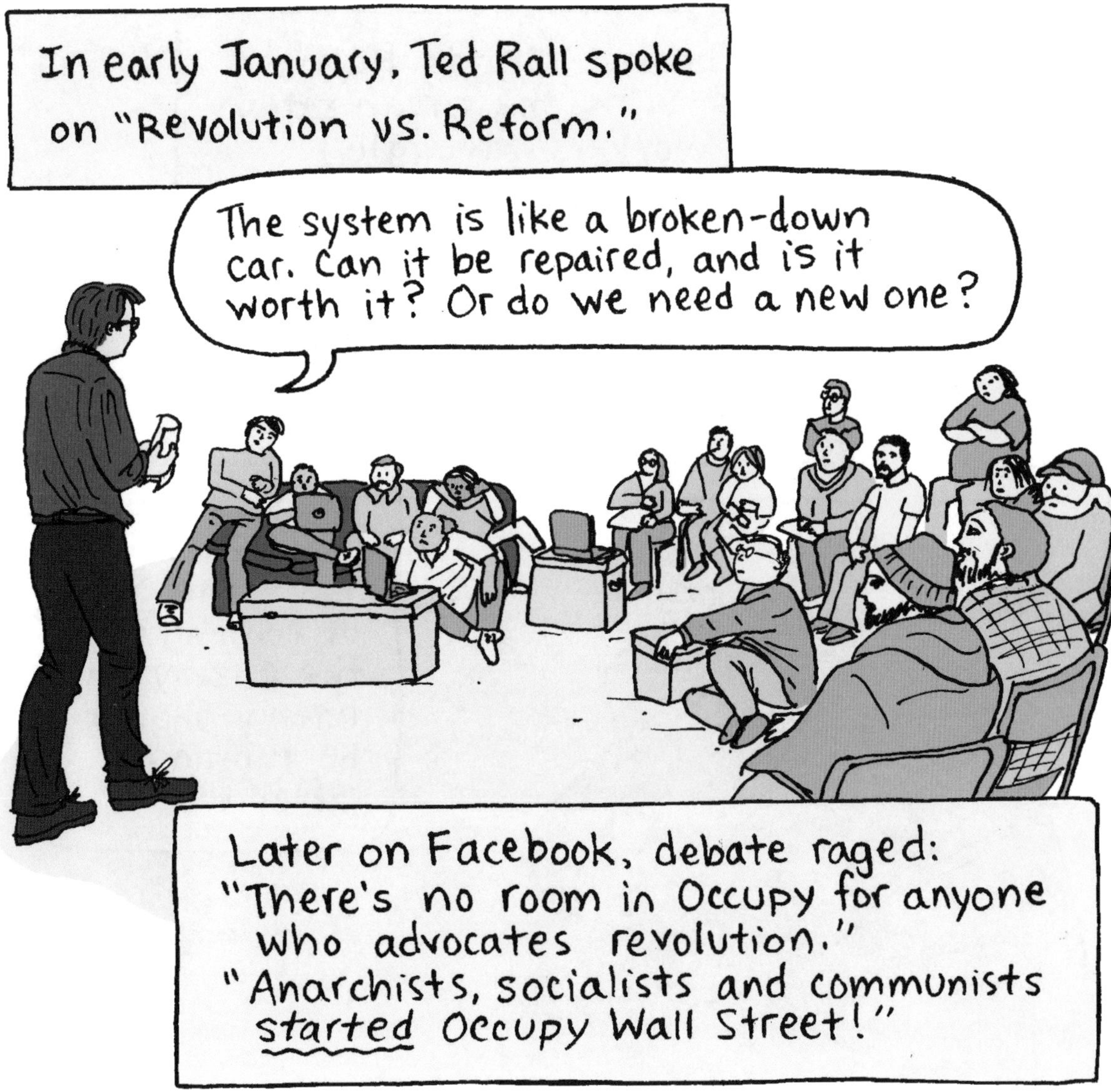
In early January, Ted Rall spoke on "Revolution vs. Reform."
The system is like a broken-down car. Can it be repaired, and is it worth it? Or do we need a new one?
Later on Facebook, debate raged: "There's no room in Occupy for anyone who advocates revolution." "Anarchists, socialists and communists started Occupy Wall Street!"

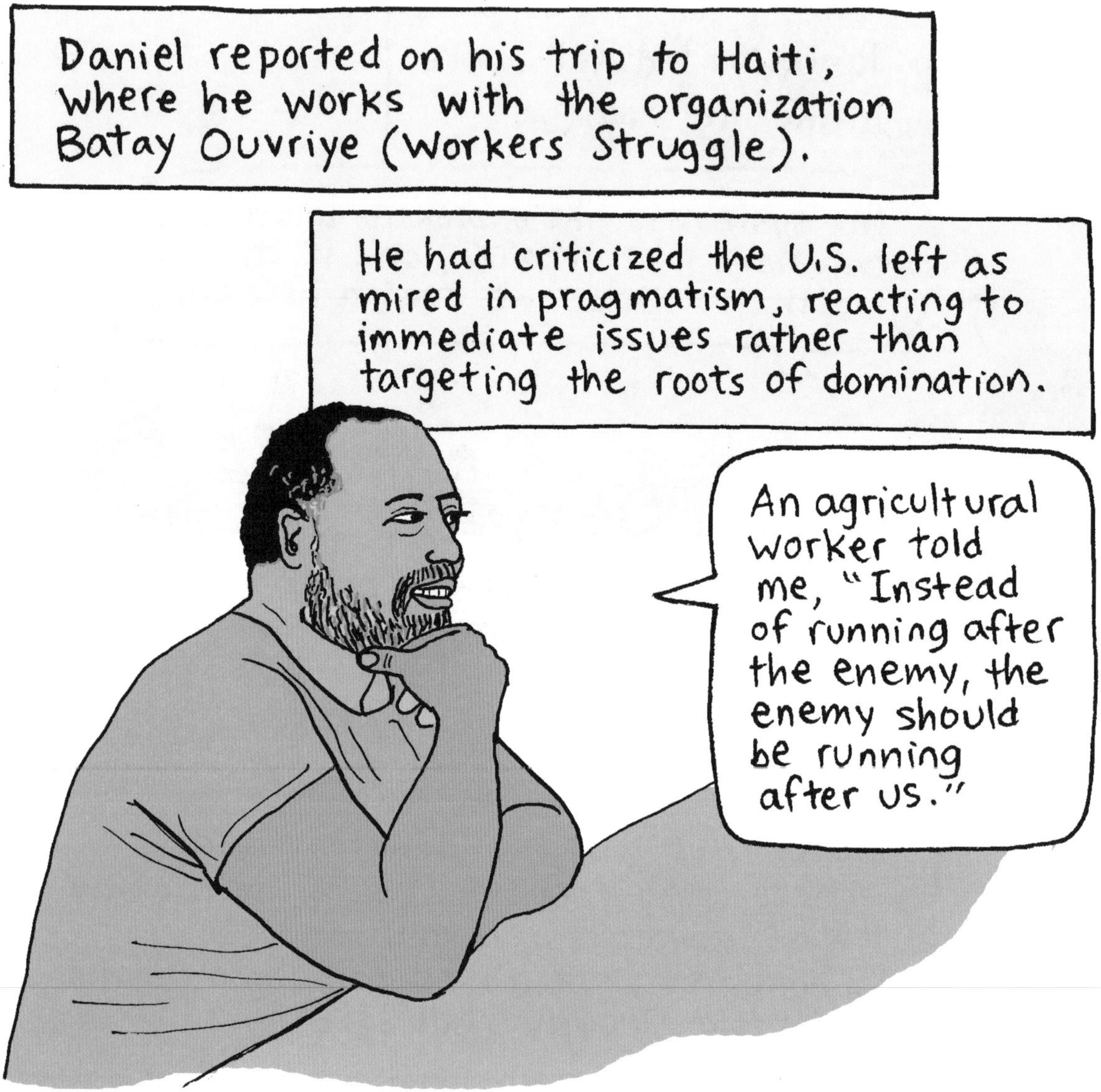
Daniel reported on his trip to Haiti, where he works with the organization Batay Ouvriye (Workers Struggle).
He had criticized the U.S. left as mired in pragmatism, reacting to immediate issues rather than targeting the roots of domination.
An agricultural worker told me, "Instead of running after the enemy, the enemy should be running after us."

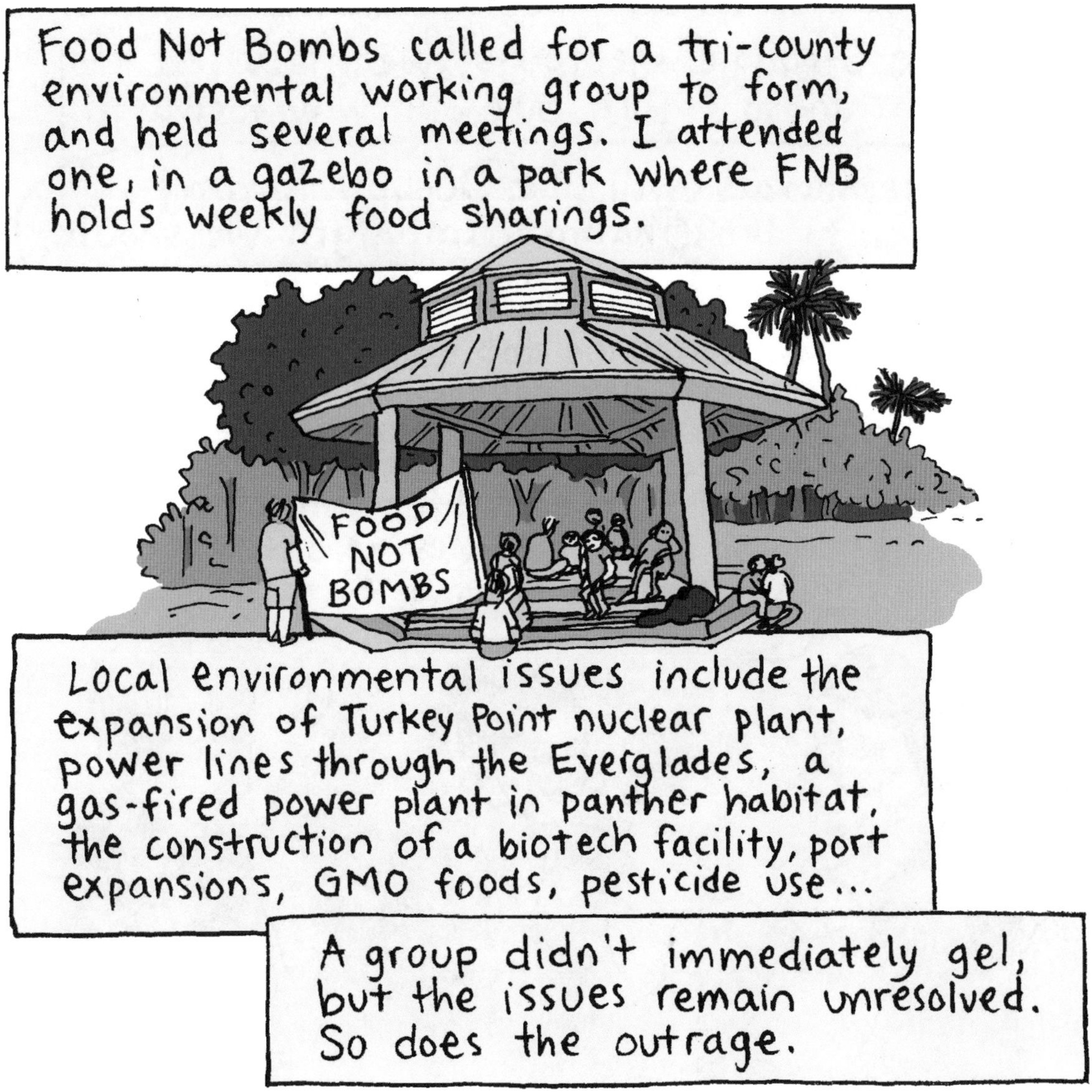
Food Not Bombs called for a tri-county environmental working group to form, and held several meetings. I attended one, in a gazebo in a park where FNB holds weekly food sharings.
FOOD NOT BOMBS
Local environmental issues include the expansion of Turkey Point nuclear plant, power lines through the Everglades, a gas-fired power plant in panther habitat, the construction of a biotech facility, port expansions, GMO foods, pesticide use...
A group didn't immediately gel, but the issues remain unresolved. So does the outrage.

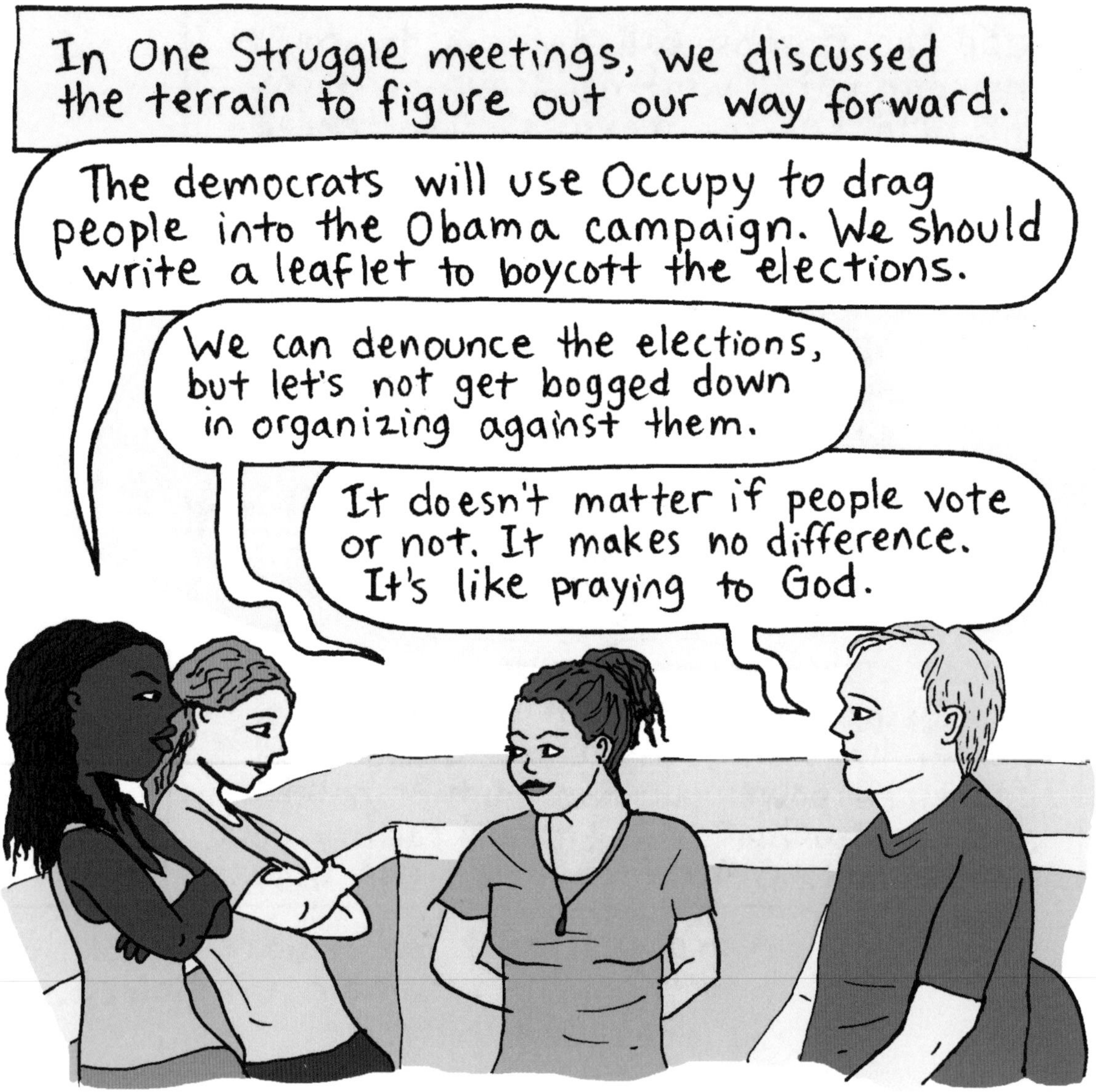
In One Struggle meetings, we discussed the terrain to figure out our way forward.
The democrats will use Occupy to drag people into the Obama campaign. We should write a leaflet to boycott the elections.
We can denounce the elections, but let's not get bogged down in organizing against them.
It doesn't matter if people vote or not. It makes no difference. It's like praying to God.

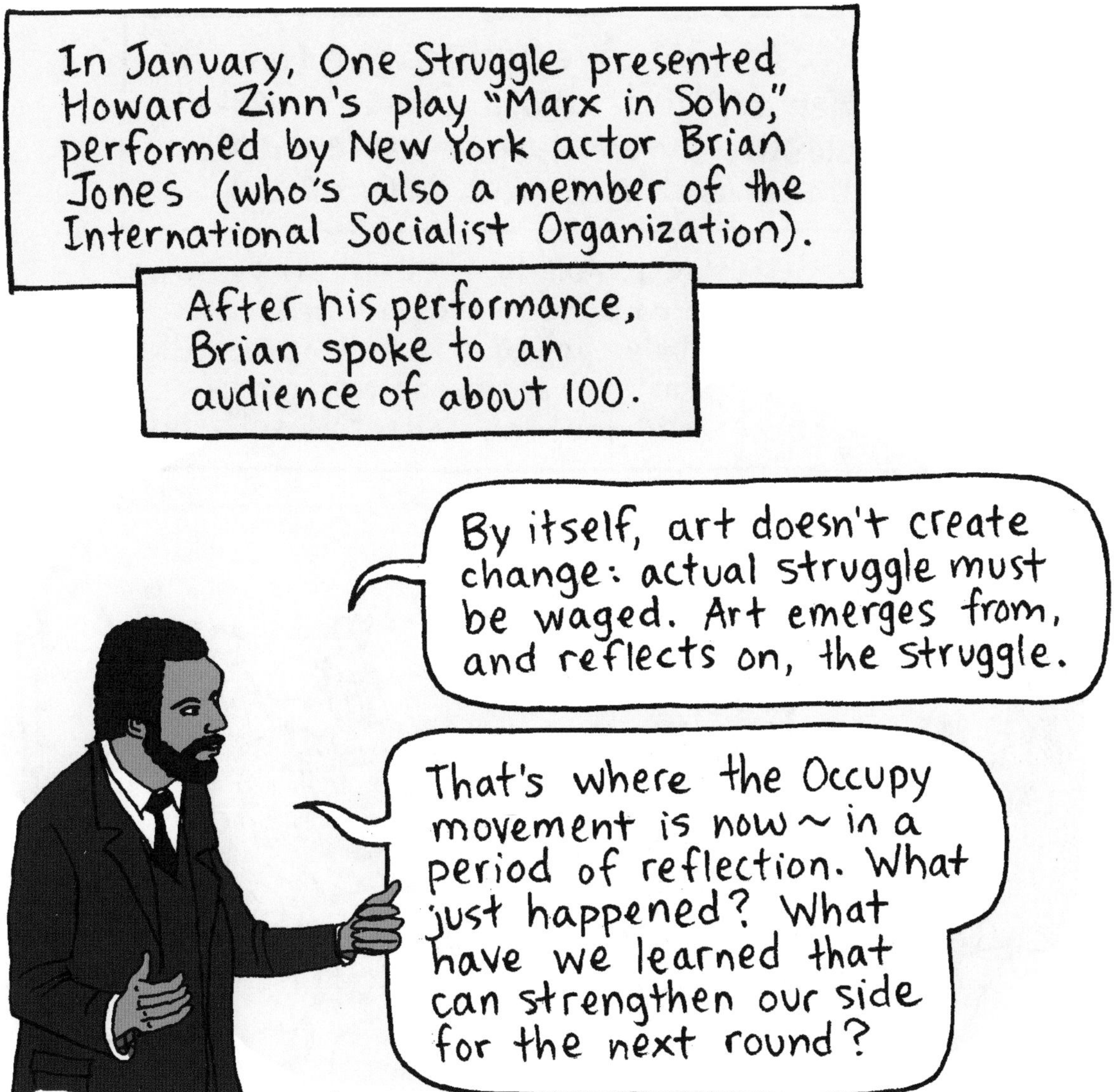
In January, One Struggle presented Howard Zinn's play "Marx in Soho," performed by New York actor Brian Jones (who's also a member of the International Socialist Organization).
After his performance, Brian spoke to an audience of about 100.
By itself, art doesn't create change: actual struggle must be waged. Art emerges from, and reflects on, the struggle.
That's where the Occupy movement is now ~ in a period of reflection. What just happened? What have we learned that can strengthen our side for the next round?

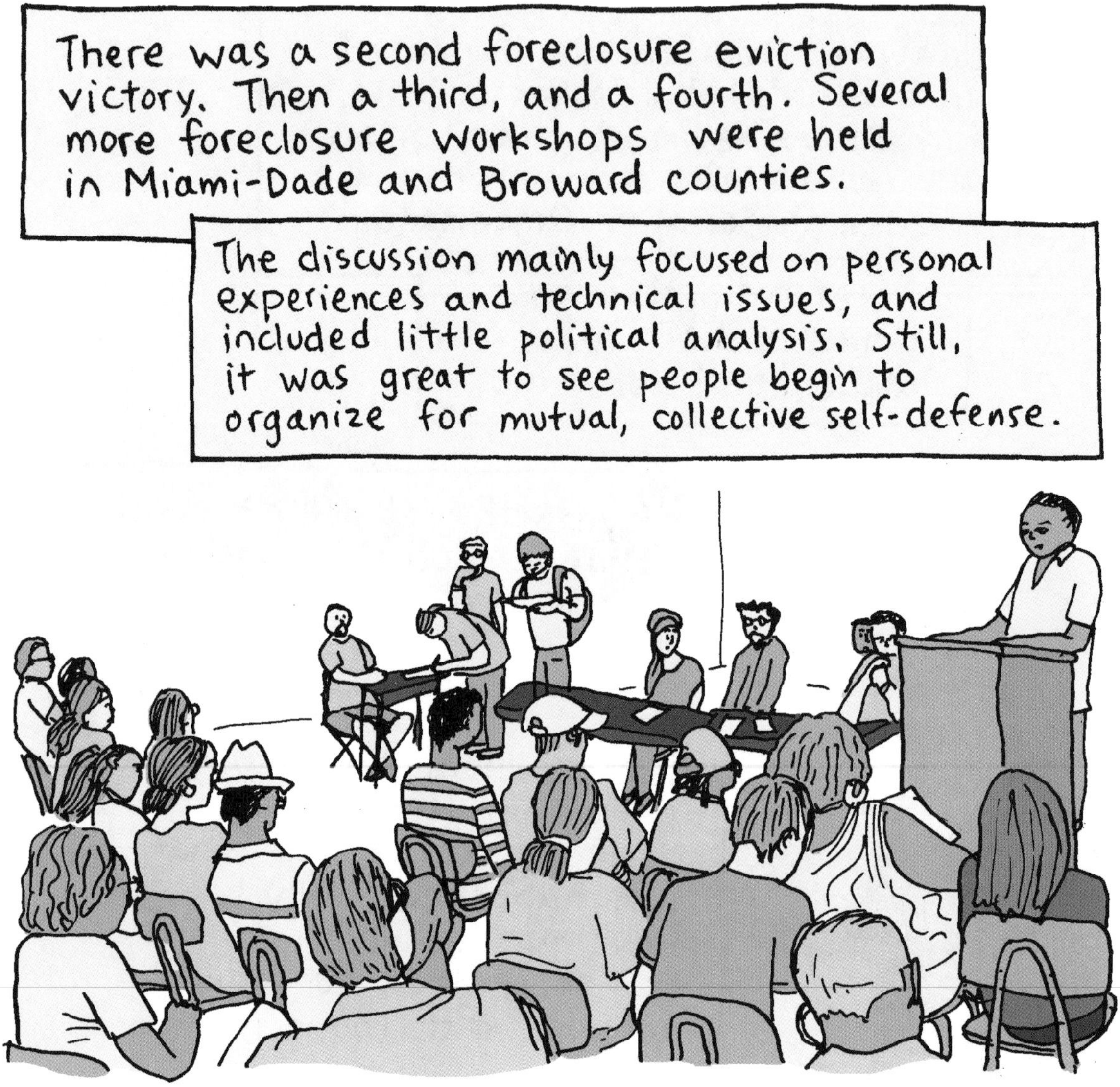
There was a second foreclosure eviction victory. Then a third, and a fourth. Several more foreclosure workshops were held in Miami-Dade and Broward counties.
The discussion mainly focused on personal experiences and technical issues, and included little political analysis. Still, it was great to see people begin to organize for mutual, collective self-defense.

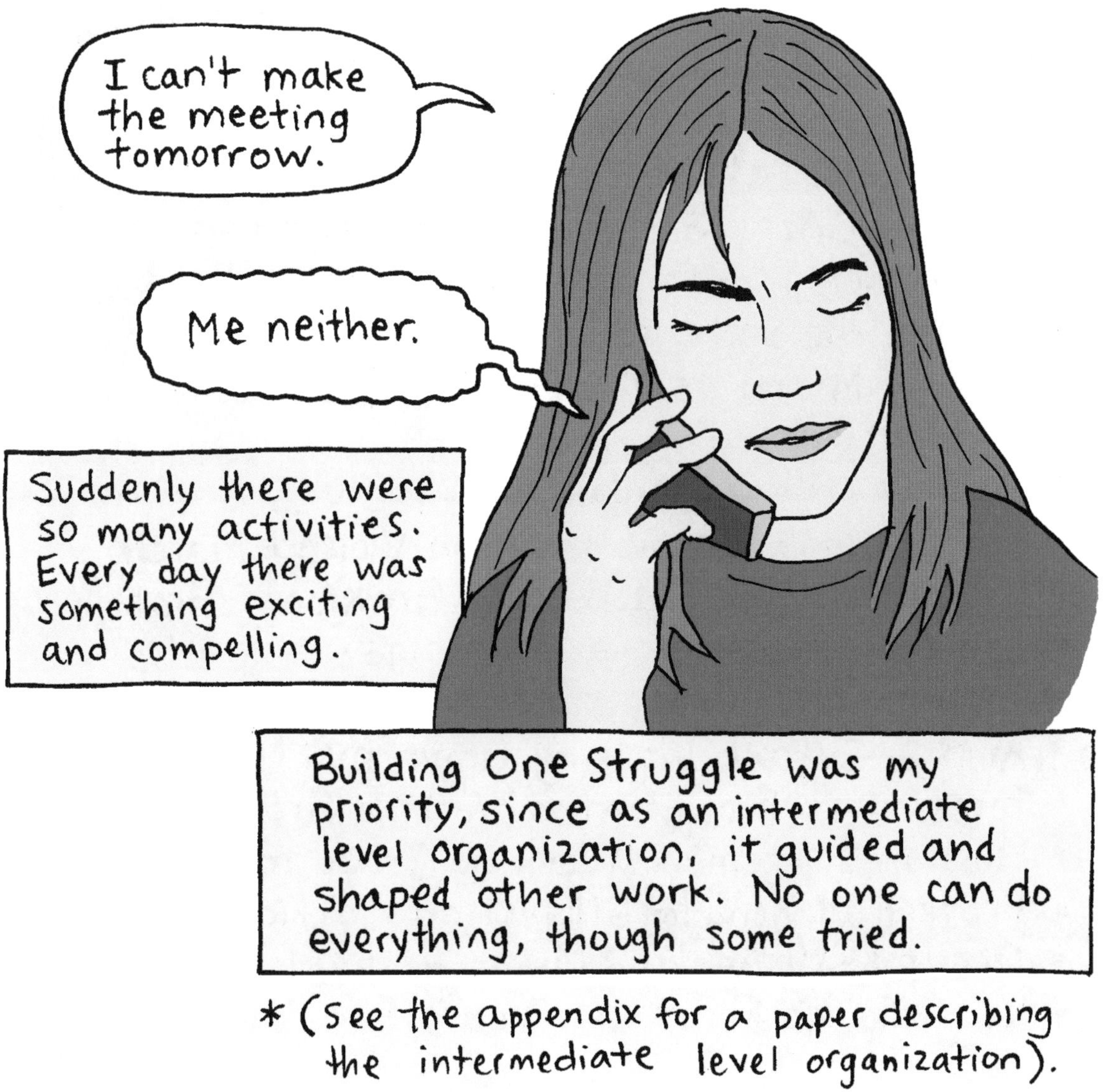
I can't make the meeting tomorrow.
Me neither.
Suddenly there were so many activities. Every day there was something exciting and compelling.
Building One Struggle was my priority, since as an intermediate level organization, it guided and shaped other work. No one can do everything, though some tried.
* (See the appendix for a paper describing the intermediate level organization).

SOME OF THE EVENTS I DIDN'T ATTEND

- Drum circle at City Hall
- Occupy GAIM (Gathering of Investors and Managers) Conference, Boca Raton Resort & Club
- Awake the State rally
- Occupy Miami vs. Occupy Fort Lauderdale soccer game
- Occupy Fort Lauderdale pool party
- King Holiday Parade and Non-Violence March
- Victor Houston Teach-in on Grassroots Strategies
- Labor Outreach Group meetings
- Direct Action Group meetings
- Arts & Culture Working Group meetings
- Foreclosure Mobilization Working Group meetings
- Mission Statement Working Group meetings
- Protest at Senator Bill Nelson's office
- Occupy FIU Art and Music Festival
- King Mango Strut New Year's Eve Parade

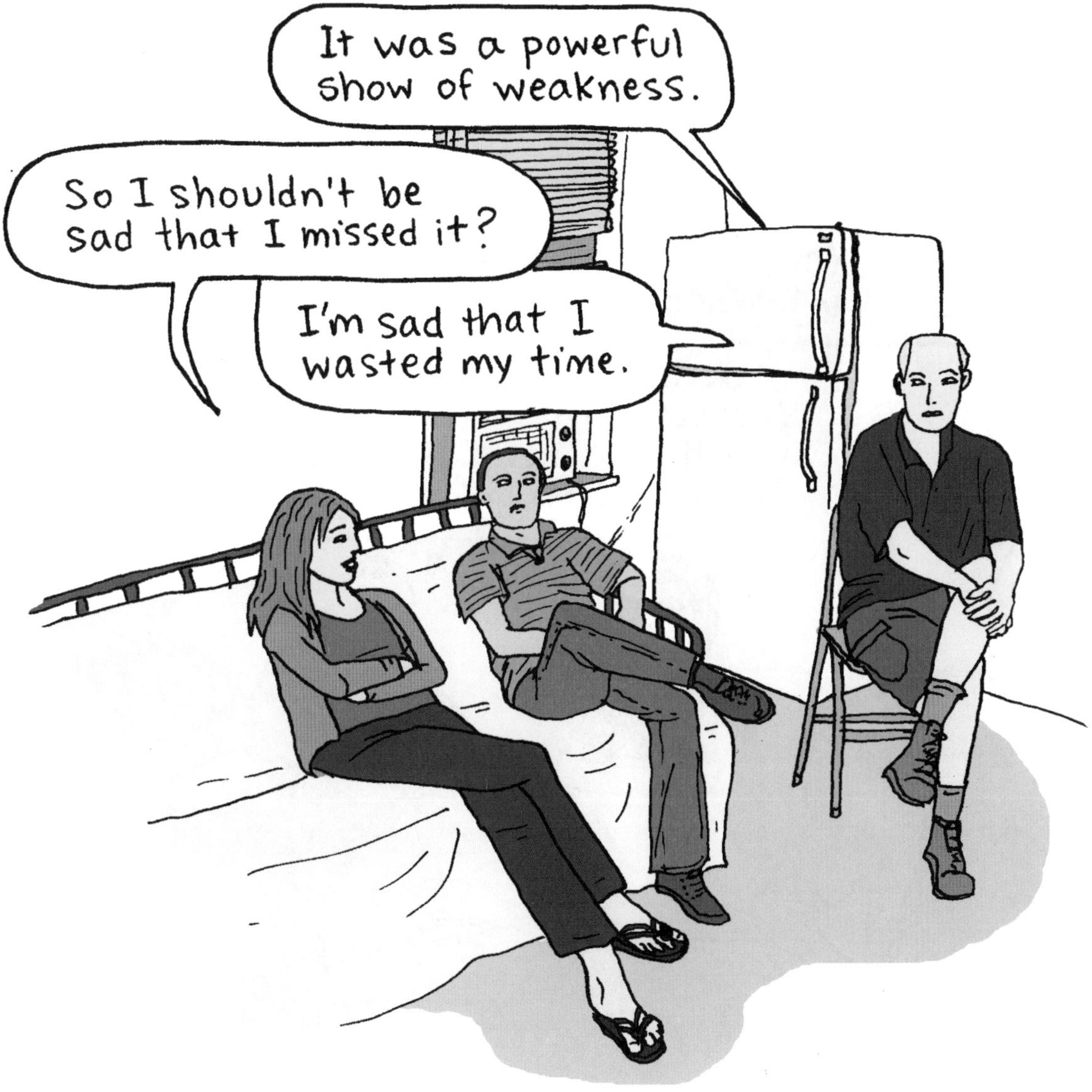
It was a powerful show of weakness.
So I shouldn't be sad that I missed it?
I'm sad that I wasted my time.

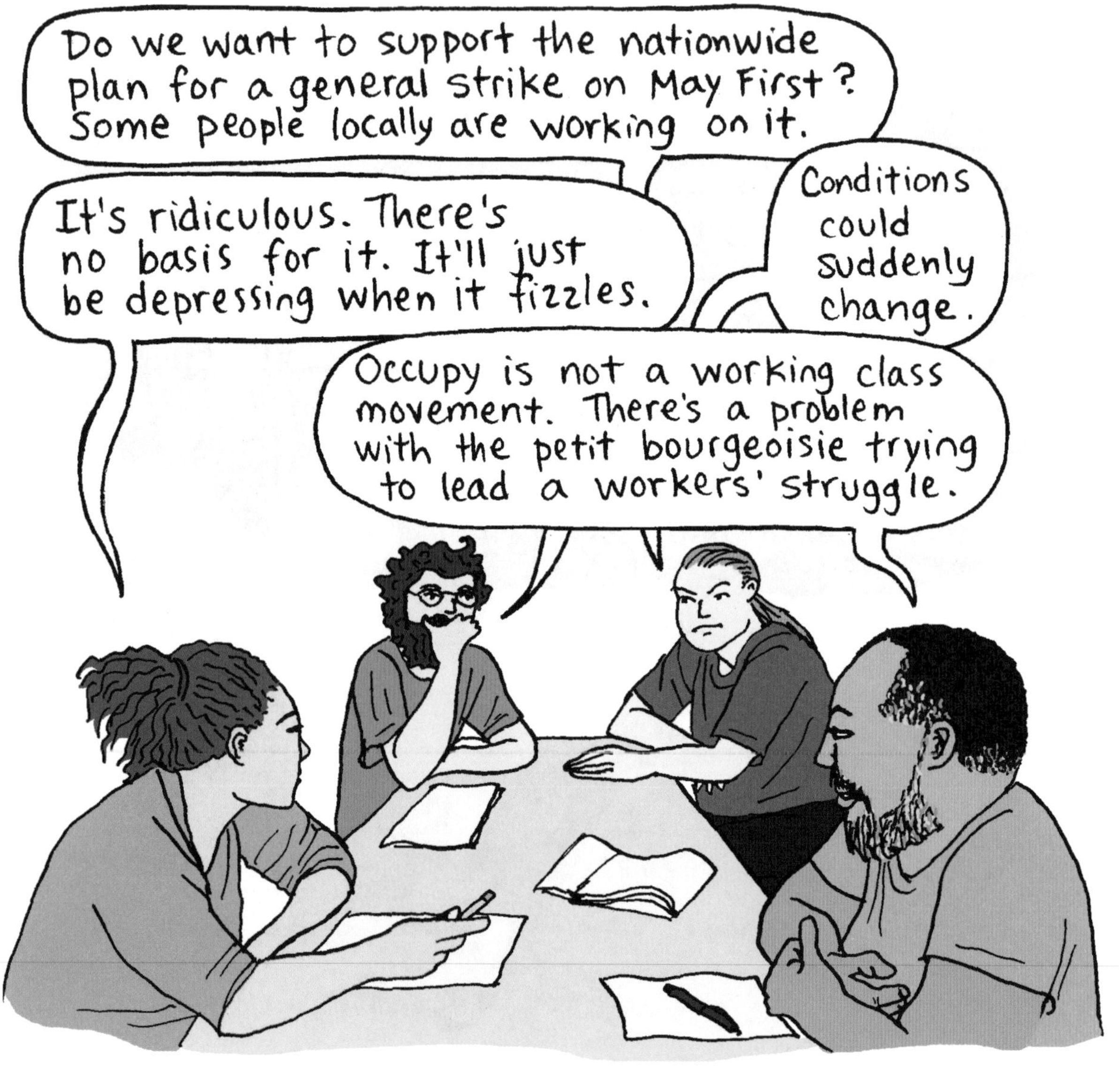
Do we want to support the nationwide plan for a general strike on May First? Some people locally are working on it.
It's ridiculous. There's no basis for it. It'll just be depressing when it fizzles.
Conditions could suddenly change.
Occupy is not a working class movement. There's a problem with the petit bourgeoisie trying to lead a workers' struggle.

The Uncertain Future

"**T**HE Occupy camps are dead," said Patches, an organizer for Occupy Miami and Fort Lauderdale's Foreclosure Working Group, the Anti-Capitalist Caucus, One Struggle, Food Not Bombs, and the Autonomous Puppet Theater (a busy man indeed), in late December.

The only ones still sleeping at the Miami camp were non-political homeless people, he reported.

This didn't surprise me. I'd been hearing about the camp's decline for weeks: sexual assaults, rampant alcohol and drug use (including an overdose), self-appointed "security" forces who were entirely too chummy with the cops, long periods of inertia and boredom, general entropy.

The Fort Lauderdale camp had disintegrated too. When the police told people to take the tents down, they complied. At both locations, activists had begun only showing up for meetings and events, and then going home.

All over the country, local arms of the state dealt with each encampment in one of two ways. The first was blunt repression. This was risky—as we saw

numerous times, raw cop violence caught on camera can backfire and cause a movement to grow. But not always. With the movement still in its infancy, and activists mostly connected loosely and informally, they couldn't achieve sufficient strength to hold their ground. Holding territory against the massive armed power of the state is impossible without comparably armed, organized, seasoned, and disciplined forces. Some protesters did fight back, and valiantly; all, in the end, gave way like oaks to chainsaws.

The second dispersal strategy—to exploit and intensify the internal contradictions of the movement itself—was more subtle and took a bit longer, but was actually smarter in that it also left a residue of frustration and demoralization.

Because many Occupy participants virtuously attempted to create the future in the present—to model a fair, free, and humane society in contrast to the nightmare that currently prevails—they worked hard to meet everyone's basic needs. Soon people were coming to the camps motivated not by the shared political concerns of the 99 percent, but to personally acquire food, shelter, and relative safety. Activists struggled to meet the needs of everyone who showed up, many who had been discarded by a heartless economy, many with mental and physical illnesses. Soon they were too busy keeping services running to focus on fighting the system. Political work devolved into social work.

One can imagine city officials chuckling over cocktails: "The malcontents complain that we don't care well enough for the riff-raff—let's see how they handle it." Rumors spread of police directing home-less people and drug users to the Occupy camps in an effort to overwhelm and divide them.

Meanwhile, championing ideals of personal free-dom and individual autonomy, occupiers have been reluctant to establish community rules and compel compliance. Violent, dominating, and disruptive peo-ple have been handled with extreme tolerance. In at least one case, a rapist was offered group counseling.

Many kept away from the camps even before they were shut down.

All over the Internet, by late December people were declaring the Occupy movement dead. Others claimed it was retrenching to bust out even stronger in the spring. In fact, no one knows what will hap-pen. But what is certain is that the structural crises and inequalities that gave rise to the global uprisings in the first place will only intensify.

Many speculate on the future direction it will take. Among the ideas being discussed (and being tried out) at the time of this writing include fore-closure eviction defense, organizing against police brutality, and taking over abandoned buildings and land to serve public needs.

These would be an advance, because they would push activity beyond self-reproduction and into the realm of mutual defense and confronting state power. To win victories, various forms of organiza-tion will need to emerge and firm up. The difficulties thus far—including the repression—have been both inevitable and could be ultimately beneficial, forc-ing the movement to evolve. We'll see if it can keep ahead of those determined to see it fail.

Occupy's once-brilliant tactic—the refusal to leave—has rapidly become obsolete. But we shouldn't mourn our retreat. The development from uprising to revolution is never linear or smooth. Ebb must follow surge, yielding ground temporarily in order to consolidate power for the next wave.

So we sit together and painstakingly attempt to construct, as they say, political unity. We assess our strengths and weaknesses, determine who is with us for what, and for how long.

Whether or not a called-for General Strike is pulled off nationally or in specific areas, there's a lot more in the proposal and planning stages: the RNC and DNC, the G8 meeting in Chicago, a planned National Occupation in DC, National Re-Occupy

Day, the Left Forum, a Deep Green Resistance national conference, an "Everything for Everyone" festival. In South Florida, there are numerous possible issues to tackle: foreclosures and evictions, the environment, student debt, austerity measures, workers' struggles. Where to dig in, and how?

We are in a life-or-death contest for the future, and our side is still struggling to emerge as a social force. In confronting our true situation and avoiding fantasies of easy victories, we can collectively decide where we need to go, and define a path that might be able to get us there.

We've begun to do the hard work required. We have a lot more to do.

As the winter draws to a close and the season turns, there is a sense of anticipation—for some fragile, for others strong—for what may burst forth in the coming spring.

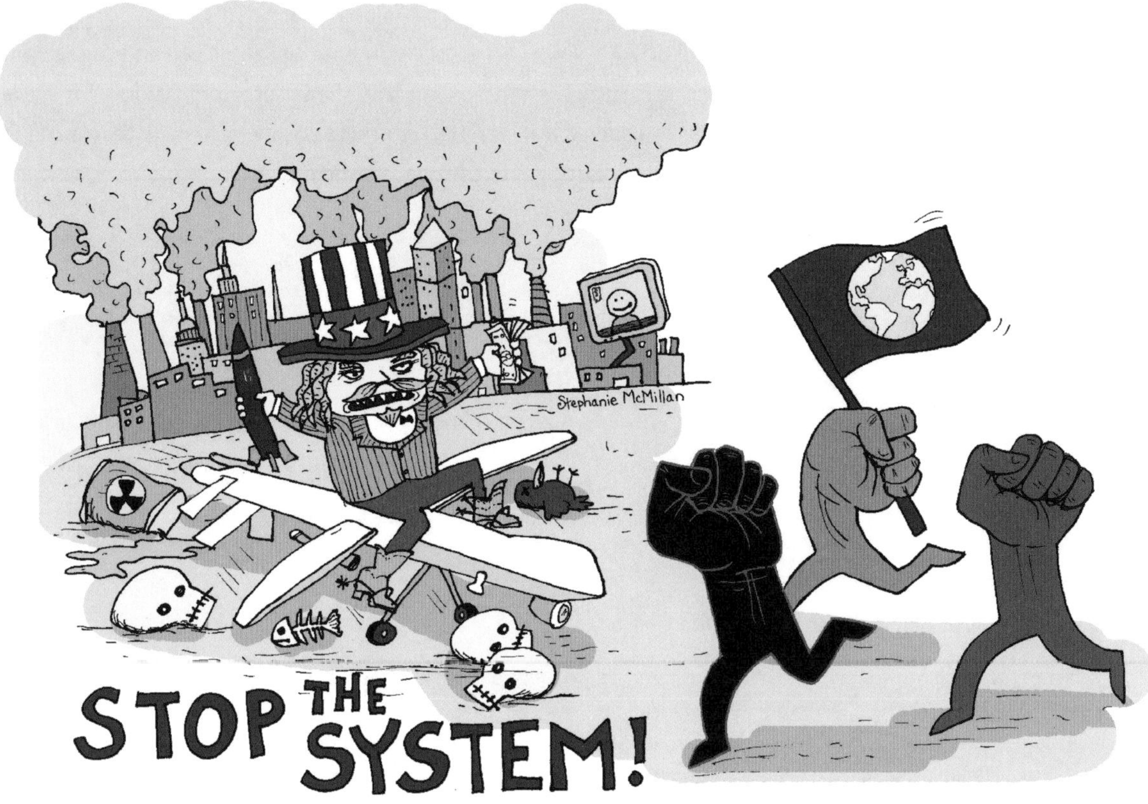
Stephanie McMillan
STOP THE SYSTEM!

Appendices

"I was an organizer before I was a musician.
I have never thought that it was the job of the artist to simply interpret. If you're not involved,
your interpretation is off, disconnected, not believable."
—BOOTS RILEY (*on Facebook*)

THE main body of this book comprises a very general overview of events and experiences; but the closer you get to any phenomenon, the more details become visible. I'm including some documents here in the back for those who want to look beyond the surface. They might not be for everyone, but for me are an important part of the work (because they both shaped and resulted from the events and experiences). Some of the following supplementary pieces are included for the record; others are specifically geared toward assisting the building of organizations.

A NOTE ON METHOD

PARTICIPATE in political activity. I also draw cartoons and write. This book is a mix of all of these, which I would not be able to keep separate even if I wanted to. I don't claim that this account encompasses "the whole truth," but that it is my interpretation of events, one of many fragments of a broad spectrum of analysis and observations about the movement—all shaped by personal idiosyncrasy, experience, and outlook.

I assembled this from what I decided to take note of, which is of course determined by what I care about and find important and interesting. It's not meant to be comprehensive. A different person might have focused less on the environmental thread of the movement and more on union organizing or the logistics of running a free public kitchen.

It is also not meant to be permanent. It captures a moment, and the feelings of that moment. But already just a few months after beginning this project, my views have evolved and I have to resist the urge to go back and make revisions. Life runs much faster than our ability to record and interpret it.

This is a work of art as much as it is a journalistic narrative. Since art is a synthesis of life, and not its exact replica, there are times when I've combined information to concentrate a moment or highlight a point. If I had doubts that a person wished to be identifiable, or couldn't remember exactly what they looked like, I changed their appearance. Attributed quotes are exact (and excerpts of speeches are only included if I actually saw them in person), but other conversations portrayed here are based on notes and an imperfect memory. Text and visual elements have been heavily edited and often condensed or recombined for clarity and aesthetic reasons. In real life I don't always wear a red shirt.

If you recognize yourself in here, please forgive the limitations of my drawing skills—you are so much cuter in real life.

NAVIGATING THE MAZE OF GROUPS

WHEN people are in motion politically, a lot of different organizational forms and combinations spring up—networks, collectives, sub-groups, front groups, sects, splits, alliances, and more. This can be confusing, but it's simply the nature of how movements develop.

Here are the main groups I talk about in this book, and how they relate to each other:

Occupy Wall Street

Adbusters, a magazine in Canada, sent out a call in July 2011 for people to descend on Wall Street in New York City on September 17 and camp out. Initially smaller than expected, the occupation took hold and expanded into hundreds of locations, and has become the most significant domestic political event of this generation so far.

Stop the Machine

Promoted in June 2011 (before the call for Occupy Wall Street was issued) by prominent activists, and begun on October 6 (after the start of OWS), this was both a loose network and an action (an ongoing protest encampment) at Freedom Plaza in Washington, DC. Though similar to the "Occupy" protests, it wasn't identical. Occupy DC and Stop the Machine coordinated actions together, but remained separate.

One Struggle

An anti-capitalist/anti-imperialist collective in South Florida (with other possible chapters forming). This is the organization I mainly identify with—my participation with other events and groupings is usually as a One Struggle member. Its "Points of Unity" document is included as an Appendix.

Anti-Capitalist Caucus

A diverse and loose network of both organized and independent anti-capitalists in South Florida, many of whom also work with One Struggle, Occupy Fort Lauderdale, and/or Occupy Miami.

PROPOSED ORIENTATION FOR AN APPROACH TO ENVIRONMENTAL ISSUES BY THE ENVIRONMENTAL COMMITTEE, OCTOBER2011.ORG

(Following is the text of an email to the national organizers):

The Environmental Committee of October2011.org met several times in person at Freedom Plaza starting on October 6. Since most of us are no longer in Washington, DC, we are keeping in contact via email. A range of diverse ideas characterize the members of our committee, but we share some commonalities as well—most of all, a sense of urgency and desire to see effective action to stop the destruction of the planet.

On our first day, with the most people present, we came to agreement on several basic principles that describe our basic collective outlook. This represents the collective effort and decision of the thirty-two people who participated in our committee. We would like to offer them to the rest of October2011, plus to other groups who may find them useful (such as Occupy formations), as foundational guidelines for formulating future decisions, actions and statements.

- We encourage a radical, rather than a liberal approach.

- The environment is the most urgent issue—if we don't solve it, nothing else will matter.

- The struggle to save the planet is deeply interconnected with social justice and other issues. It's impossible to address it outside the context of our social/political/economic structure.

- Change must happen at all levels, from the personal to the systemic.

- We embrace a range of strategies and believe it's important to be mutually supportive even of those who approach the struggle differently.

- As we carry out our actions, we do not intend to ask permission from the system, or its representatives, institutions, or apologists.

- Direct action should be part of our strategy.

- Everyone should pledge to act to the maximum of their ability, and be willing to make personal sacrifices in the interests of Earth.

- Dominator/industrialized nations should assume a large share of the responsibility to fix ecological problems, and assist the rest of the world in mitigating their effects.

- We acknowledge that we live on stolen land, and must take leadership from non-colonized, indigenous, land-based communities.

- We insist that greenwashing strategies be eliminated from the environmental movement.

- We need to develop a sustainable way of life based on steady-state, no-growth, local economies (negative growth until the Earth is healed).

- We feel a special, specific urgency to stop the Keystone XL tar sands pipeline. We pledge to resist all attempts to build the pipeline, and encourage others to make this pledge.

ONE STRUGGLE: POINTS OF UNITY

October 2010

Capitalism/imperialism is an economic system constructed for the purpose of theft and accumulation of wealth for those in power, regardless of what it does to the rest of humanity and the planet. Its built-in drive for profit has caused measureless human misery all over the world, and is threatening the very existence of life on Earth.

Social struggles against oppression—including but not limited to patriarchy, racism, homophobia, oppression of immigrants, the ongoing theft of land, and domination of indigenous people—plus the fight against imperialist wars and international domination, as well as the fight to save the planet from ecocide, are all interconnected.

We support the fight against imperialist wars and international domination, as well as the struggle of the popular masses in all dominated countries against their own dominant classes and against global capitalism, and for self-determination.

It is all ONE STRUGGLE.

The mission of One Struggle is to participate in the construction of combative mass popular organizations and mass popular democratic movements by engaging in the struggles of these dominated classes in which we belong. We will engage in these struggles from a non-sectarian perspective.

We will share information, build solidarity and coordinate activities among those involved in social justice, anti-imperialist, and environmental struggles, so that we can strengthen our fight against our common enemy: the global capitalist system.

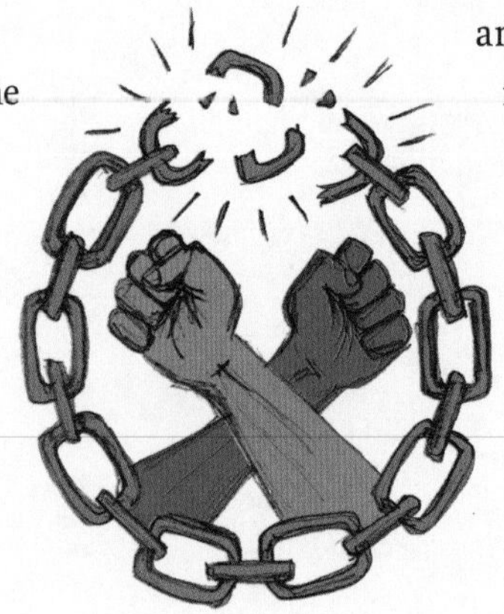

THE DANGER OF POPULISM

EXCERPTS from One Struggle internal document (not finalized)

... Through history, powerful movements for social and economic liberation have been co-opted and diverted by populism with very reactionary, repressive results, such as the rise of the Nazis in Germany and the Ayatollah Khomeini in Iran, the election of the imperialist puppet Martelly ("Sweet Micky") in Haiti, and the ascendency of the Muslim Brotherhood within the struggle against Mubarak in Egypt.

... Populism is a way of thinking that doesn't acknowledge the fact that we live in a system of class domination—that the capitalist class exploits the working class, and uses the middle classes to stabilize this social inequality. Instead, populist rhetoric masks this reality by contrasting more vague economic/social divisions, commonly "the people vs. the elite." In other words, populism hides class struggle. Some commonly populist concepts in use are: the dispossessed, disenfranchised, oppressed, 99% ... concepts that describe a general condition without addressing its root cause and core contradictions.

The majority of people in the US consider themselves "middle class," even many who actually belong to the working class. The concept of middle class itself is often constructed empirically in order to defray class contradictions. Thus there is not widespread consciousness of working class anti-capitalist interests—fundamentally, that capitalism must be eliminated and that the ruling class (large capitalists and their high-level representatives) are an enemy to be defeated.

Instead, the petit bourgeoisie ("middle class"), which has some privileges and advantages within this system, tends to promote its own interests as universal. Vague terms such as "freedom," "democracy," and "fairness" are not given context. What does it mean to have "freedom" and "democracy" if we are trapped in a system characterized by capitalist class dictatorship, a system that is fundamentally exploitative and oppressive?

The danger, then, is that when the petit bourgeoisie achieves the partial reforms that it wants, it can then snuggle back under the wing of the ruling class, and end up abandoning the working class and even turn against it. This strangles the process of liberation and turns it into its opposite.

The ruling class understands this very well, and leans on the petit bourgeoisie to divert the overall struggle back into the framework of the system. In South Africa, for example, as soon as the interests of the petit bourgeoisie and ruling classes were satisfied, they quickly moved to squash the workers' struggle for total emancipation, by claiming that the workers were promoting instability against the newly reformed state. And so we see that even decades after the end of apartheid, the conditions of the vast majority of South Africans have not changed. A similar process occurred in Nicaragua after the fall of Somoza.

. . . Global capitalism is a system that is structured upon, enforces, and reproduces domination. *It is our enemy.* Our goal must be to liberate ourselves by eliminating this exploitative system altogether. We must keep this uppermost in mind—and learn our history and political theory—if we are to avoid being the unwitting foot-soldiers of any of the fractions of the capitalist class. The struggle against opportunism must be linked with the struggle against populism in order for our struggles to advance.

TOWARD AN ANTI-CAPITALIST/
ANTI-IMPERIALIST MASS MOVEMENT:
Organizing at the Intermediate Level

One Struggle, September 2011

Mass movements cannot be conjured from thin air or willed into being, no matter how correct our ideas or determined our hearts. They arise in response to intolerable social problems, congeal through collective practice and theoretical work, and harden through continuous, escalating struggle.

In the US, as in many parts of the world, the 1960s saw the birth of a radical mass movement with revolutionary currents running through it. It didn't burst onto the scene fully formed, but developed through twists and turns, suffering painful lessons, betrayals, mistakes, and defeats on the way. It also celebrated victories which, like waves pushed by storm winds, grew ever larger and more powerful until the idea of revolution rose in the public consciousness as a tangible possibility.

As the movement found its footing, participants became skilled in tactics and honed their strategies. Small and vague collectives coalesced and matured into national, multi-level, unified fighting machines.

When the Vietnam War ended, the sense of personal urgency dissipated for many in the US. The declining waves of struggle ultimately beat themselves out on the barren shore of the 1980s bubble economy. The pretense of growth based on debt was enough to bribe much of the population into passivity. The loss of socialism in China and the collapse of the Soviet Union (which, their own natures aside, had acted as counterweights to US hegemony) broke the spirits of most of the rest.

Today the global system faces a convergence of crises, but this time there is no economic growth (real or pretend) on the horizon. The system shows no viable possibilities for a future. Capitalism is played out.

Yet the ruling class hangs onto power, squeezing the last bits of profit out of us and the natural world, not hesitating to kill us in the process. If we're to save ourselves and the planet, we must eliminate the capitalist/imperialist system once and for all.

Opposing the system can, and does, take many forms. Many types of organizations are arising and will arise, with different visions of the future and different strategies on getting there. Some will contribute positively to the overall project; others will commit errors of varying degrees of severity. Diversity in our approaches and ideas is our strength, and mutual respect and non-sectarianism will help us learn from one another, and advance hand-in-hand.

Together, each contributing in our own way, and in tandem with our independent work, we can build a movement strong enough to accomplish the one essential task we all share: to end capitalism/imperialism.

We need to build organizations to magnify our power.

Organizations are structured relationships between people who understand that collective power can affect society on a level that atomized individuals can not. Organizations begin with two people and a plan, and go through a process of development as surely as we all go through the stages of infancy, youth and maturity. As the system cracks apart, it intensifies the suffering of all of us living inside the thrashings of its final stage. In response to this new level of urgency to find a way out and create alterna-tives, people are exploring many possible courses of action. Small, loosely defined collectives are spring-ing up all over.

How will they coalesce into a combative mass movement capable of sweeping away the entire system of global capitalism?

We're still at the initial stage of the current round of systemic crisis-and-response, attempting to come into being as a social force. Since a mass movement cannot spring whole into existence, but will instead be forged through practice we have yet to perform, we should organize on a basis corresponding to our current situation and the measure of our forces. To lay the groundwork for a mass movement, we can start with a preliminary type of organization: the Interme-diate Level.*

The intermediate level organization is a tool with which we can build a mass movement. It can create

---

* The concept was implemented in 1979 by the Workers Committee of Rockland County (NY), as well as by a group of Haitian revolutionaries to build a mass move-ment based among workers and peasants during the fall of Duvalier. More recently, it has been articulated in a paper "The Intermediate Level Analysis," by S. Nappalos for Miami Autonomy and Solidarity (posted on 11/24/11 at: http://miamiautonomyandsolidarity.wordpress. com/2010/11/24/the-intermediate-level-analysis/). The South Florida group One Struggle was initiated on the basis of the intermediate level concept in 2010.

more favorable conditions for mass struggle, and be in place when mass struggle does erupt, to maximize its effectiveness and provide continuity through its inevitable ebbs and flows.

The intermediate level organization is neither a revolutionary organization nor a mass organization, but has characteristics distinct from both. As its name implies, it operates between the two, structurally and ideologically, and links them. Because it isn't well-defined in popular consciousness, it is often confused with one or the other level.

These categories, defined by levels of consciousness and commitment, are not rigid, and a group can blend them or change from one to another according to circumstances. Their relationship is dialectical, each level acting upon and influencing the others. Their boundaries are permeable, with individuals able to move from one level to another, or to operate in more than one at a time. Some of their elements differ only in degree or emphasis. The levels are generally characterized as follows:

Revolutionary organization

- A high level of theoretical, ideological, and political unity
- A common long-term goal, a comprehensive strategy, and a detailed plan to implement that strategy
- Continuously developing methods of work, and systematic summation of that work

- A process, honed through practice, of collectively shaping ideas, direction, and policies
- A membership of cadre who have dedicated their lives to the struggle
- A structure that is configured to withstand repression

Mass organization

- Unity based on common interests to achieve a specific goal (such as a union fighting for higher wages, or a coalition to stop a war)
- Ideologically and politically broad, often vague or populist
- A simple goal and/or strategy, usually limited to one issue, often short-term
- Membership requirements are loose, and expectations are not strict
- A basically open structure—anyone can join

Intermediate organization

- A level of unity that defines and opposes the system as a whole, yet refrains from defining a specific strategy for eliminating it (thus is able to embrace members with various theories)
- A goal of uniting all who can be united for a medium-range goal (the precise content of which is not fixed, but dependent upon historical circumstances and the changing level of class consciousness among the masses—for example, it could

currently be to defeat global capitalism) without attempting to unify on long-term goals (such as the precise form of a future society)

- Collectivity in developing common plans and tactics for achieving the medium-range goal
- Non-sectarian and mutually supportive
- Continuously improve methods and practice through collective summation
- A membership with some level of accountability and commitment beyond "weekend warrior"
- A semi-open or invitation-only (but not clandestine) structure

The revolutionary level is principle

The revolutionary level is indispensible and ultimately determinate—without its presence, the other two tend to lose themselves in the murky dead ends of spontaneity, such as reformism and economism. This does not mean that the intermediate level is a front group for revolutionaries—care must be taken to avoid inadvertently forming a top-down bureaucratic structure. Each level must function autonomously and to its own fullest potential.

The intermediate level addresses limitations of the other levels

The revolutionary organization and the mass organization each faces specific obstacles during periods of low struggle, such as that from which we are currently emerging.

- Revolutionary organizations strain to connect with masses who are largely unreceptive. While the global system is still intact and appears strong, it's difficult for people to imagine that the alternatives presented by revolutionaries are possible to implement. Revolutionary organizations, as they struggle to retain their declining membership and their political identity during unfavorable periods, can either become rigid and dogmatic (increasing their isolation), or they can water themselves down in an effort to be more appealing, and be absorbed into the dominant political structure.
- Mass organizations are, under this system, usually dominated by institutionalized bureaucracies (ie,: unions and NGOs) whose very functions are to divert the discontent of the masses into themselves and into compromise with capital. Many of them are funded by capitalist entities, turning political organizing into jobs involving social work or charity, and the organized into passive recipients of assistance. The non-funded ones tend to lack continuity: they are able to mobilize people for brief spurts but then lose support as issues fade. Mass organizations, by providing no analysis of the systemic nature of problems, are unable to break the system's ideological hegemony. Currently they

are hobbled by a lack of class consciousness and swamped by liberalism and reformism.

An intermediate level organization addresses these obstacles from both directions, and prepares militants to potentially work in all levels. It has two basic functions:

· to build a combative, continuously advancing mass movement that unites all who can be united to fight against the system
· to locate and train radicals who might also organize at the revolutionary level**

Organizing explicitly at the intermediate level can prevent the problems that occur when a group calling itself either a revolutionary or a mass organization is, in reality, mushing the levels together. Though the intermediate level organization is not widely understood, it is widely practiced (usually unknowingly). If a group proclaims to be revolutionary but hasn't yet achieved the degree of unity and commitment that revolutionary practice requires, then it

is in fact an intermediary organization. If a group is attempting to build a mass organization but doesn't yet have a mass base, then it is in fact an intermediate level organization.

Confusion about levels leads to problems. For example, if revolutionary-minded people are working in an intermediate level organization but treat it as revolutionary, they tend to push for a higher level of unity than is appropriate, and don't fully value or take into account the ideological diversity that is present. There lies the danger of replacing genuine unity with pressure to conform. Revolutionaries can, if not careful, end up dominating an intermediate level group, preventing the less experienced people from developing their skills and knowledge, and blocking the free flow and exchange of new ideas.

Often those who do mass organizing are, in reality, also intermediate level organizers who are generating temporary mass mobilizations rather than the movements they are aiming for. With their higher levels of commitment and medium-range (as opposed to short-term) goals, intermediate level organizations can remain in existence through the ebb and flow of mass struggles. They can provide continuity during dry periods, and continuously work to bring people into motion. Their goal should be to constantly draw in new people to replace themselves as organizers at the mass level.

If intermediate level people work within mass

** For our present purposes, this term is general and applies to any organization with a long-term goal of social transformation, whether this involves insurrection, overthrow, dismantling, seizing, smashing, or any other type of activity that results in a fundamental shift in power relations.

organizations but treat them as intermediate, they also can make the mistake of pushing for a higher level of unity than is appropriate for that particular work. Instead they can (and should) work autonomously within mass struggles as an intermediate tendency, representing their own distinct political level within the mass movement. In this way they can avoid being swamped by the liberalism and reformism characteristic of today's mass organizations.

Organizations advance in an ongoing process

As the system goes deeper into crisis, as its cracks widen and struggle erupts in society, people become increasingly radicalized. Mass organizations become more robust and more explicitly political—in effect, they become the intermediate level. As this occurs, the intermediate level gives way to them and dissolves into them. New intermediate levels then form at yet higher levels, in a continuous process that, like a conveyor belt, pulls people in the direction of revolutionary consciousness and organizational forms.

At the same time, revolutionary organizations also advance, working toward more refined bases of theoretical, ideological, and political unity. As events escalate, and as organizations ever more effectively express and embody the demands of the increasingly class-conscious masses, these organizations can grow and coalesce into a powerful social force capable of leading fundamental social transformation.

Events are moving rapidly, and we need to be out there, everywhere, collectively sparking and fanning the mass struggles that are necessary to end the nightmare of global capitalism. We need as many people as possible to be prepared and able to quickly respond when mass struggle does erupt (which will likely be sudden and surprising). We need to forge strong, competent organizations and movements that cannot be shaken, derailed, or pacified. We can contribute to this process now by building organizations at the intermediate level.

MOBILIZATIONS AND MASS MOVEMENTS

One Struggle, December 2010

This is a discussion of two approaches employed in organizing at the mass level: mobilizations and mass movements. Mobilizations typically entail calling on people to participate in rallies, protests, and other actions. A mass movement pushes dialogue and strategizing from the revolutionary or intermediate levels to the mass level, building organization and consciousness through continuity of practice.

Mobilizations and organized mass movements are two distinct and essential tools we must wield in our fight to defeat capitalism. They exist in dialectical relation to one another, with the organized mass movement as the main goal. Mobilizations have two roles: they are both a method to build a movement, and they are the outward expression of the organized movement.

The needs of the mass movement should determine the ways in which people are mobilized, and in turn, mobilizations must perennially consolidate and reinforce our efforts to build the movement. The organized movement is the point—any mass mobilizations that do not contribute to building and strengthening it are meaningless activist endeavors that lead nowhere.

Mobilization is the collective response, spontaneous or organized, of the dominated and/or oppressed masses to either oppose measures taken by the dominant classes (defensive), or to make demands that are in their interests (active).

Types of Mobilization:

- **Defensive**: This is the response (organized or spontaneous) by the dominated and/or exploited masses to reactionary measures taken by the dominant classes in general, or by the capitalist class in the US.

- **Active**: This is the demand (organized or spontaneous) by the dominated and/or exploited masses for political, social, and economic rights. These popular demands pressure the system to change, and while they expose the oppressive nature of the system, these struggles also contain the inherent danger of being co-opted by the system without changing its fundamental exploitative nature, by winning changes in bourgeois law and objectively enlarging bourgeois democracy. Historical examples include the achievement of voting rights for women, the Civil Rights struggle, and the fight for workers rights such as a higher minimum wage and the eight-hour day.

The active mobilization might be used to win some concessions or to "make our voices heard" —in other words, to popularize the struggle more broadly in society. The demands might be partial (presented in stages less than total transformation). If they are, for example, in a workplace, they might be directed at one or a group of industries, and could be local or national. These demands have the potential to affect local industries or even entire societies.

- **Spontaneous:** Collective spontaneous mobilizations are usually short-lived, with limited demands. Within these types of mobilizations, there is a dialectical relationship between combativity and political consciousness, with combativity being the dominant and determinant aspect. This is a problem because the participants have not adequately defined the nature of the enemy, their demands, and their long-term objectives. This makes them vulnerable to being easily pacified and having their demands easily recuperated. Also, when political consciousness is not in command of combativity, a mobilization can become self-defeating and even, in the final analysis, a gift to the bourgeois propaganda machine.
- **Organized:** Collective organized responses are more defined, with an appropriate balance between political consciousness and combativity. The participants' understanding of the enemy is deepening, and becomes increasingly rational. They develop the methods to build organization, the capacity to advance, the ability to retreat to defend gains, and to handle repression. This type of mobilization fosters determination and stamina, and can better endure the test of time.

Mobilization does not happen by magic. It is the masses' response to atrocity or to intolerable conditions. Even if this response is combative, and might appear radical, it could be limited to a demand for reforms and stay stuck in reformism.

It is very difficult to discuss mobilizations separately from the organizational capacity of mass movements. We must also examine the role of the revolutionary and intermediary level organizations in relation to mass movements. Before we define and elaborate on these organizational forms and their relationships, we will discuss two tools of mobilization: agitation and propaganda.

- **Agitation:** This expresses an issue in a concise manner and calls people to action. Agitational materials include leaflets, posters, radio, television, social networking, and other media. Their purpose is to bring issues to the attention of the people through active presence in popular neighborhoods, workplaces, and schools as well as to spread them beyond direct contact by using communications technologies like the Internet. Agitation seeks to arouse the outrage of the masses, and to connect with people who are already outraged. Raising political consciousness, though undertaken, is secondary to fostering combativeness.

- **Propaganda:** This is aimed at raising political consciousness by revealing the underlying reality of an issue through theoretical analysis. Propaganda materials include newspapers and newsletters, web sites and discussion forums, conferences and debates, and one-on-one discussions. Their purpose is to facilitate the masses' collective understanding of the internal contradictions that give rise to external (or visible) manifestations of phenomena, and to engage in political dialogue with the masses to move discussions forward on questions relating to revolutionary transformation.

Agitation and propaganda foster a dialectical relationship between the popular masses and the organizational structures (mass, intermediary, and revolutionary organizations). These structures must be comprised of the masses (the classes, fractions of classes, and social categories) they aim to organize. The purpose of agitation and propaganda is to construct and develop organizations at all levels.

The purpose, in turn, of these organizations is to facilitate autonomous collective power, capacity, and consciousness at all levels.

For agit/prop to be effective at mobilization, it must express the character of the dominated and/or exploited classes that it is directed to. We must, at all organizational levels, be very aware of whom we are addressing and the interrelations between the various classes. For example, many students have a middle class background, while another large sector of students have parents who are in the working class and/or the social category of working people, and some students are working people themselves. To be effective, agit/prop must take these factors into consideration.

In creating effective agit/prop, organizations are well-advised to implement the Mass Line, which is an organizing method that bases itself on the principle "from the masses, to the masses." This means participating in the struggles of the masses, basing our practice on their concerns and ideas (as well as objective conditions), and bringing to these struggles our understanding of the nature of the system and the goal of transformation.

This back-and-forth relationship between the organized level and the masses can help us avoid these common errors:

- Tailgating the masses (expressing the lowest common denominator and weakening our demands)
- Sending wrong messages

- Making erroneous calls for action that don't correspond to the mood of the people or objective conditions
- Over- or underestimating the capacity of the masses or sectors we are trying to mobilize
- Misunderstanding the conditions, or the relative strength and weaknesses of the popular forces in relation to the enemy
- Proposing pompous slogans that don't connect with people, with long-term demoralizing and demobilizing effects
- Falsely inflating the struggle through exaggeration, which inevitably leads to deflating it

Goals are long-term aims; priorities are immediate activities along the path to our goals. We should not confuse the two, but always be clear about the dialectical relationship between them. Once we define our goals, we can work out our priorities. Mobilizations are priorities— they are mainly a tactic to gather forces (keeping in mind both quantitative and qualitative concerns) to build organized mass movements.

The mobilizations of students in the 1960s did not clearly define goals, or demarcate the line between goals and priorities. As a result, the mobilizations ended up becoming the movement themselves, rather than being an integral (yet distinct) element in constructing the movement. This resulted in the compartmentalization of the mobilizations into various political organizations that became isolated from the masses, and the dissolution of the mass movement.

Mobilizations can represent the interests of a variety of classes, and must be differentiated accordingly. Lately, reactionary mobilizations have been defending the interests of different sectors of the capitalist class in the US, represented by the competition between the Republican and Democratic parties. The contradictions between these sectors are secondary to their commonality—there is no road to revolution, nor even the possibility of significant reform, within the current capitalist/imperialist framework. Even when mobilizations appear populist, if they represent any fractions of the capitalist class they are, today, inherently reactionary. This is true of both the Democrats' recent One Nation rally, and the right-wing Tea Party mobilization.

We must define a political line to divert the vast sections of the masses who are currently being led by these reactionary classes. We must win them over to our side, while avoiding the pitfalls of class collaborationism and opportunism/populism. When we initiate mobilizations with the goal of constructing mass democratic organizations and combative mass movements, our orientation must be anti-exploitation, anti-domination, and anti-imperialist.

The role of organized structures:

The revolutionary level and the mass level are interdependent and at the same time autonomous. To survive, they must relate to each other dialectically, each affecting and helping the other to realize its potential and aims.

Two aspects of their relative autonomy must be understood:

· The autonomous practice of the revolutionary level in pursuing its particular objectives
· The presence of the revolutionary level within the mass organization

Here we will discuss only the latter. When working within the mass level, the revolutionary has several objectives:

· To struggle against reformist tendencies. There is a thin line separating the struggle for reforms, and having a reformist political orientation, or line. The danger of recuperation by the bourgeoisie of struggles for reforms is constant, since most reforms, if won, will become bourgeois laws.
· To build political rapprochement with the masses to define which mobilizations for reforms are a priority. These mobilizations are not a goal in themselves—they are tactical in nature and in content, and their goal is to constantly weaken the system and strengthen the revolutionary potential of the organized masses. These are perennial under capitalism.
· To expose the fact that at this stage of imperialism, capitalism has reached its peak and is reactionary to the core, and can not reform itself. To make demands for reforming it is useless.
· To participate in the construction of combative mass organizations, in a manner that takes into account their purpose in the present and future. In the pre-revolutionary stage, they act as instruments of struggle against exploitation and domination. In the post-revolutionary period, they will be instruments of power against the defeated capitalist class that is struggling to regain ascendancy.

The conceptualization of these mass organizations is not pre-determined, but will unfold during the process of struggle. As instruments of struggle and power, they need to be constructed in forms that are highly democratic, if they are to be resilient and creative enough to challenge and defeat the dominant system. The underpinning and fundamental elements of power must be popular democratic structures and practice.

The masses must control all organized structures. Trust must be built between the revolutionaries and the masses. Accountability will be essential in theory and in practice.

Errors to avoid:

- Revolutionaries should avoid the vanguardist mentality that would lead them to attempt to bureaucratically control mass organizations, or mechanically take leadership of them. If this error is made, the mass level structure will rapidly become a front organization, the masses will abandon it, and it will degenerate into a head without a body.
- We must avoid confusing the two levels. Instead we must conceptualize the two levels in our theoretical model, and respect their relative autonomy. If we make the error of bringing revolutionary level discussion into the mass level, we render the latter obsolete and sterile. This would have the consequence of depleting the mass levels, since the democratic structures for its views to manifest would no longer exist.

The intermediary level

The objective of the intermediary level is to participate alongside and in some unity with the revolutionary level (but short of that level) to construct mass level organizations. The intermediary level is comprised of large political organizations organizing within the popular classes and/or social categories, with the goal of building combative mass organizations, and participating as the most politically advanced detachments of their classes in the struggle against exploitation and domination, in the ways most appropriate to the current historical period.

Points for further reflection and future elaboration:

- At what point the intermediary level organization becomes a mass organization.
- When this happens, what happens to the initial or most advanced core?
- How to avoid being a front group.
- Be theoretically aware of the moment we are in, and appropriately navigate the inevitable waxing and waning of opportunity.
- Identifying the classes and social categories to organize. This should reflect the social origin of the initial core and/or the class position of the initial core.
- Build a democratic structure of functioning from the start. (This doesn't necessarily mean that the organization is open). The intermediary level/large political organizations are the embryonic constructions of mass organizations as instruments of struggle and instruments of power.
- Unity should be built around theoretical models, rather than around individuals.

Each of the points addressed in this presentation should be further developed as part of a theoretical model to be produced and constantly questioned. The objective of this piece is to lay the groundwork for constructing combative mass organizations.

ACKNOWLEDGMENTS

Thank you to:

· Editors Matt Bors and Tjeerd Royaards, for hiring me to create the initial part of this book as a piece for the Cartoon Movement

· Dan Simon for envisioning the project as a book, and the rest of Seven Stories Press including Gabe Espinal, Crystal Yakacki, Ruth Weiner, Elizabeth DeLong, Anne Rumberger, Stewart Cauley, Eleanor Blair, Veronica Liu, and Beth Kessler

· One Struggle (http://onestrugglesouthflorida.wordpress.com)

· Deep Green Resistance

· Christine McMillan, for all her support

· Derrick Jensen and Ted Rall, who have helped and encouraged me in more ways than I could possibly list

· Max Wilbert and Bruce Stanley, for photographic references

· Jim Sanders, for the concept of cities as labor camps

· Jill Marr, Elisabeth James and Sandy Dijkstra of the Sandra Dijkstra Literary Agency

· Heartfelt appreciation for every one of my comrades, near and far; past, present and future; known and unknown.